P9-EET-160

Home and Child Life in Colonial Days

Abridged from
Home Life in Colonial Days
and *Child Life in Colonial Days*
by ALICE MORSE EARLE

The Macmillan Company, New York
Collier-Macmillan Ltd., London

Home and Child Life in Colonial Days

Edited by

SHIRLEY GLUBOK

Special photography by
Alfred Tamarin

The Macmillan Company
866 Third Avenue, New York, N.Y. 10022
Collier-Macmillan Canada Ltd., Toronto, Ontario

Library of Congress catalog card number: 69–11295
Printed in the United States of America

10 9 8 7 6 5 4 3 2

FRONTISPIECE:
Mrs. Noah Smith and her children, by Ralph Earl (1751–1801)
(The Metropolitan Museum of Art, Bequest of Edgar William Garbisch and Bernice Chrysler, 1964)

Contents

Introduction

It is two generations since Alice Morse Earle wrote *Home Life in Colonial Days* (1898) and *Child Life in Colonial Days* (1899), two of her sixteen published books on early America. She was moved to write her first work after hearing her grandfather relate the customs of colonial times. Alice Morse Earle was proud of her colonial ancestry and was in close touch with the people who knew and experienced the traditions of early America. Until her time there had been little study of colonial America and certainly very little written about it. Our young country was too busy living history to be interested in writing it.

There was no dictionary containing the words for some of the utensils or tools that were brought out of the cellar or attic by her friends, descendants of colonial families, and no printed information on these objects. Mrs. Earle had to get the names from "old-time country folk," and thus rescued the words from oblivion.

In her foreword to *Home Life in Colonial Days* Mrs. Earle calls the illustrations "rare relics of past days . . . symbols of years of careful research, patient investigation, and constant watchfulness." To find the obsolete domestic articles that were used by every household, she rescued a variety of strangely shaped bits and pieces "from the lofts of woodsheds, under attic eaves, in dairy cellars, out of old trunks and sea-chests from mouldering warehouses."

Mrs. Earle was indefatigable in her research

and left no subject untouched. However, her books were not written as works of formal scholarship but as reminiscences of bygone days. They are noteworthy for fostering the renewed interest in our colonial past that was developing toward the close of the nineteenth century.

I have tried to consolidate and abridge the two volumes without losing Mrs. Earle's intimate, personal style. By taking advantage of the great advances in photography since her time, I have been able to replace most of the original illustrations with new pictures.

While the author sometimes describes events and objects of the nineteenth century, I have attempted to stay within the colonial period. Illustrations of later objects have been used only when earlier ones were not available.

I appreciate the help of all the museums, libraries, and historical societies who gave us their valuable advice. Thanks to Elizabeth Coleman, Assistant Curator, Department of Decorative Arts, The Newark Museum, Robert E. P. Hendrick, Assistant Curator, Department of Decorative Arts, The Brooklyn Museum, and especially to Jay Cantor.

Shirley Glubok

New York City
November, 1968

Home and Child Life in Colonial Days

Chapter I

Homes of the Colonists

When the first settlers landed on American shores they found a land magnificent with forest trees of every size and variety, but they had no sawmills, and few saws. There was plenty of clay and ample limestone, yet they could have no brick and no mortar; grand boulders of granite and rock were everywhere, yet there was not a single facility for cutting, drawing, or using the stone. These men,

Mount Vernon, built in 1735 (The New York Public Library, Stokes Collection)

in need of immediate shelter, were baffled by pioneer conditions, and had to turn to many poor expedients, and be satisfied with rude covering.

The homes of the Indians were copied by the English settlers, being ready adaptations of natural resources. Wigwams in the South were made of plaited rush or grass mats; of deerskins pinned on a frame; of tree boughs rudely piled into a cover. Bark wigwams were the most easily made; they could be quickly pinned together on a light frame. In 1626 there were thirty home buildings of Europeans on the island of Manhattan, and all but one of them were of bark.

But these houses did not satisfy English men and women. They began to build what Roger

Stadt House, New York City, built 1642 (The Metropolitan Museum of Art, Gift of Charles Allen Munn, 1924. Photograph by Alfred Tamarin)

Williams called English houses. These houses had a single room on the ground, called the fire room, with a vast chimney at one end. A so-called staircase, usually a narrow ladder, led to a sleeping loft above. Some of those houses were made of whole logs, but with clapboards nailed over the chinks and cracks. Others were of a lighter frame covered with clapboards, or in Delaware with boards pinned on perpendicularly. Soon this house was doubled in size and comfort by having a room on either side of the chimney.

Each settlement generally copied the houses which the owners had known in Europe. In New York, settled by the Dutch, the first permanent houses were Dutch in shape, such as may still be seen in Holland.

Inside the houses were the heavy timbers of the frame. The summer-piece was the large beam in the middle from end to end of the ceiling; the joists were crossbeams. These were not covered with plaster as nowadays but showed in every ceiling.

Some New York houses had patterns of colored

brick set in the front. Dutch houses were set close to the sidewalk with the gable-end to the street, and these ends were often of brick, while the rest of the walls were of wood. The roofs were notched like steps, called corbel roof. They were high and steep, surmounted usually in Holland fashion with weather vanes in the shape of horses, lions, geese, sloops, fish, or a rooster, which was a favorite Dutch weather vane. There were metal gutters sticking out from every roof almost to the middle of the street; this was most annoying to passers-by in rainy weather, who were deluged with water. The cellar windows had small loop-holes with shutters. The windows were always small; some had only sliding shutters, others had but two panes or quarrels of glass, as they were called, only six or eight inches square.

Weathervane, about 1715 (Abby Aldrich Rockefeller Folk Art Collection, Williamsburg, Virginia)

The front doors were cut across horizontally into two parts and in early days were hung on leather hinges instead of iron.

In the upper half of the door were two round bull's-eyes of heavy greenish glass, which let faint rays of light enter the hall. The door opened with a latch and often had a knocker. Every house had a porch or "stoep" flanked with benches, which were constantly occupied in the summer evenings in the city and village alike. Dutch farmhouses were a single straight story, with two more stories in the high, in-curving roof. They had doors and stoops like the townhouses, and the windows had heavy board shutters.

The cellar and the garret were the most useful

rooms in the house; they were storerooms for all kinds of substantial food. In the attic by the chimney was the smokehouse filled with hams, bacon, smoked beef, and sausages.

In Virginia and Maryland there were at first few sawmills, and the houses were universally built of undressed logs. Nails were costly, as were all articles manufactured of iron; hence many houses were built with wooden pins and pegs. Hinges were of leather; the shingles on the roof were sometimes pinned or were held in place by "weight timbers." The doors had latches with strings hanging outside. When the string was pulled within doors the house was securely locked. When persons abandoned houses, they sometimes set them on fire in order to gather up the nails from the ashes. To prevent this destruction, the government of Virginia gave to each planter who was leaving his house as many nails as the house was estimated to have, provided the owner would not burn the house down.

Later, when boards could be readily obtained, the favorite dwelling place in the South was a frame building with a great stone or log-and-clay chimney at either end. The house was usually set on sills resting on the ground. The partitions were sometimes covered with a thick layer of mud which dried into a sort of plaster and was whitewashed. The roofs were covered with cypress shingles.

When prosperity and wealth came to the South through the speedily profitable crops of tobacco, the houses improved. There was not only the spacious mansion house for the planter with its pleasant porch, but separate buildings in which were a kitchen, cabins for the Negro servants and the overseer, a stable, barn, coach house, henhouse, smokehouse, dove cote, and milk room. There was seldom an icehouse. The only means for the preservation of meats in hot weather was by water constantly pouring into and through a box house erected over the spring that flowed near the house. Sometimes a brew house was also found for making home-brewed beer, and a tool house for storing tools and farm implements. Some farms had a cider mill. Often there was a spinning house where servants could spin flax and wool. This usually had one room containing a handloom on which coarse bagging could be woven, and homespun for the use of the servants. A very beautiful example of a splendid and comfortable Southern mansion such as was built by wealthy planters in the middle of the eighteenth century has been preserved for us at Mount Vernon, the home of George Washington.

North of Virginia through Pennsylvania, "the Jerseys," and Delaware, the servant cabins and detached kitchen disappeared, and many of the houses were of stone and mortar. A clay oven stood by each house.

For half a century nearly all New England houses were cottages. Many had thatched roofs. Seaside towns set aside for public use certain reedy lots between salt marsh and low-water mark, where thatch could be freely cut. The catted chimneys were of logs plastered with clay, or platted, that is, made of reeds and mortar. Since wood and hay were stacked in the streets, all the early towns suffered much from fires, and soon laws were passed forbidding the building of these unsafe chimneys. As brick was imported or made and stone was quarried, there was certainly no need to use such dangerous materials. Fire wardens were appointed who peered around in all the kitchens and hunted for what they called foul chimney hearts. They ordered flag roofs and wooden chimneys to be removed and replaced with stone or brick. In Boston every housekeeper had to own a fire ladder, and ladders and buckets were kept in the church. Salem kept its "fire-buckets and hook'd poles" in the townhouse. Soon in all towns each family owned fire buckets made of heavy leather and marked with the owner's name or initials. The entire town constituted the fire company. As soon as a fire alarm was given, everyone ran at once to the scene of the fire. All who owned buckets carried them, and if any person was delayed, he flung his fire buckets from the window into the street, where someone in the running crowd seized them and carried them on. On reaching the fire, the people formed a double line from the fire to the river or pond, or well. The buckets, filled with water, were passed from hand to hand, up one line of persons to the fire, while the empty ones went down the other line. Boys were stationed on the "dry lane." Thus a constant supply of water was carried to the fire. If any person attempted to pass through the line, or hinder the work, he promptly got a bucketful or two of water poured over him. When the fire was over, the fire warden took charge of the buckets. Some hours later the owners appeared, picked out their own buckets from the pile, carried them home, and hung them up by the front door, ready to be seized again for use at the next alarm of fire.

Many of these old fire buckets are still preserved and are deservedly cherished heirlooms, for they represent the dignity and importance due a householding ancestor. They were a valued and costly possession, being made of the best leather. They were often painted not only with the name of the owner, but with family mottoes, crests, or appropriate inscriptions, sometimes in Latin. In these fire buckets were often kept, tightly rolled, strong canvas bags in which valuables could be thrust and carried from the burning building.

The first fire engine made in this country was for the town of Boston. It was made about 1650 by Joseph Jencks, the famous old ironworker in Lynn. It was doubtless very simple in shape, as were its successors until well into this century. The first fire engine used in Brooklyn, New York, was made in 1785 by Jacob Boome. Relays of men at both handles worked the clumsy pump. The water supply for this engine was still only through the lanes of fire buckets except in rare cases.

By 1670 the Plymouth and Bay colonies had

Firebucket, late 18th century (The Firefighting Museum of the Home Insurance Company)

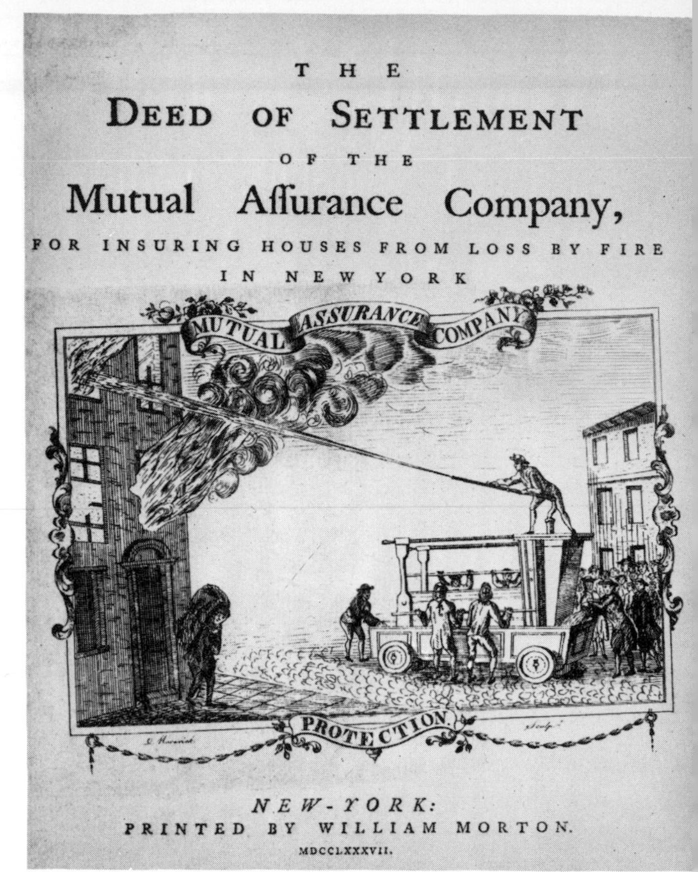

THE

DEED OF SETTLEMENT

OF THE

Mutual Affurance Company,

FOR INSURING HOUSES FROM LOSS BY FIRE

IN NEW YORK

NEW-YORK:

PRINTED BY WILLIAM MORTON.

MDCCLXXXVII.

Fighting a fire in New York, 1787 (The New York Public Library, Stokes Collection)

houses of two stories, which were frequently built with the second story jutting out a foot or two over the first, and sometimes with the attic story still further extending over the second story. This overhang is popularly supposed to have been built for the purpose of affording a convenient shooting place from which to repel the Indians. This is, however, a historic fable. The overhanging second story was a common form of building in England in the time of Queen Elizabeth, and the Massachusetts and Rhode Island settlers simply and naturally copied their old homes. The roofs of many of these new houses were steep and were shingled with handmade shingles. The walls between the rooms were of clay mixed with chopped straw. Sometimes the walls were whitened with a wash made of powdered clamshells. The ground floors were occasionally of earth, but puncheon floors were common in the better houses. The well-smoothed timbers were sanded in careful designs with clean beach sand.

A later form of many houses was two stories or two and a half stories in front, with a peaked roof that sloped down nearly to the ground in the back over an ell covering the kitchen, added in the shape known as a lean-to, or, as it was called by country folk, the linter. This sloping roof gave the one element of picturesqueness which redeemed the prosaic ugliness of these bare-walled houses.

The next roof form built from early colonial days was the gambrel roof. This resembled on two sides the mansard roof of France in the seventeenth century, but was gabled at two ends. The gambrel roof had a certain grace of outline, especially when joined with lean-tos and other additions.

House of Parson Capen, Topsfield, Massachusetts, 1683

The birthplaces of John Quincy and John Adams, photograph taken about 1930 (The Society for the Preservation of New England Antiquities)

The windows of the first houses had oiled paper to admit light. A colonist wrote back to England to a friend who was soon to follow, "Bring oiled paper for your windows." In 1629 glass was ordered for windows. This glass was set in the windows with nails; the sashes were often narrow and oblong, of diamond-shaped panes set in lead, and opening up and down the middle on hinges. Long after the large towns and cities had glass windows, frontier settlements still had heavy wooden shutters. They were a safer protection against Indian assault, as well as cheaper. It is asserted that in the province of Kennebec, now the state of Maine, there was not, even as late as 1745, a house that had a square of glass in it.

Few of the early houses in New England were painted, or colored, as it was called, either without or within. Painters do not appear in any of the early lists of workmen.

There was one external and suggestive adjunct of the earliest pioneer's home which was found in nearly all the settlements built in the midst of threatening Indians. Some strong houses were always surrounded by a stockade, or "palisado," of heavy, well-fitted logs, which thus formed a garrison in time of danger. In the valley of Virginia each settlement consisted of houses set in a square, connected from end to end of the outside walls by stockades with gates; thus forming a closed front. On Manhattan Island there were stockades. The whole town plot of Milford, Connecticut, was enclosed in 1645, and the Indians taunted the settlers by shouting, "White men all same like pigs." At one time in Massachusetts, twenty towns proposed an all-surrounding palisade. The progress and condition of our settlements can be traced in our fences. As Indians disappeared, the solid row of pales gave place to a long fence, which served to keep out predatory animals. When dangers from Indians or wild animals entirely disappeared, boards being still not over-plenty, there came the double-rail fence: two rails, held in place one above the other at each joint by four crossed sticks. It was a boundary and would keep in cattle. It was said that every fence should be horse high, bull proof, and pig tight. Then came stone walls, showing a thorough clearing and taming of the land. The succeeding half-high stone wall—a foot or two high with a single rail on top—showed that stones were not as plentiful in the fields as in early days. The snake fence, or Virginia fence, so common in the Southern states, utilized the second growth of forest trees. The split-rail fence, four or five rails in height, was set at intervals with posts pierced with holes to hold the ends of the rails. These were used to some extent in the East;

but our Western states were fenced throughout with rails split by sturdy pioneer rail-splitters, among them young Abraham Lincoln. Board fences showed the day of the sawmill and its plentiful supply; the wire fences of today equally prove the decrease of our forests and our wood and the growth of our mineral supplies and manufacture of metals. Thus, even our fences might be called historical monuments.

Window with leaded glass panes, 17th century (The Metropolitan Museum of Art, Gift of Mrs, J. Insley Blair, 1947)

As social life in Boston took on a little of the aspect of court life in the circle gathered around the royal governors, the pride of the wealthy found expression in handsome and stately houses. These were copied and added to by men of wealth and social standing in other towns. The Province House, built in 1679, the Frankland House in 1735, and the Hancock House, all in Boston; the Shirley House in Roxbury, the Wentworth Mansion in New Hampshire, are good examples. They were dignified and simple in form, and have borne the test of centuries. These houses never erred in overornamentation, being scant of interior decoration except in two or three principal rooms and the hall and staircase. The paneled step ends and soffits, the graceful newels and balusters of those old staircases continue as models to this day. Outside, the front door was the sole point of ornamentation. Many colonial doors had door latches or knobs of heavy brass; nearly all had a knocker of wrought iron or polished brass.

The King-Hooper House in Danvers, Massachusetts, closely resembled the Hancock House.

This house, built by Robert Hooper in 1745, was for a time the refuge of the royal governor of Massachusetts—Governor Gage—and hence is sometimes called General Gage's Headquarters. When the Minutemen marched past the house to Lexington on April 18, 1775, they stripped the lead from the gate posts. "King Hooper" angrily denounced them, and a Minuteman fired at him as he entered the house. The bullet passed through the panel of the door, and the hole may still be seen. Hence, the house has been often called The House of the Front Door with the Bullet Hole.

King-Hooper House, Danvers, Massachusetts, built in 1754 (The Society for the Preservation of New England Antiquities)

Chapter II

The Light of Other Days

The first and most natural way of lighting the houses of the American colonists both in the North and in the South was by the pine knots of the fat pitch pine, which were found everywhere in the forests. And a very good light this candlewood furnished.

Pitch pine also produced tar, which was one of the most valuable trade products of the colonists. So much tar was made by burning the pines on the banks of the Connecticut, that as early as 1650

Bedroom from a house in Springfield, Massachusetts, built by Ruebin Bliss in 1754 (The Brooklyn Museum)

the towns had to prohibit the using of candlewood for tar-making if gathered within six miles of the Connecticut River, though it could be gathered by families for illumination and fuel.

To avoid smoke in the room, and on account of the pitchy droppings, the candlewood was usually burned in a corner of the fireplace on a flat stone. The knots were sometimes called pine-torches. Lighting was an important item of expense in any household; and the single candle would often be frugally extinguished during the long family prayers each evening. Every family laid in a good supply of this light wood for winter use, and it was said that a prudent New England farmer would as soon start the winter without hay in his barn as without candlewood in his woodshed.

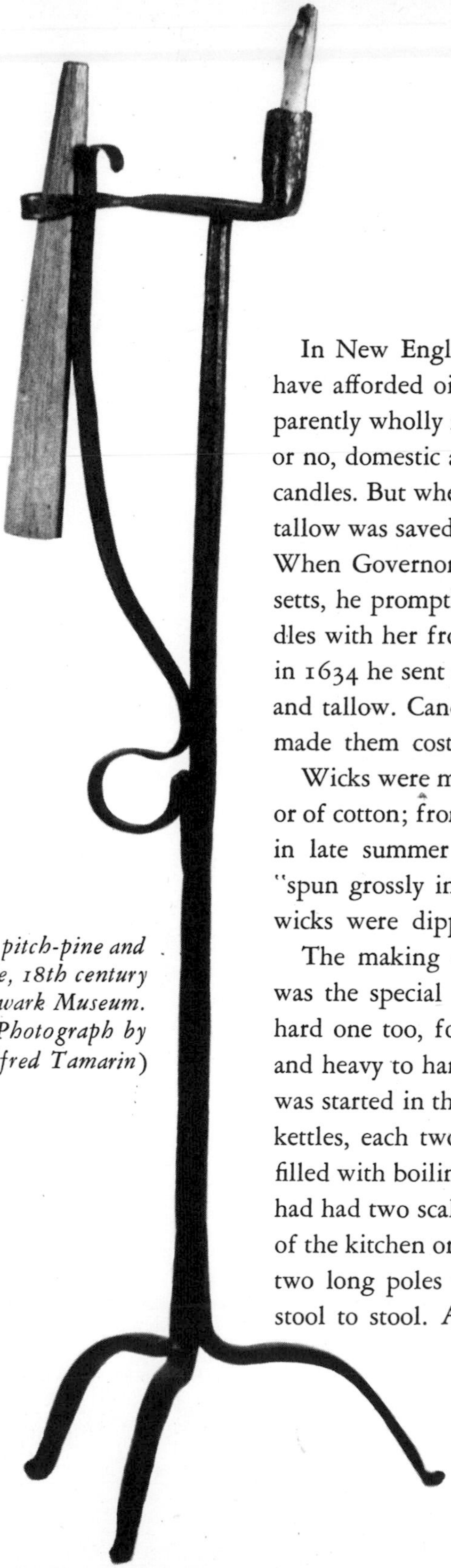

In New England the abundance of fish could have afforded oil for lamps. But fish oil was apparently wholly neglected, though there were few, or no, domestic animals to furnish tallow to make candles. But when cattle increased, every ounce of tallow was saved as a precious and useful treasure. When Governor Winthrop arrived in Massachusetts, he promptly wrote to his wife to bring candles with her from England when she came. And in 1634 he sent over for a large quantity of wicks and tallow. Candles cost fourpence apiece, which made them costly luxuries for the colonists.

Wicks were made of loosely spun hemp or tow, or of cotton; from milkweed the children gathered in late summer the silver silkdown which was "spun grossly into candle wicke." Sometimes the wicks were dipped into saltpeter.

The making of the winter's stock of candles was the special autumnal household duty, and a hard one too, for the great kettles were tiresome and heavy to handle. At an early hour a good fire was started in the kitchen fireplace under two vast kettles, each two feet, perhaps, in diameter, half filled with boiling water and melted tallow, which had had two scaldings and skimmings. At the end of the kitchen or in an adjoining and cooler room, two long poles were laid from chair to chair or stool to stool. Across these poles were placed at

Holder for pitch-pine and candle, 18th century (The Newark Museum. Photograph by Alfred Tamarin)

regular intervals, like the rounds of a ladder, smaller sticks about fifteen or eighteen inches long, called candle rods. These poles and rods were kept from year to year, either in the garret or up on the kitchen beams.

To each candle rod were attached about six or eight carefully straightened candlewicks. The wicking was twisted strongly one way; then doubled; then the loop was slipped over the candle rod, when the two ends, of course, twisted the other way around each other, making a firm wick. A rod, with its row of wicks, was dipped in the melted tallow in the pot, and returned to its place across the poles. Each row was thus dipped in regular turn; each had time to cool and harden between the dips, and thus grew steadily in size. If allowed to cool fast, they of course grew quickly, but were brittle, and often cracked. Hence a good worker dipped slowly but, if the room was fairly cool, could make two hundred candles for a day's work. Some could dip two rods at a time. The tallow was constantly replenished, as the heavy kettles were used alternately to keep the tallow constantly melted, and were swung off and on the fire. Boards or sheets of paper were placed under the rods to protect the snowy, scoured floors.

Candles were also run in molds which were groups of metal cylinders, usually made of tin or pewter. The larger size made two dozen candles, but its companion, the smaller mold, making six candles, was more commonly seen. Each wick was attached to a wire or a nail placed across the open

Candlestick, 18th century, and snuffer, about 1800 (The Newark Museum. Photograph by Alfred Tamarin)

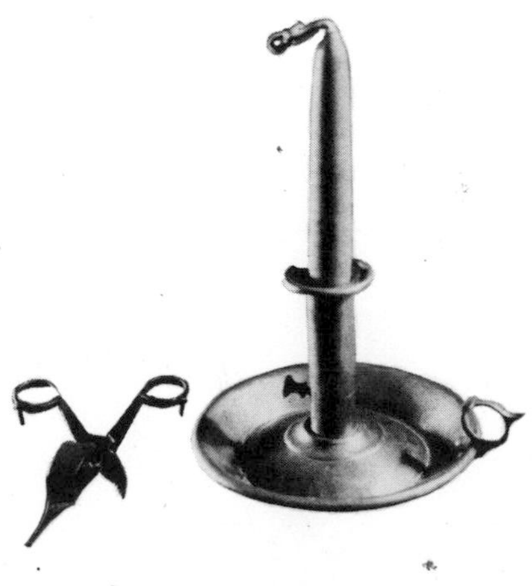

Candle rods and candles, early 19th century (The Newark Museum. Photograph by Alfred Tamarin)

top of the cylinder and hung down in the center of each individual mold. The melted tallow was poured in carefully around the wicks.

Wax candles also were made. They were often shaped by hand by pressing bits of heated wax around a wick. Farmers kept hives of bees as much for the wax as for the honey, which was in much demand for sweetening, when "loaves" of sugar were so high priced. Deer suet, moose fat, and bear's grease were all saved in frontier settlements and carefully melted into tallow for candles. Every particle of grease rescued from pot liquor, or fat from meat, was utilized for candlemaking. Rushlights were made by stripping part of the outer bark from common rushes, thus leaving the pith bare, then dipping them in tallow or grease, and letting them harden.

The precious candles thus tediously made were

carefully packed in candle boxes with compartments, covered over, and set in a dark closet, where they would not discolor and turn yellow. A metal candle box, hung on the edge of the kitchen mantel shelf, always held two or three candles to replenish those which burned out in the candlesticks.

A natural and apparently inexhaustible material for candles was found in all the colonies in the waxy berries of the bayberry bush. In 1748 a Swedish naturalist, Professor Kalm, wrote an account of the bayberry wax:

"The candle-berry tree or bayberry bush . . . grows abundantly in a wet soil, and seems to thrive particularly well in the neighborhood of the sea. The berries look as if flour had been strewed on them. They are gathered late in Autumn, being ripe about that time, and are thrown into a kettle or pot full of boiling water; by this means their fat melts out, floats at the top of the water, and may be skimmed off into a vessel; with the skimming they go on till there is no tallow left. The tallow, as soon as it is congealed, looks like common tallow or wax, but has a dirty green color. By being melted over and refined it acquires a fine and transparent green color. This tallow is dearer than common tallow, but cheaper than wax. Candles of this do not easily bend, nor melt in summer as common candles do; they burn better and slower, nor do they cause any smoke, but yield rather an agreeable smell when they are extinguished."

A valuable material which was once used for making candles was stored in the blunt heads of whales. This material is termed Sperma-Coeti in the most ancient reference in New England records. It was asserted that one of these spermaceti candles gave out more light than three tallow candles and had four times as big a flame. Soon their manufacture and sale amounted to large numbers, and materially improved domestic illumination.

All candles, whatever their material, were carefully used by the economical colonists to the last bit by a little wire frame of pins and rings called a save-all. Candlesticks of various metals and shapes were found in every house, as well as sconces, which were also called candle arms, or prongs. Candlebeams were rude chandeliers, a metal or wooden hoop with candleholders. Snuffers to trim the candles and snuffer trays were always seen.

Though there was plenty of whale and fish oil to burn, lamps were not extensively used in America for many years. Betty lamps, shaped much like antique Roman lamps, were the earliest form. They were small, shallow receptacles, two or three

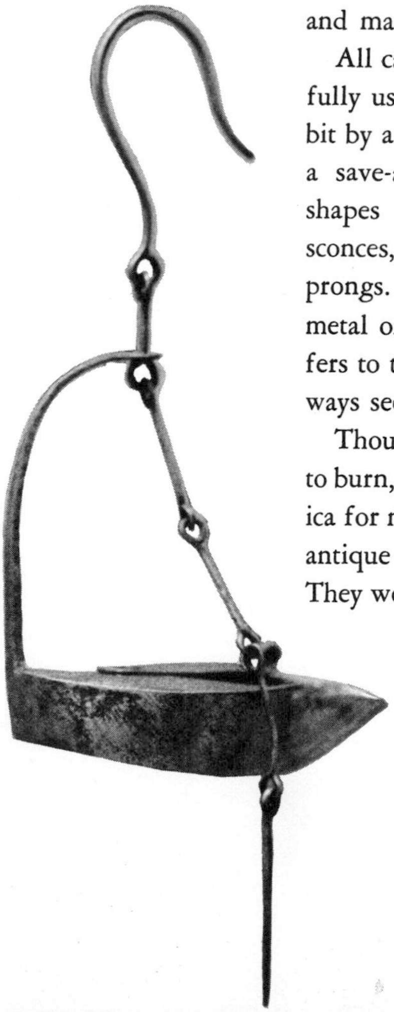

Betty lamp, early 19th century (The New-York Historical Society. Photograph by Alfred Tamarin)

inches in diameter and about an inch in depth; either rectangular, oval, round, or triangular in shape, with a projecting nose or spout an inch or two long. They usually had a hook and chain by which they could be hung on a nail in the wall, or on the round in the back of chair; sometimes there was also a smaller hook for cleaning out the nose of the lamp. They were filled with tallow, grease, or oil, while a piece of cotton rag or coarse wick was so placed that, when lighted, the end hung out on the nose. From this wick, dripping dirty grease, rose a dull, smoky, ill-smelling flame.

Phœbe lamps were similar in shape, though

Phoebe lamps, early 18th century (The New-York Historical Society. Photograph by Alfred Tamarin)

some had double wicks, that is, a nose at either side.

Pewter was a favorite material for lamps, as it was for all other domestic utensils. It was specially in favor for the lamps for whale oil and the "Porter's fluid," that preceded petroleum. A rare form is a pewter lamp with clear bull's-eyes of unusually pure glass, which gave what was truly a brilliant light for the century of its use.

Glass lamps of many simple shapes shared popularity for a long time with the pewter lamps; as pewter gradually disappeared from household use, these glass lamps monopolized the field. They were rarely of cut or colored glass, but were pressed glass of commonplace form and quality.

For many years the methods of striking a light were very primitive, just as they were in Europe. If by ill fortune the fire in the fireplace became wholly extinguished through carelessness at night, someone, usually a small boy, was sent to the house of the nearest neighbor, bearing a shovel or covered pan, or perhaps a broad strip of green bark, on which to bring back coals for relighting the fire. Nearly all families had some form of a flint and steel—a method of obtaining fire which has been used from time immemorial. This always required a flint, a steel, and a tinder of some vegetable matter to catch the spark struck by the concussion of flint and steel. This spark was then blown into a flame. Among the colonists scorched linen was a favorite tinder to catch the spark of fire, and all the old cambric handkerchiefs, linen underwear, and worn sheets of a household were carefully saved for this purpose. The flint, steel, and tinder were usually kept together in a circular tinderbox; it was a shape universal in England and America. This had an inner flat cover with a ring, a flint, a horseshoe-shaped steel, and an upper lid with a place to set a candle-end in, to carry the newly acquired light. Soon there was an improvement on this tinderbox, by which sparks were obtained by spinning a steel wheel with a piece of cord, somewhat like spinning a humming top, and making the wheel strike a flint fixed in the side of a little trough full of tinder. This was an infinite advance in convenience on the first tinderbox. This box was called in the South a mill. Then some person invented strips of wood dipped in sulphur and called spunks. These readily caught fire and retained it, and were handy to carry light to a candle or pile of chips.

Another way of starting a fire was by flashing a little powder in the pan of an old-fashioned gun. Sometimes this fired a twist of tow, which in turn started a heap of shavings.

Chapter III

The Kitchen Fireside

The kitchen in all the houses of all the colonies was the most cheerful and picturesque room in the house. The walls were often bare, the rafters dingy; the windows were small, the furniture meager; but the kitchen had a warm, glowing heart that spread light and welcome and made the poor room a home. In the houses of the first settlers the chimneys and fireplaces were vast in size,

Kitchen fireplace, about 1800 (The Newark Museum. Photograph by Alfred Tamarin)

sometimes so big that the forelogs and backlogs for the fire had to be dragged in by a horse and a long chain; or a hand sled was kept for the purpose. Often there were seats within the chimney on either side. At night children could sit on these seats and there watch the sparks fly upward and join the stars which could plainly be seen up the great chimney throat.

But as the forests disappeared under the waste of burning for tar, for potash, and through wanton clearing, the fireplaces shrank in size. Benjamin Franklin, even in his day, could write of "the fireplaces of our fathers."

The inflammable catted chimney of logs and clay, hurriedly and readily built by the first settlers, soon gave place in all houses to vast chimneys of stone, built with projecting inner ledges, on which rested a bar about six or seven or even eight feet from the floor, called a lug pole (lug meaning to carry) or a back bar. This was made of green wood, and thus charred slowly—but it charred surely in the generous flames of the great chimney heart. Many annoying and some fatal accidents came from the collapsing of these wooden back bars. The destruction of a dinner sometimes was attended with the loss of a life. Later the back bars were made of iron. On them were hung iron hooks or chains with hooks of various lengths called pothooks, trammels, hakes, pot hangers, pot claws, pot clips, pot brakes, pot crooks. Folding trammels nine feet long were found in an old Narragansett chimney heart. On these hooks, pots and kettles could be hung at varying heights over the fire. The iron swinging crane was a Yankee invention of a century after the first settlement, and it proved a convenient and graceful substitute for the back bar.

Some Dutch houses had an adaptation of a Southern method of housekeeping in the use of a detached house called a slave kitchen, where the meals of the Negro house and farm servants were cooked and served. The fireplace itself sometimes went by the old English name, clavell-piece. Often a large plate of iron, called the fire back or fire plate, was set at the back of the chimney, where the constant and fierce fire crumbled brick and split stone. These iron backs were often cast in a handsome design.

In New York the chimneys and fireplaces were Dutch in shape. A calico or linen valance was hung on the edge of the mantel shelf, a pretty and cheerful fashion seen in some English as well as Dutch homes.

Another Dutch furnishing, the alcove bedstead, much like a closet, seen in many New York kitchens, was replaced in New England farm kitchens by the "turn-up" bedstead. This was a strong frame filled with a network of rope which was fastened at the bed head by hinges to the wall. By night the foot of the bed rested on two heavy legs; by day the frame with its bed furnishings was hooked up to the wall and covered with homespun curtains or doors. This was the sleeping place of the master and mistress of the house, chosen because the kitchen was the warmest room in the house.

Over the fireplace and across the top of the room were long poles on which hung strings of peppers, dried apples, and rings of dried pumpkin. And the favorite resting place for the old queen's arm or fowling piece was on hooks over the kitchen fireplace.

On the pothooks and trammels hung what formed in some households the costliest house furnishing—the pots and kettles. Often these kettles were worth three pounds apiece. In many inventories of the states of the settlers the brassware formed an important item. The great brass and copper kettles often held fifteen gallons. The vast iron pot—desired and beloved of every colonist—sometimes weighed forty pounds and lasted

Fireback, 1703 (The Metropolitan Museum of Art, Gift of Mrs. J. Insley Blair, 1947)

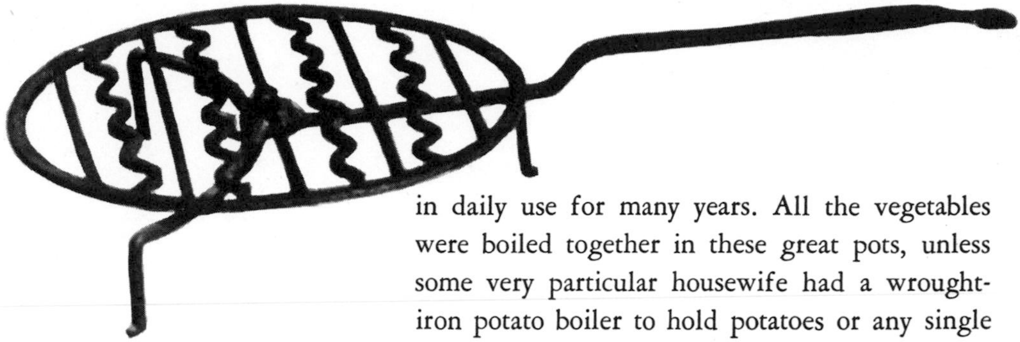

Gridiron, 18th century (The Newark Museum. Photograph by Alfred Tamarin)

in daily use for many years. All the vegetables were boiled together in these great pots, unless some very particular housewife had a wrought-iron potato boiler to hold potatoes or any single vegetable in place within the vast general pot.

Chafing dishes and skimmers of brass and copper were also cheerful discs to reflect the kitchen firelight.

Very little tin was seen, either for kitchen or table utensils. Governor Winthrop had a few tin plates, and some Southern planters had tin pans, others "tynnen covers." Tin pails were unknown; and the pails they did own, either of wood, brass, or other sheet metal, had no bails, but were carried by thrusting a stick through little ears on either side of the pail. Latten ware was used instead of tin; it was a kind of brass.

There was a distinct characteristic in the house furnishing of olden times. It was a tendency for the main body of everything to set well up, on legs which were strong enough for adequate support of the weight, yet were slender in appearance. Chests of drawers, Chippendale sideboards, four-post bedsteads, dressing cases, were set, often a foot high, in a tidy fashion; thus they could all be thoroughly swept under. This same peculiarity of form extended to cooking utensils. Pots and kettles had legs, gridirons had legs, skillets had legs; and further appliances in the shape of trivets, which were movable frames, took the place of legs. The necessity for the stilting up of cooking utensils was a very evident one; it was necessary to raise the body of the utensil above the ashes and coals of the open fireplace. If the bed of coals and burning logs were too deep for the skillet or pot legs, then the utensil must be hung from above by the ever ready trammel.

Often in the corner of the fireplace there stood a group of trivets, or three-legged stands, of varying heights, through which the exactly desired proximity to the coals could be obtained.

Even toasting forks, and similar frail utensils of wire or wrought iron, stood on tall, spindling legs, or were carefully shaped to be set up on trivets. They usually had, also, long, adjustable handles, which helped to make endurable the blazing heat of the great logs. All such irons as waffle irons had far longer handles than are seen on any cooking utensils in these days of stoves and ranges, where the flames are covered and the housewife shielded. Gridirons had long handles of wood or iron, which could be fastened to the shorter stationary handles.

Toasting rack, late 18th century (The Newark Museum. Photograph by Alfred Tamarin)

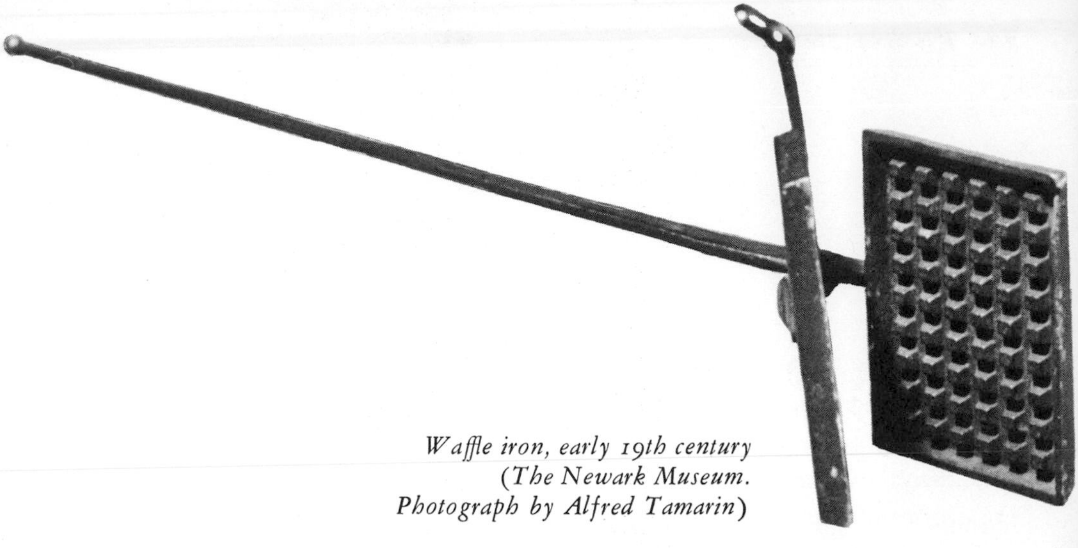

Waffle iron, early 19th century (The Newark Museum. Photograph by Alfred Tamarin)

An accompaniment of the kitchen fireplace, found not in farmhouses but among luxury-loving townfolk was the plate warmer.

An important furnishing of every fireplace was the andirons. In kitchen fireplaces these were usually of iron, and the shape known as gooseneck was common. Cob irons were the simplest form, and merely supported the spit; sometimes they had hooks to hold a dripping pan. A common name for the kitchen andirons was fire-dogs; and creepers were low, small andirons, usually used with the tall fire-dogs. The kitchen andirons were simply for use to help hold the logs and cooking utensils. But other fireplaces had handsome fire-dogs of copper or brass, cast or wrought in handsome devices. These were a pride and delight to the housewife.

A primitive method of roasting a joint of meat or a fowl was by suspending it in front of the fire by a strong hempen string tied to a peg in the ceiling, while someone—usually an unwilling child—occasionally turned the roast around. Sometimes the sole turnspit was the housewife, who, every time she basted the roast, gave the string a good twist, and thereafter it would untwist, and then twist a little again, and so on until the vibration ceased, when she again basted and started it. As the juices sometimes ran down in the roast and left the upper part too dry, a double string-roaster was invented, by which the equilibrium of the joint could be shifted. A jack was a convenient and magnified edition of the primitive string, being a metal suspensory machine. A still further glorification was the addition of a revolving power which ran by clockwork and turned the roast with regularity; this was known as a clock-jack. A smoke-jack was run somewhat irregularly by the pressure of smoke and the current of hot air in the chimney. These were noisy and creaking and not regarded with favor by old-fashioned cooks.

We are apt to think of the turnspit dog as a

Plate warmer, 18th century (The Mount Vernon Ladies Association of the Union, Mount Vernon, Virginia)

Clock-jack, about 1830
(The Staten Island Historical Society. Photograph by Alfred Tamarin)

creature of European life, but we had them here in America—little low, bowlegged, patient souls, trained to run in a revolving cylinder and keep the roasting joint turning before the fire. Mine host Clark of the State House Inn in Philadelphia in the first half of the eighteenth century advertised in Benjamin Franklin's *Pennsylvania Gazette* that he had for sale "several dogs and wheels, much preferable to any jacks for roasting any joints of meat."

A frequent accompaniment of the kitchen fireplace in the eighteenth century, and a domestic luxury seen in well-to-do homes, were the various forms of the "roasting kitchen," or Dutch oven. These succeeded the jacks. They were a boxlike arrangement, open on one side, which when in use was turned to the fire. Like other utensils of the day, they often stood up on legs, to bring the open side before the blaze. A little door at the back could be opened for convenience in basting the roast. These kitchens came in various sizes for roasting birds or joints, and in them bread was occasionally baked. The bake kettle, which in some communities was also called a Dutch oven, was preferred for baking bread. It was a strong kettle, standing on stout, stumpy legs, and when in use was placed among the hot coals and closely covered with a strong metal, convex cover on which coals were also closely heaped.

Dutch oven, about 1830 (The Staten Island Historical Society. Photograph by Alfred Tamarin)

When the great stone chimney was built, there was usually placed on one side of the kitchen fireplace a brick oven which had a smoke uptake into the chimney—and an ash pit below. The great door was of iron. This oven was usually heated once a week. A great fire of dry wood, called oven wood, was kindled within it and kept burning fiercely for some hours. This thoroughly heated all the bricks. The coals and ashes were then swept out, the chimney draft closed, and the oven filled with brown bread, pies, pots of beans, etc. Sometimes the bread was baked in pans, sometimes it was baked in a great mass set on cabbage leaves or oak leaves. In some towns an autumn harvest of oak leaves was gathered by children to use throughout the winter. The leaves were strung on sticks. This was called going aleafing.

By the oven side was always a long-handled shovel known as a peel or slice, which sometimes had a rack or rest to hold it; this implement was a necessity in order to place the food well within the glowing oven. The peel was sprinkled with meal, great heaps of dough were placed thereon, and by a dexterous twist they were thrown on the cabbage or oak leaves. A bread peel was a universal gift to a bride; it was significant of domestic utility and plenty, and was held to be luck-bearing. During Thanksgiving week the great oven had a fire built in it every morning, and every night it was well filled and closed till morning.

On one side of the kitchen often stood a dresser on which was placed in orderly rows the cheerful pewter and scant earthenware of the household.

In Dutch households plate racks, spoon racks, knife racks—all hanging on the wall—took the place of the New England dresser.

In some houses, on each chimney piece were hooks to hang firearms, and at one side curious little drawers were set for pipes and tobacco. Hanging on a nail alongside the tobacco drawer, or shelf, would usually be seen a pipe tongs, or smoking tongs. They were slender little tongs, usually of iron or steel; with them the smoker lifted a coal from the fireplace to light his pipe. The tongs owned and used by Captain Joshua Wingate, of Hampton, New Hampshire, who lived from 1679 to 1769, had a handle unlike any other I have seen, having one end elongated, knobbed, and ingeniously bent S-shaped into convenient form to press down the tobacco into the bowl of the pipe. Some old-time pipe tongs were in the form of lazy tongs. A companion of the pipe tongs on the kitchen mantel was what was known as a comfortier—a little brazier of metal in which small coals could be handed about for pipe-lighting. An unusual luxury was a comfortier of silver. These were found among the Dutch settlers.

The Pennsylvania Germans were the first to use stoves. These were of various shapes. A curious one, seen in houses and churches, was of sheet metal, box shaped; three sides were within the house, and the fourth, with the stove door, outside the house. Thus what was really the back of the stove projected into the room, and when the fire was fed it was necessary for the tender to go out of doors. There is no doubt that their evident economy and comfort suggested to Benjamin Franklin the "New Pennsylvania Fireplace," which he invented in 1742, in which both wood and coal could be used and which was somewhat like the heating apparatus which we now call a Franklin stove, or heater.

Among the English settlers the kitchen was, too often, the only comfortable room in the house in winter weather. Indeed, the discomforts and inconveniences of a colonial home could scarcely be endured today; of course these culminated in the wintertime, when icy blasts blew fiercely down the great chimneys and rattled the loosely fitting windows. Children suffered bitterly in these cold houses. The rooms were not warm three feet away from the blaze of the fire. Cotton Mather and Judge Samuel Sewall both tell in their diaries of the ink freezing in their pens as they wrote within the chimney side. One noted that, when a great fire was built on the hearth, the sap forced out of the wood by the flames froze into ice at the end of the logs. The bedrooms were seldom warmed and, had it not been for the deep feather beds and heavy bed curtains, would have been unendurable. In Dutch and some German houses, with alcove bedsteads and sleeping on one feather bed with another for cover, the Dutch settlers could be far warmer than any English settlers, even in four-post bedsteads curtained with woolen.

Water froze immediately if left standing in bedrooms. President John Adams so dreaded the bleak New England winter and the ill-warmed houses that he longed to sleep like a dormouse every year, from autumn to spring. In the Southern colonies, during the fewer cold days of the winter months, the temperature was not so low, but the houses were more open and lightly built than in the North. They were without cellars and had fewer fireplaces; hence the discomfort from the cold was as great.

The first chilling entrance into the ice-cold bed of a winter bedroom was sometimes mitigated by heating the inner sheets with a warming pan. This usually hung by the side of the kitchen fireplace, and when used was filled with hot coals, thrust within the bed, and constantly and rapidly moved back and forth to keep from scorching the bed linen. The warming pan was a circular metal pan about a foot in diameter, four or five inches deep, with a long wooden handle and a perforated metal cover, usually of copper or brass, which was kept highly polished and formed, as it hung on the wall, one of the cheerful kitchen discs to reflect the light of the glowing fire.

Warming pan, late 18th century (The Newark Museum. Photograph by Alfred Tamarin)

Chapter IV

The Serving of Meals

The dining table of the colonists was a long, narrow board, sometimes but three feet wide with no legs attached to it. It was laid on supports or trestles, shaped usually something like a sawhorse. Thus it was literally a board, and was called a table-board, and the linen cover used at meals was not called a tablecloth, but a board-cloth or board-clothes.

As smoothly sawed and finished boards were

Wooden plate, about 1800; pewter knife and fork, early 19th century; and spoon, late 18th century (The Newark Museum. Photograph by Alfred Tamarin)

not so plentiful at first in the colonies, all such boards were carefully treasured, and used many times to avoid sawing others by the tedious and wearying process of pit sawing. Hence portions of packing boxes, or chests which had carried stores from England to the colonies, were made into table-boards.

The old-time board-cloth was in no way inferior in quality or whiteness to present table linen. The linen tablecloth was either of holland, huckaback, dowlas, osnaburg, or lockram—all heavy and comparatively coarse materials—or of fine damask, just as today; some of the handsome board-cloths were even trimmed with lace.

The colonists had plenty of napkins. They had

need of them, for when America was first settled forks were almost unknown to English people—being used for eating in luxurious Italy alone. So hands had to be constantly employed for holding food, instead of forks, and napkins were therefore as constantly necessary. The first fork brought to America was for Governor John Winthrop in Boston in 1633, and it was in a leather case with a knife and a bodkin. Thirty or forty years later a few two-tined iron and silver forks were brought across the water and used in New York and Virginia, as well as Massachusetts. The first mention of a fork in Virginia is in an inventory dated 1677. The salt cellar, or saler, as it was first called, was the centerpiece of the table. It was often large and high, of curious device in silver, and was then called a standing salt. Guests of honor were seated "above the salt," that is, near the end of the table where sat the host and hostess side by side; while children and ordinary guests were placed "below the salt," that is, below the middle of the table.

"A great silver salt" was given to Harvard University in 1644, when the new seat of learning was but eight years old. At the table it divided graduates, the faculty, and such, from the undergraduates. This rich gift was inscribed with the name of the giver, Mr. Richard Harris. Often salt cellars had a small projecting arm attached to one side, over which a folded napkin could be thrown to be used as a cover, not only to preserve cleanliness,

Silver salt, by Jacobus Vanderspiegel, about 1690 (The Brooklyn Museum)

but in earlier days to prevent the ready introduction of poison.

There are some very entertaining and curious old English books which were written in the sixteenth century to teach children correct and elegant manners at the table, as well as helpful ways to serve others. These books are called *The Babees Boke, The Boke of Nurture, The Boke of Curteseye,* etc. From them we learn that the only kind of table furnishings used at that time were cups to drink out of, spoons and knives to eat with, chafing dishes to serve hot food, chargers for display and for serving large quantities of food, salt cellars, and trenchers for use as plates.

One of the most important articles for setting the table was the trencher. These were made of wood, and often were only a block about ten or twelve inches square and three or four deep, hollowed down into a sort of bowl in the middle.

In this the food was placed—porridge, meat, vegetables, etc. Each person did not have even one of these simple dishes; usually two children, or a man and his wife, ate out of one trencher. This was a custom in England for many years. So great a warrior and so prominent a man in the Massachusetts Bay Colony as Miles Standish used wooden trenchers at the table, as also did all the early governors. For many years college boys at Harvard ate out of wooden trenchers at the college mess table.

I have seen a curious old table top, or tableboard, which permitted diners seated at it to dispense with trenchers or plates. It was of heavy oak about six inches thick, and at intervals of about eighteen inches around its edge were scooped out deep, bowl-shaped holes about ten inches in diameter in which each individual's share of the dinner was placed. After each meal the top was lifted off the trestles, thoroughly washed and dried, and was ready for the next meal.

Poplar wood is an even, white, and shining wood. Poplarwood trenchers and plates were used on the table and were really attractive dishes. From earliest days the Indians made and sold many bowls and trenchers of maplewood knots. Bottles were made also of wood, and drinking cups and "noggins," which were a sort of mug with a handle. Wood furnished many articles for the table to the colonist, just as it did in later days on our Western frontiers, where trenchers of wood and plates of birch bark were seen in every log cabin.

The word tankard was originally applied to a heavy and large vessel of wood banded with metal, in which to carry water. Smaller wooden drinking tankards were subsequently made and used throughout Europe, and were occasionally brought here by the colonists. Commonplace tankards of staves were not so rare as the beautiful carved and hooped tankards which were found in some homes.

The chargers, or large round platters found on every dining table, were of pewter. Some were so big and heavy that they weighed five or six pounds apiece. In colonial times what was called a garnish of pewter, that is, a full set of pewter platters, plates, and dishes, was the pride of every good housekeeper and also a favorite wedding gift. It was kept as bright and shining as silver. One of the duties of children was to gather a kind of horsetail rush which grew in the marshes and, because it was used to scour pewter, was called scouring rush.

Pewter bottles of various sizes were sent to the Massachusetts Bay Colony in 1629. Governor Endicott had one, but they were certainly far from common. Dram cups, wine mugs, and funnels of pewter were also occasionally seen but scarcely formed part of ordinary table furnishings. Metheglin cans and drinking mugs of pewter were found on nearly every table. Pewter was used in the wealthiest homes both in the North

Wooden tankard, 18th century (The Metropolitan Museum of Art, Gift of Mrs. Russell Sage, 1909)

Pewter porringer, 18th century (The Newark Museum. Photograph by Alfred Tamarin)

and South and was preferred by many who owned rich china. Among the pewter-lovers was the Revolutionary patriot John Hancock, who hated the clatter of the porcelain plates.

Porringers of pewter, and occasionally of silver, were much used at the table, chiefly for children to eat from. These were a pretty little shallow circular dish with a flat, pierced handle. Some had a "fishtail" handle and are said to be Dutch. These porringers were in many sizes, from tiny little ones two inches in diameter to those eight or nine inches across. When not in use many housekeepers kept them hanging on hooks on the edge of a shelf, where they formed a pretty and cheerful decoration.

The small porringers are sometimes called posnets, which is an old-fashioned word that may originally have referred to a posset cup.

All the colonists had spoons, and certainly all needed them, for at that time much of their food was in the form of soup and "spoon meat," such as had to be eaten with spoons when there were no forks. Meat was usually made into hashes or ragouts; thick stews and soups with chopped vegetables and meats were common, as were hotch pots. The cereal foods, which formed so large a part of English fare in the New World, were more frequently boiled in porridge than baked in loaves. Many of the spoons were of pewter. Worn-out pewter plates and dishes could be recast into new pewter spoons. The molds were of wood or iron.

Pewter spoons in rack, 1729 (The Newark Museum. Photograph by Alfred Tamarin)

A still more universal spoon material was alchymy, also called occamy, alcamy, arkamy, etc., a metal never used now, which was made of a mixture of pan brass and arsenicum. Wooden spoons, too, were always seen. In Pennsylvania and New York laurel was called spoonwood, because the Indians made pretty white spoons from that wood to sell to the colonists. Horn was an appropriate and available material for spoons. Many Indian tribes excelled in the making of horn spoons.

Every family of any considerable possessions or owning good household furnishings had a few silver spoons; nearly every person owned at least one. At the time America was settled the common form of silver spoon in England had what was known as a baluster stem and a seal head; the assay mark was in the inner part of the bowl. But the fashion was just changing, and a new and much altered form was introduced which was made in large numbers until the reign of George I. This shape was without a doubt the very one in which many of the spoons of the first colonists were made; and wherever such spoons are found, if they are genuine antiques, they may safely be assigned a date earlier than 1714. The handle was flat and broad at the end, where it was cleft in three points which were turned up, that is, not toward the back of the spoon. This was known as the "hind's-foot handle." The bowl was a perfectly regular ellipse and was strengthened by continuing the handle in a narrow tongue of rat-tail, which ran down the back of the bowl. The succeeding fashion, in the early part of the eighteenth century, had a longer elliptical bowl. The end of the handle was rounded and turned up at the end, and it had a high sharp ridge down the middle. This was known as the old English shape and was in common use for half a century. About the period of our Revolutionary War the bowl became egg-shaped and the end of the handle was turned down instead of up. The rattail, which extended down the back of the bowl, was shortened into a drop. Apostle spoons, and monkey spoons for extraordinary use were occasionally made, and a few are still preserved.

Silver tankard,
by Benjamin Burt, 1760
(The Metropolitan Museum of Art, Gift of Charles K. Davis, 1946)

Families of consequence had usually a few pieces of silver besides their spoons and the silver salt. Some kind of drinking cup was the usual form. Persons of moderate means often owned a silver cup. In early inventories and lists appear the names of a large variety of silver vessels: tankards, beer bowls, beakers, flagons, wine cups, wine bowls, wine cans, tasters, caudle cups, posset cups, dram cups, punch bowls, tumblers, mugs, dram bottles, two-eared cups and flasks. Virginians and Marylanders in the seventeenth century had much more silver than New Englanders. Some Dutch merchants had ample amounts. It was deemed a good and safe investment for spare money. Bread baskets, salvers, muffineers, chafing dishes, casters, milk pitchers, sugar boxes, candlesticks, appear in inventories at the end of the century. A tankard or flagon, even if heavy and handsome, would be placed on the table for everyday use; the other pieces were usually set on the cupboard's head for ornament.

There was a great desire for glass, a rare novelty to many persons at the date of colonization. The English were less familiar with its use than settlers who came from continental Europe. The establishment of glass factories was attempted in early days in several places, chiefly to manufacture sheet glass, but with slight success. Little glass was owned in the shape of drinking vessels, and probably none was used generally on the table during the first few years. Glass bottles were certainly a great rarity and were bequeathed with special mention in wills, and they are the only form of glass vessel named. The earliest glass for table use was greenish in color, like coarse bottle glass, and poor in quality, sometimes decorated in crude designs in a few colors. Bristol glass in the shape of mugs and plates was next seen. It was opaque, a milky white color, and was coarsely decorated with vitrifiable colors in a few lines of red, green, yellow, or black, occasionally with initials, dates, or scriptural references.

Though shapes were varied, and the number was generally plentiful, there was no attempt made to give separate drinking cups of any kind to each individual at the table. Blissfully ignorant of the existence of microbes, germs, and bacteria, our sturdy and unsqueamish forbears drank contentedly in succession from a single vessel, which was passed from hand to hand, and lip to lip, around the board. Even when tumbler-shaped glasses were seen in many houses—flipglasses, they were called—they were of communal size (some held a gallon) and all drank from the same glass. The great punch bowl, not a very easy vessel to handle when full, was passed up and down as freely as though it were a loving cup, and all drank from its brim. At college tables, and even at tavern boards, where table neighbors might be strangers, the flowing bowl and foaming tankard were passed serenely from one to another and replenished to pass again.

Leather was perhaps the most curious material used. Pitchers, bottles, and drinking cups were made of it. Great jugs of heavy black leather, waxed and bound, and tipped with silver, were used to hold metheglin, ale, and beer and were a very substantial, and at times a very handsome vessel. The use of great leather jacks led to the amusing belief that the English drank their ale out of their boots. These leather jugs were commonly called black jacks, and the larger ones were bombards. Giskin was still another and rarer name.

Drinking cups were sometimes made of horn. A handsome one used in colonial days on Long Island for "quince drink," a potent mixture of hot rum, sugar, and quince marmalade, or preserves, has a base of silver, a rim of silver, and a cover of horn tipped with silver. A stirrup cup of horn, tipped with silver, was used to "speed the parting guest." Occasionally the whole horn, in true mediaeval fashion, was used as a drinking cup. Often they were carved with considerable skill.

Gourds were plentiful on the farm and gathered with care so that the hard-shelled fruit might be shaped into simple drinking cups. Silver cups were made in the shape of these gourds. The ships that brought "lemmons and raysins of the sun" from the tropics to the colonists, also brought coconuts. Since the thirteenth century the shells of coconuts have been mounted with silver feet and "covercles" in a goblet shape and been much sought after by Englishmen. Mounted in pewter, and sometimes in silver, or simply shaped with a wooden handle attached, the shell of the coconut was a favorite among the English settlers.

Popular drinking mugs of the English from which they specially drank their mead, metheglin, and ale, were the stoneware jugs which were made in Germany and England in the sixteenth and seventeenth centuries in great numbers. An English writer in 1579 spoke of the English custom of drinking from "pots of earth, of sundry colors and moulds, whereof many are garnished with silver, or leastwise with pewter." Many Boston colonists had "stone juggs," "fflanders juggs," "tipt juggs." What were known as "Fulham juggs" were also much prized. The most interesting ones are the Georgius Rex jugs, those marked with a crown, the initials G. R., or a medallion head of the first of the English Georges. One of these jugs has a Revolutionary bullet imbedded in its tough old side and is not even cracked. Many of them had pewter or silver lids which are now missing. Some

Stoneware jug, by John Crolius, 1775 (The Metropolitan Museum of Art, Rogers Fund, 1934)

have the curious hound handle which was so popular with English potters.

There was no china in common use on the table and little was owned even by persons of wealth throughout the seventeenth century, either in England or America. Delft ware was made in several factories in Holland at the time the Dutch settled in New Netherland; but even in the towns of its manufacture it was not used for tableware. The pieces were usually of large size, what were called state pieces, for cabinet and decorative purposes. The Dutch settlers, however, had "purslin cupps" and earthen dishes in considerable quantities toward the end of the century. The earthen was possibly Delft ware, and the "Purslin" India china by that time was largely imported from Holland. Some Portuguese and Spanish pottery was imported but was not much desired, as it was ill fired and perishable. It was not until Revolutionary times that china was a common table furnishing; then it began to crowd out pewter. The sudden and enormous growth of East India commerce, and the vast cargoes of Chinese pottery and porcelain wares brought to American ports soon provided ample china for every housewife. In the Southern colonies beautiful isolated pieces of porcelain, such as vast punch bowls, often were found in the homes of opulent planters; but there, as in the North, the first china for general table use was the handleless tea cup, usually of some Canton ware.

A long narrow bench without a back, called a

form, was placed on each side of the table. Children in many households were not allowed to sit, even on these uncomfortable forms, while eating. Many times they had to stand by the side of the table during the entire meal. In some families children stood behind their parents and other grown persons, and food was handed back to them from the table. In other houses they stood at a side table and, trencher in hand, ran over to the great table to be helped to more food.

The chief thought on the behavior of children at the table, which must be inferred from all the accounts we have of those times, is that they were to eat in silence, as fast as possible (regardless of indigestion), and leave the table as speedily as might be.

It certainly conveys an idea of the demeanor of children of colonial days to read what was enjoined upon them in a little book of etiquette which was apparently widely circulated and doubtless carefully read. Instructions as to behavior at the table run thus:

"Never sit down at the table till asked, and after the blessing. Ask for nothing; tarry till it be offered thee. Speak not. Bite not thy bread but break it. Take salt only with a clean knife. Dip not the meat in the same. Hold not thy knife upright but sloping, and lay it down at right hand of plate with blade on plate. Look not earnestly at any other that is eating. When moderately satisfied leave the table. Sing not, hum not, wiggle not.

Spit no where in the room but in the corner. . . .

"Eat not too fast nor with Greedy Behavior. Eat not vastly but moderately. Make not a noise with thy Tongue, Mouth, Lips, or Breath in Thy Eating and Drinking. Smell not of thy Meat; nor put it to Thy Nose; turn it not the other side upward on Thy Plate."

A certain formality existed at the table of more fashionable folk. Children were given a few drops of wine in which to drink the health of their elders. In one family the formula was, "Health to papa and mamma, health to brothers and sisters, health to all my friends." In another, the father's health only was named. Sometimes the presence of grandparents at the table was the only occasion when children joined in health-drinking.

In Virginia the table furnishings were similar to those in New England, but there were greater contrasts in table appointments. There were more silver and richer food. When dinners of some state were given in the larger towns, the table was not set or served like the formal dinner of today, for all the sweets, pastry, vegetables, and meats were placed on the table together, with a grand decorative ornament in the center. At one period, when pudding was part of the dinner, it was served first. There was considerable formality in portioning out the food, especially in carving, which was regarded as much more than a polite accomplishment, even as an art. Carving had its own proper terms such as "break that Goose," "thrust that Chicken," "spoil that Hen," "pierce that Plover."

There were few state dinners, however, served in the American colonies, even in the large cities. There were even few dinners of many courses; not always were there many dishes. There were still seen in many homes primitive forms of serving and eating meals. In some homes an abundant dish, such as a vast bowl of suppawn and milk, a pumpkin stewed whole in its shell, or a savory and mammoth hotchpot was set on the table-board. From this well-filled receptacle each hungry soul, armed with a long-handled pewter or wooden spoon, helped himself, sometimes ladling his great spoonfuls into a trencher or bowl, just as frequently eating directly from the bountiful dish with a spoon that came and went from dish to mouth without reproach, or thought of ill manners.

By the time that newspapers began to carry advertisements—about 1750—we find many more articles for use at the table. Sugar bowls were called sugar boxes and sugar pots; milk pitchers were milk jugs, milk ewers, and milk pots. Vegetable dishes were called basins, pudding dishes twifflers, small cups were called sneak cups.

Near the close of the dinner, a deep wicker, wooden, or metal basket, called a voider, was passed around, and into it the persons at the table placed their trenchers, napkins, and the crumbs from the table.

Chapter V

Food and Drink

All the early explorers and travelers in America turned to the forests for food. Deer were plentiful everywhere, and venison was offered by the Indians to the first who landed from the ships. Some families lived wholly on venison for nine months of the year. In Virginia vast numbers of red and fallow deer were destroyed ruthlessly by a system of fire-hunting in which tracts of forests

Needlework picture, detail, about 1740 (The Metropolitan Museum of Art, Pulitzer Fund, 1939)

were burned over by starting a continuous circle of fire miles around, which burned in toward the center of the circle; thus the deer were driven into the middle and killed. This wholesale slaughter was not for venison, but for the sake of the valuable hides. They were used to make the durable and suitable buckskin breeches and jackets worn by the settlers; and they were also exported to Europe in large numbers. A tax was placed on hides for the support of William and Mary College.

In Georgia in 1735 the Indians sold a deer for sixpence. Deer were just as abundant in the more northern colonies. At Albany a stag was sold readily by the Indians for a jackknife or a few iron

Wild turkey, by John J. Audubon. From Birds of America, *1827–1838* (*The New-York Historical Society*)

nails. The deer in winter came and fed from the hog pens of Albany swine. Even in 1695, a quarter of venison could be bought in New York City for ninepence. At the first Thanksgiving, in 1621, the Indians brought in five deer to the colonists for their feast.

That year there was also "great store of wild turkies." These beautiful birds of gold and purple bronze were at first plentiful everywhere. They came in flocks of a hundred and they weighed thirty or forty pounds each.

Wild turkeys were caught in turkey pens, enclosures made of poles about twenty feet long, laid one above another, forming a solid wall ten feet high. This was covered with a close pole and brush roof. A ditch was dug beginning about fifteen feet away from the pen, sloping down and carried under one side of the pen and opening up into it through a board in which a hole was cut just large enough for a turkey to pass through. Corn was strewn the whole length of the ditch. The turkeys followed the ditch and the corn up through the hole into the pen, and held their heads too high ever to find their way out again. Often fifty captives would be found in the morning.

From Maine to Virginia vast flocks of pigeons were seen. Some years pigeons were so plentiful that they were sold for a penny a dozen in Boston.

Boys learned "to prate" for pigeons, that is, to imitate their call. This was useful in luring them within gun shot. A successful method of pigeon-shooting was learned from the Indians. A covert was made of green branches with an opening in the back by which the hunter could enter. In front of this covert, at firing distance, a long pole was raised up on two crotched sticks eight or ten feet from the ground, set so that a shot from the booth would rake the entire length of the pole; hence the crotch nearest the booth was a trifle lower than the other, at the same angle that the gun barrel would take.

To lure pigeons from a flock to settle on this pole, live pigeons were used as decoys. They were temporarily blinded in a cruel manner. A hole was pierced in the lower eyelid, a thread inserted, and the eyelid drawn up and tied over the eye. A loop was put over one leg and a fine cord tied to it. The pigeon called the long flyer had a long cord, and by his fluttering attracted pigeons from a flock. The short flyer with shorter cord lured pigeons flying low. The hoverer was tied close to the end of a small pole set on an upright post. This pole was worked by a string, and by moving the pigeon up and down it appeared to be hovering as if to alight. The hunter, loudly prating, sat hidden behind his three blind, fluttering, terrified decoys. Then came a beautiful flash and gleam of color and life and graceful motion, as with a swish of reversed wings a row of gentle creatures lighted on the fatal pole. In a second came the report of the gun, and the ground was covered with the fluttering, maimed, and dead bodies. Fifty-two at one shot were killed by a Lexington man named William Locke. Other methods of pigeon-killing were by snaring them in "twitch-ups"; also in a pigeon-bed, baited, over which a net was thrown on the feeding birds.

Pheasant, partridge, woodcock, and quail abounded; plover, snipe, and curlew were in the marsh woods. In fact, in Virginia every bird familiar to Englishmen was found except peacock and domestic fowl.

Wild hare and squirrels were so plentiful that they became pests, and so much grain was eaten by them that bounties were paid in many towns for the heads of squirrels.

In hunting and fishing colonial boys doubtless found one of their greatest amusements. But these sports were also hard work and were engaged in for profit as well as for pleasure. The scattered sheepfolds and grazing pastures at first had to be zealously guarded from wild animals; wolves were everywhere the most hated and most destructive beasts. They were caught in many ways—in wolf pits, in log pens, in log traps. Heavy mackerel hooks were tied together, dipped in melted tallow, which hardened in a bunch and concealed the hooks, and tied to a strong chain. If the wolf swallowed the hooks without any chain attached, it would kill him, but he might die in the depths of the forest and his head could not be brought in to secure the bounty. In old town lists are the names of many boys with "wolf-money set to their credit."

A wolf rout or wolf drive, which was like the old English "drift of the forest," was a ring of men and boys armed with guns surrounding a large tract of forest. The wary wolves scented their enemies afar and retreated before them to the center of a circle, and many were killed. Squirrels and hares were hunted in the same way. Once a year in many places they had shooting matches in which every living wild creature was prey, and a prize was given to the one bringing in the most birds' heads and animals' tails. From the woods came a sweet food store, one specially prized because sugar was so scarce—wild honey, which the colonists eagerly gathered everywhere from hollow tree trunks. Curiously enough, it was claimed that bees were not native in America, but were brought over by the English; that the Indians had no name for them and called them English flies.

Governor Berkeley of Virginia, writing in 1706, called the maple the sugar tree. He said:

"The Sugar-Tree yields a kind of Sap or Juice which by boiling is made into Sugar. This juice is drawn out, by wounding the Trunk of the Tree, and placing a Receiver under the Wound. It is said that the Indians make one Pound of Sugar out of eight Pounds of the Liquor. It is bright and moist with a full large Grain."

The sugar-making season was hailed with delight in colonial days for it gave men and boys a chance to spend several nights a-gypsying in the woods. The maple trees were tapped as soon as the sap began to run in the trunk and showed at the end of the twigs; this was in late winter if mild, or in the earliest spring. A notch was cut in the trunk of the tree at a convenient height from the ground, usually four or five feet, and the running sap was guided by setting in the notch a semicircular basswood spout cut and set with a special tool called a tapping gauge. In earlier days the trees were "boxed," that is, a great gash cut across the side and scooped out and down to gather the sap. This often proved fatal to the trees and was abandoned. A trough, usually made of a butternut log about three feet long, was dug out, Indian fashion, and placed under the end of the spout. These troughs were made deep enough to hold about ten quarts. In later years a hole was bored in the tree with an augur; and sap buckets were used instead of troughs.

Sometimes these troughs were left in distant sugar camps from year to year, turned bottom side up, through the summer and winter. It was more thrifty and tidy, however, to carry them home and store them. When this was done, the men and boys began work by drawing the troughs and spouts and provisions to the woods on hand sleds. Sometimes a mighty man took in a load on his back.

Maple sugar mold,
19th century
(The Newark Museum.
Photograph by Alfred Tamarin)

The owner of the camp selected the trees and drove the spouts, while the boys placed the troughs. Then the snow had to be shoveled away on a level spot about eighteen or twenty feet square in which strong forked sticks were set twelve feet apart. Or the ground was chosen so that two small low-spreading and strong trees could be trimmed and used as forks. A heavy green stick was placed across from fork to fork, and the sugaring-off kettles, sometimes five in number, hung on it. Then dry wood had to be gathered for the fires. As the sap collected in the troughs it was gathered in pails or buckets which, hung on a sap-yoke across the neck, were brought to the kettles and the sap set a-boiling down. When there was a "good run of sap," it was usually necessary to stay in the camp overnight. Many times the campers stayed several nights. As the "good run" meant milder weather, a night or two was not a bitter experience.

If the camp were near enough to any group of farmhouses to have visitors, the last afternoon and evening in camp was made a country frolic. Great sled-loads of girls came out to taste the new sugar, to drop it into the snow to candy, and to have an evening of fun.

Long before the full riches of the forests were tested the colonists turned to another food supply —the sea.

The early voyagers and colonists came to the New World to find gold and furs. The gold was not found by them nor their children's children in the land which is now the United States till over two centuries had passed and the gold mines of California were opened. The furs were at first found and profitably gathered, but the timid fur-bearing animals were soon exterminated near the settlements. There was, however, a vast wealth ready for the colonists on the coast of the New World which was greater than gold, greater than furs; it was *fish.* The sea, the rivers, the lakes teemed with fish. Not only was there food for the settlers, but for the whole world, and all Europe desired fish to eat. Captain John Smith, the explorer, famous in history as the friend of Pocahontas, went to New England in 1614 to search for whale, and instead he fished for cod. He secured sixty thousand in one month, and he wrote to his countrymen, "Let not the meanness of the word *fish* distaste you, for it will afford as good gold as the mines of Guiana or Potosi, with less hazard and charge, and more certainty and facility." This promise of wealth has proved true a thousandfold. Smith wrote home to England full accounts of the fisheries, of the proper equipment of a fishing vessel, of the methods of fishing, the profits, all in a most enticing and familiar style. He said in his *Description of New England:*

"What pleasure can be more than to recreate themselves before their owne doores in their owne boates, upon the Sea, where man, woman, and childe, with a small hooke and line by angling, may take diverse sorts of excellent fish, at their pleasure? And is it not pretty sport to pull up twopence, sixpence, or twelvepence, as fast as you can hale and veare a line? If a man worke but three days in seaven hee may get more than hee can spend unless hee will be excessive."

His accounts and similar ones were so much read in England that when the Puritans asked King James of England for permission to come to America, and the king asked what profit would be found by their emigration, he was at once answered, "Fishing." Whereupon he said in turn, "In truth 'tis an honest trade; 'twas the apostles' own calling." Yet in spite of their intent to fish, the first English ships came but poorly provided for fishing, and the settlers had little success at first even in getting fish for their own food. Elder Brewster of Plymouth, who had been a courtier in Queen Elizabeth's time and had seen and eaten many rich feasts, had nothing to eat at one time but clams. Yet he could give thanks to God that he was "permitted to suck of the abundance of the seas and the treasures hid in the sand." The Indian Squanto showed the Pilgrims many practical methods of fishing, among them one of treading out eels from the brook with his feet and catching them with his hands. And every ship brought in either cod hooks and lines, mackerel hooks and lines, herring nets, seines, shark hooks, bass nets, squid lines, eel pots, coils of rope and cable, "drails, barbels, pens, gaffs," or mussel hooks.

Over two hundred kinds of fish were caught in New England waters. Lobsters were plentiful enough to prevent starvation. At Salem, many of them weighed twenty-five pounds apiece. In 1623, when the ship *Anne* arrived from England bringing many of the wives and children of the Pilgrims who had come in the first ships, the only feast of welcome that the poor husbands had to offer the newcomers was "a lobster or a piece of fish without bread or anything else but a cup of spring water." Patriarchal lobsters five and six feet long were caught in New York Bay. In Virginia waters lobsters were caught, and vast crabs, often a foot in length and six inches broad, with a long tail and many legs. One of these crabs furnished a sufficient meal for four men.

Strachey, in his *Historie of Travaile into Virginia,* says he saw oysters in Virginia that were thirteen inches long. Fortunately for the starving Virginians, oyster banks rose above the surface at ebb tide at the mouth of the Elizabeth River, and in 1609 a large number of these famished Virginia colonists found in these oyster banks a means of preservation of life.

As might be expected of any country so intersected with arms of the sea and fresh-water streams, Virginia at the time of settlement teemed with fish. The Indians killed them in the brooks by striking them with sticks, and it is said the colonists scooped them up in frying pans. Horses ridden into the rivers stepped on the fish and killed them.

The New York rivers and bays were also full of fish; among them sturgeon, beloved of the Indians and despised of Christians, and terrapin, not despised by anyone.

While other fish were used everywhere for

food, cod was the great staple of the fishing industry. By 1633 Dorchester and Marblehead had started fisheries for trading purposes. Sturgeon also was caught at a little later date, also bass and alewives.

The regulation of fish weirs or traps soon became an important matter in all towns where streams let alewives up from the sea. The New England ministers took a hand in promoting and encouraging the fisheries. Fishermen were excused from military training, and portions of the common stock of corn were assigned to them. The General Court of Massachusetts exempted "vessels and stock" from "country charges" (which were taxes) for seven years. Seashore towns assigned free lands to each boat to be used for stays and flakes for drying. As early as 1640 three hundred thousand dried codfish were sent to market from New England.

Codfish consisted of three sorts, "marchantable, middling, and refuse." The first grade was sold chiefly to Roman Catholic Europe, to supply the constant demands of the fast days of that religion, and also those of the Church of England; the second was consumed at home or in the merchant vessels of New England; the third went to the West Indies and was often called Jamaica fish. The dun-fish or dumb-fish, as the word was sometimes written, were the best; so called from the dun color. Fish was always eaten in New England for a Saturday dinner, which was considered not complete without dun-fish being served.

Of course the first fishing vessels had to be

built and sent from England. Some carried fifty men. They arrived on the coast in early spring, and by midsummer sailed home. The crew had for wages one-third share of the fish and oil; another third paid for the men's food, the salt, nets, hooks, lines, etc.; the other third went to the ship's owners. This system was not carried out in New England. There, each fisherman worked on "his own hook"—and it was literally his own hook. A tally was kept of the fish caught by each man, and the proceeds of the trip were divided in proportion to the number of fish each caught. When there was a big run of fish, the men never stopped to eat or sleep, but when food was held to them gnawed it off while their hands were employed with the fish lines. With every fishing vessel that left Gloucester and Marblehead, the chief centers of the fishing industries, went a boy of ten or twelve to learn to be a skilled fisherman. He was called a "cut-tail," for he cut a wedge-shaped bit from the tail of every fish he caught, and when the fish were sorted out the cut tails showed the boy's share of the profit.

For centuries, fish was plentiful and cheap in New England. The price of salmon was less than a penny a pound and shows the low estimation in which it was held in the early years of the eighteenth century.

Shad were profoundly despised; it was even held to be somewhat disreputable to eat them. The story is told of a family in Hadley, Massachusetts, who were about to dine on shad, that, hearing a knock at the door, would not open it till the platter holding the obnoxious shad had been hidden. At first shad was fed chiefly to hogs. Two shad for a penny was the ignoble price in 1733, and it was never much higher until after the Revolution. After shad and salmon acquired a better reputation as food, the falls of various rivers became great resorts for American fishermen as they had been for the Indians. Both kinds of fish were caught in scoop nets and seines below the falls. Men came from a distance and loaded horses and carts with the fish to carry home.

Salted fish was carefully prepared and amiably regarded in New England and New York. The ling and herring of the old countries of Europe gave place in America to cod, shad, and mackerel. The greatest pains were taken in preparing, drying, and salting the plentiful fish.

Near the waters were the magnificent tribes of marine fowl that had peopled for centuries the waters of the New World. The Chesapeake and its tributaries furnished each autumn vast feeding grounds of wild celery and other aquatic plants to millions of birds. The firearms of Captain John Smith and his two companions were poor things compared with those of today, but with their three shots they killed a hundred and forty-eight ducks at one firing. The splendid wild swan wheeled and trumpeted in the clear autumn air; the wild geese flew there in their beautiful V-shaped flight; duck in all the varieties known to modern sportsmen—canvasback, mallard, widgeon, redhead, oxeye, dottrel—rested on the Chesapeake waters in vast flocks a mile wide and seven miles long. Governor

Corn pestle, about 1800
(The Staten Island Historical Society. Photograph by Alfred Tamarin)

Berkeley named also brant, shell drake, teal, and blewings. The sound of their wings was said to be "like a great storm coming over the water."

Indian corn was a native of American soil at the settlement of this country and under full cultivation by the Indians. Its abundance, adaptability, and nourishing qualities not only saved the colonists' lives, but altered many of their methods of living, especially their manner of cooking and their tastes in food.

One of the first things that every settler in a new land has to learn is that he must find food in that land; that he cannot trust long to any supplies of food which he has brought with him, or to any fresh supplies which he has ordered to be sent after him. He must turn at once to hunting, fishing, and planting to furnish him with food. This was quickly learned by the colonists in America except in Virginia, where they had sad starving times before all were convinced that corn was a better crop for settlers than silk or any other which could not be eaten. Powhatan, the father of the Indian princess Pocahontas, was one of the first to "send some of his People that they may teach the English how to sow the Grain of his Country." In 1608 Captain John Smith, ever quick to learn, got two Indians to show him how to break up and plant forty acres of corn, which yielded him a good crop. A succeeding governor of Virginia, Sir Thomas Dale, assigned small farms to each colonist and encouraged and enforced the growing of corn. Soon many thousand bushels were raised. There was a terrible Indian massacre in 1622, for the careless colonists, in order to be free to give their time to the raising of that new and exceedingly alluring and high-priced crop, tobacco, had given the Indians firearms to go hunting game for them. The lesson of easy killing with powder and shot, when once learned, was turned with havoc upon the white men. The following year comparatively little corn was planted, as the luxuriant foliage made a perfect ambush for the Indians. There was, of course, scarcity and famine as the result; and a bushel of corn meal became worth twenty to thirty shillings. The planters were each compelled by the magistrates the following year to raise an ample amount of corn to supply all the families, and to save a certain amount for seed as well. There has been no lack of corn since that time in Virginia.

The stores brought over by the Pilgrims were poor and inadequate enough; the beef and pork were tainted, the fish rotten, the butter and cheese corrupted. European wheat and seeds did not mature well. Soon, as Governor Bradford says in his now famous *Log-Book* "the grim and grizzled face of starvation stared" at them. The readiest supply to replenish the scanty larder was fish, but the English made surprisingly bungling work over fishing, and soon the most unfailing and valuable supply was the native Indian corn, or "Guinny wheat," or "Turkie wheat," as it was called by the colonists.

Famine and pestilence had left eastern Massachusetts comparatively bare of inhabitants at the time of the settlement of Plymouth; and the vacant cornfields of the dead Indian cultivators were taken and planted by the weak and emaciated Plymouth men, who never could have cleared new fields. From the teeming sea, in the April run of fish, was found the needed fertilizer. From this planting sprang not only the most useful food, but the first and most pregnant industry of the colonists.

The first fields and crops were communal, and the result was disastrous. The third year, at the sight of the paralyzed settlement, Governor Bradford wisely decided, as did Governor Dale of Virginia, that "they should set corne every man for his owne particuler, furnishing a portion for public officers, fishermen, etc., who could not work, and in that regard trust to themselves." Thus personal energy succeeded communal inertia; Bradford wrote that women and children cheerfully worked in the fields to raise corn which should be their very own.

The Indians taught the colonists much more than the planting and raising of corn; they showed them also how to grind the corn and cook it in many palatable ways. The various foods made from Indian corn are still called with Indian names, such as hominy, pone, suppawn, samp, succotash. These cereal foods were found in every home in every colony and were a suitable diet for young children.

The Indian method of preparing maize or corn

was to steep or parboil it in hot water for twelve hours, then to pound the grain in a mortar or a hollowed stone in the field till it was a coarse meal. It was then sifted in a rather closely woven basket, and the large grains which did not pass through the sieve were again pounded and sifted.

Samp and samp porridge were soon abundant dishes. Samp is Indian corn pounded to a coarsely ground powder. It was often pounded in olden times in a primitive and picturesque Indian mortar made of a hollowed block of wood or a stump of a tree which had been cut off about three feet from the ground. The pestle was a heavy block of wood shaped like the inside of the mortar and fitted with a handle attached to one side. This block was fastened to the top of a young and slender tree which was bent over and thus gave a sort of spring which pulled the pestle up after being pounded down on the corn. This was called a sweep and mortar mill. They could be heard at a long distance.

Two New Hampshire pioneers made clearings about a quarter of a mile apart and built houses. There was an impenetrable gully and thick woods between the cabins. The blazed path was a long distance around, so the wives of the settlers seldom saw each other. It was a source of great comfort and companionship to them both that they could signal to each other every day by pounding on their mortars. And they had an ingenious system of communication which one spring morning summoned one to the home of the other,

"The Miller" from Little Jack of All Trades, *1813* (*Old Sturbridge Village*)

where she arrived in time to be the first to welcome fine twin babies.

After these simple stump and sapling mortars were abandoned elsewhere they were used on Long Island, and it was jestingly told that sailors in a fog could always know on what shore they were, when they could hear the poundings of the samp mortars on Long Island.

Crude hand mills, called quernes, or quarnes, next were used. Some are known as samp mills. Windmills followed of which the Indians were much afraid, dreading "their long arms and great teeth biting the corn in pieces" and thinking some evil spirit turned the arms.

The first windmill erected in America was one built and set up by Governor Yeardley in Virginia in 1621. Millers had one-sixth of the meal they ground for toll.

Suppawn was another favorite of the settlers, and was an Indian dish made from Indian corn; it was a thick corn meal and milk porridge. It was soon seen on every Dutch table; for the Dutch were very fond of all foods made from all kinds of grain, and it is spoken of by all travelers in early New York.

The Swedish scientist Professor Kalm told that the Indians gave him "fresh maize-bread, baked in an oblong shape, mixed with dried huckleberries, which lay as close in it as raisins in a plum pudding."

Roger Williams said that "sukquttahhash" was "corn seethed like beans." "Succotash" we now apply to corn cooked with beans. Pones were the red men's appones.

The love of the Indians for "roasting ears" was quickly shared by the white man. In Virginia a series of plantings of corn were made from the first of April to the last of June to afford a three months' succession of roasting ears.

It seemed very curious to read in Governor Winthrop's journal, written in Boston about 1630, that when corn was "parched," as he called it, it turned inside out and was "white and floury within"; and to think that then little English children were just learning what popcorn was.

Hasty pudding had been made in England of wheat flour or oatmeal and milk, and the name was given to boiled puddings of corn meal and water. It was not a very suitable name, for corn meal should never be cooked hastily but requires long boiling or baking. The hard Indian pudding slightly sweetened and boiled in a bag was everywhere made.

There was one way of eating corn which shows

us how useful and necessary corn was, and how much all depended on it. This preparation of corn was called nocake or nookick. An old writer named Wood thus defined it:

"It is Indian corn parched in the hot ashes, the ashes being sifted from it; it is afterwards beaten to powder and put into a long leatherne bag trussed at the Indian's backe like a knapsacke, out of which they take three spoonsful a day."

It was held to be the most nourishing food known and in the smallest and most condensed form. Both Indians and white men usually carried it in a pouch when they went on long journeys and mixed it with snow in the winter and water in summer. It was sweet, toothsome, and hearty. With only this nourishment the Indians could carry loads "fitter for elephants than men." So it is not surprising that the Pilgrims could keep alive on what is said was at one time of famine their food for a day—five kernels of corn apiece.

We may be sure the colonial councils thought corn of value when they took it for taxes, made it legal currency just like gold and silver, and forbade anyone to feed it to pigs.

There are many other interesting facts connected with the early culture of corn: finding hidden in caves or "caches" in the ground the Indian's corn which he had stored for seed; the sacred "corn-dances" of the Indians; that the first patent granted in England to an American was to a Philadelphia woman for a mill to grind a kind of hominy; of the great profit to the colonists in corn raising, for the careless Indians always ate up all their corn as soon as possible, then had to go out and trap beavers in the woods to sell the skins to the colonists for corn· to keep them from starving.

Many games were played with the aid of kernels or corn: fox and geese, checkers, "hull gull, how many," and games in which the corn served as counters. One of the few scenes of gaiety in the lives of the colonists was the corn harvest.

Some of the preparation of corn fell upon the boys; it was their regular work all winter in the evening firelight to shell corn from the ears by scraping them on the iron edge of the wooden shovel or on the fire peel. Many families of moderate means fastened the long-handled frying pan across a tub and drew the corn ears across the sharp edge of the handle of the pan. Other farmers set the edge of a knife blade in a piece of wood and scraped on the back of the blade. In some households the corn was pounded into hominy in wooden mortars.

When the corn was shelled, the cobs were not carelessly discarded or disregarded. They were stored often in a lean-to or loft in the kitchen ell; from thence they were brought down in skepes or boxes about a bushel at a time; and after being used by the children as playthings to build "cob houses," were employed as light wood for the fire. They had a special use in many households for smoking hams, and their smoke was deemed to impart a specially delightful flavor to hams and bacon.

One special use of corn should be noted. By order of the government of Massachusetts Bay in 1623, it was used as ballots in public voting. At annual elections of the governors' assistants in each town, a kernel of corn was deposited to signify a favorable vote upon the nominee, while a bean signified a negative vote; "and if any freeman shall put in more than one Indian corn or bean he shall forfeit for every such offence Ten Pounds."

The food brought in ships from Europe to the colonies was limited by the imperfect methods of transportation which then existed. Nothing like refrigerators were known; no tinned foods were even thought of. The settlers turned at once to the food supplies found in the new home. In addition to corn, fish, and game, there were many other bountiful and good foods, among them pumpkins, or pompions, as they were first called.

The pumpkin has sturdily kept its own place on the New England farm, varying in popularity and use, but always of value as easy to grow, easy to cook, and easy to keep in a dried form. Yet the colonists did not welcome the pumpkin with eagerness, even in times of great want. Stewed pumpkins and pumpkin bread were coarse ways of using the fruit for food. Pumpkin bread—made of half Indian meal—was not very pleasing in appearance. The Indians dried pumpkins and strung them for winter use, and the colonists fol-

Potato boiler, mid 19th century (The Staten Island Historical Society. Photograph by Alfred Tamarin)

lowed the Indian custom. In Virginia, Indians boiled beans, peas, corn, and pumpkins together, and the colonists liked the dish. In the trying times at "James-Citty," the plentiful pumpkins played a great part in providing food supplies for the starving Virginians.

Squashes were also native vegetables. The name is Indian, which the English spelled in wonderful and varied ways; for example "askutasquashes," "squantersquashes," "squontorsquashes," and "isquoukersquashes."

Potatoes were known to New Englanders, but were rare and when referred to were probably sweet potatoes. It was a long time before potatoes were much liked. It was believed by many persons that if a man ate them every day, he could not live seven years. In the spring all that were left on hand were carefully burned, for many believed that if cattle or horses ate these potatoes they would die. They were first called, when carried to England, Virginia potatoes; then they became much liked and grown in Ireland; then the Irish settlers in New Hampshire brought them back to this continent, and now they are called, very senselessly, Irish potatoes. Many persons fancied the balls were what should be eaten, and said they "did not much desire them." A fashionable way of cooking them was with butter, sugar, and grape juice; this was mixed with dates, lemons, and mace; seasoned with cinnamon, nutmeg, and pepper; then covered with a frosting of sugar—and you had to hunt well to find the potato.

In the Carolinas the change in English diet was effected by the sweet potato. This root was cooked in various ways: it was roasted in the ashes, boiled, made into puddings, used as a substitute for bread, made into pancakes which a foreigner said tasted as though composed of sweet almonds, and was so plentiful that even the slaves fed upon it.

Beans were abundant, and were baked by the Indians in earthen pots just as we bake them today. The settlers planted peas, parsnips, turnips, and carrots, which grew and thrived. Huckleberries, blackberries, strawberries, and grapes grew wild. Apple trees were planted at once and grew well in New England and the Middle states. Twenty years after the Roman Catholic settlement of Maryland the fruitful orchards were conspicuously flourishing.

In 1634 everybody in New England could have apple, pear, and quince tarts instead of pumpkin pies. They made apple slump, apple mose, apple crowdy, apple tarts, mess apple pies, and puff apple pies. A Swedish parson, writing home in 1758 an account of the settlement of Delaware, said:

"Apple-pie is used through the whole year, and when fresh apples are no longer to be had, dried ones are used. It is the evening meal of children. House-pie, in country places, is made of apples neither peeled nor freed from their cores, and its crust is not broken if a wagon wheel goes over it."

The making of a portion of the autumn's crop of apples into dried apples, applesauce, and apple butter for winter was preceded in many country homes by an apple paring. The apples intended for drying were strung on linen thread and hung on the kitchen and attic rafters. The following day the stout crane in the open fireplace was hung with brass kettles which were filled with the pared apples, sweet and sour in proper proportions, the sour at the bottom since they required more time to cook. If quinces could be had, they were added to give flavor, and molasses or boiled-down pungent "apple molasses" was added for sweetening. As there was danger that the sauce would burn over the roaring logs, many housewives placed clean straw at the bottom of the kettle to keep the apples from the fiercest heat. Days were spent in preparing the winter's stock of applesauce, but when done and placed in barrels in the cellar, it was always ready for use, and when slightly frozen was a keen relish. Apple butter was made of the pared apples boiled down with cider.

Wheat did not at first ripen well, so white bread was for a time rarely eaten. Rye grew better, so bread made of "rye-an'-injun," which was half rye meal, half corn meal, was used instead. Bake shops were so many in number in all the towns that it is evident that housewives in towns and villages did not make bread in every home but bought it at the baker's.

At the time when America was settled, no European peoples drank water for a constant beverage. The English drank ale, the Dutch beer, the French and Spanish light wines, for everyday use. Hence it seemed to the colonists a great trial and even a very dangerous experiment to drink water in the New World. They were forced to do it, however, in many cases; and to their surprise found that it agreed with them very well and that their health improved.

As cows increased in number and were cared for, milk of course was added to the everyday fare. In 1630 milk cost in Salem but a penny a quart. Milk became a very important part of the food of families in the eighteenth century. In 1728 a discussion took place in the Boston newspapers as to the expense of keeping a family "of middling figure." These writers all named only bread and milk for breakfast and supper. Milk and hasty pudding, milk and stewed pumpkin, milk and baked apples, milk and berries, were variations. In winter, when milk was scarce, sweetened cider diluted with water was used instead. Sometimes bread was soaked with this mixture. It is said that children were usually very fond of it.

Comparatively few New England families in the seventeenth century owned churns; of course families of wealth ate butter, but it was not common. Butter was worth from threepence to sixpence a pound. As cattle increased the duties of the dairy grew. The care of cream and making of butter was in the eighteenth century the duty of every good wife and dame in the country, and usually in the town.

Wooden churn, 18th century (The Metropolitan Museum of Art, Gift of Mrs. Russell Sage, 1909)

Cheese was plentiful and good in all the Northern colonies. It was also an unending care from the time the milk was set over the fire to warm and then to curdle; through the breaking of the curds in the cheese basket; through shaping into cheeses and pressing in the cheese press, placing them on the cheese ladders, and constantly turning and rubbing them.

The manuscript cooking recipe-book of many an ancient dame shows the great care she took in family cooking. English methods of cooking at the time of the settlement of this country were very complicated and laborious. It was a day of hashes, ragouts, soups, hotchpots, etc. In almost every sixteenth century recipe for cooking meat, appear some such directions as these: "Y-mynce it, smyte them on gobbets, hew them on gobbets, chop on gobbets, hew small, dyce them, skern them to dyce, kerf it to dyce, grind all to dust,

Cheese press, early 19th century (The Staten Island Historical Society. Photograph by Alfred Tamarin)

smyte on peces, parcel-hem; hew small on morselyen, hack them small, cut them on culpons." Great amounts of spices were used, even perfumes; and as there was no preservation of meat by ice, perhaps the spices and perfumes were necessary.

Of course the colonists were forced to adopt simple ways of cooking, but as towns and commerce increased there were many kitchen duties which made much tedious work. Many pickles, spiced fruits, preserves, candied fruits and flowers, and marmalades were made.

Preserving was a very different art from canning fruit today. There were no hermetically sealed jars, no chemical methods, no quick work about it. Vast jars were filled with preserves so rich that there was no need of keeping the air from them; they could be opened, that is, the paper cover taken off, and used as desired; there was no fear of fermentation, souring, or molding.

The housewives pickled samphire, fennel, purple cabbage, nasturtium buds, green walnuts, lemons, radish pods, barberries, elder buds, parsley, mushrooms, asparagus, and many kinds of fish and fruit. They candied fruits and nuts, made many marmalades and quiddonies, and a vast number of fruit wines and cordials. Even their cakes, pies, and puddings were most complicated, and humble households were lavish in the various kinds they manufactured and ate.

They collared and potted many kinds of fish and game, and they salted and soused. Salted meat was eaten, and very little fresh meat; for there were no means of keeping meat after it was killed. Every well-to-do family had a "powdering tub," in which meat was "powdered," that is, salted and pickled. Many families had a smokehouse, in which beef, ham, and bacon were smoked.

Perhaps the busiest month of the year was November—called "killing time." When the chosen day arrived, oxen, cows, and swine which had been fattened for the winter's stock were slaughtered early in the morning, that the meat might be hard and cold before being put in the pickle. Sausages, rolliches, and headcheese were made, lard tried out, and tallow saved.

A curious and quaint domestic implement or utensil found hanging on the walls of some kitchens was what was known as a sausage gun. The sausage meat was forced out through the nozzle into the sausage cases. A simpler form of sausage stuffer has also been seen, much like a tube-and-piston garden syringe; though it is possible that the latter utensil was really a syringe gun, such as

Sausage gun, 19th century
(The New-York Historical Society.
Photograph by Alfred Tamarin)

once was used to disable hummingbirds by squirting water upon them.

Sausage meat was thus prepared in New York farmhouses. The meat was cut coarsely into half-inch pieces and thrown into wooden boxes about three feet long and ten inches deep. Then its first chopping was by men using spades which had been ground to a sharp edge.

There were many families that found all their supply of sweetening in maple sugar and honey; but housewives of dignity and elegance desired to have some supply of sugar, certainly to offer visitors for their dish of tea. This sugar was always loaf sugar, and truly loaf sugar; for it was purchased in great loaves or cones which averaged in weight about nine to ten pounds apiece. One cone would last thrifty folk for a year. This pure clear sugar cone always came wrapped in a deep blue-purple paper, of such unusual and beautiful tint and so color laden that in country homes it was carefully saved and soaked to supply a dye for a small amount of the finest wool. The cutting of this cone of sugar into lumps of equal size and regular shape was distinctly the work of the mistress and daughters of the house. It was too exact and too dainty a piece of work to be entrusted to clumsy or wasteful servants. Various simply shaped sugar shears or sugar cutters were used.

Sweetmeats for the enticement of children consisted of "Sucket, Surrip, Grene Ginger, and Marmalade, Bisket, Cumfet, and Carraways as fine as can be made." A sucket was dried sweetmeat such as candied orange peel. A caraway was a sweet cake with caraway seeds. Apples and caraways were a favorite dish. Comfits were highly flavored, often scented with strong perfumes like musk and bergamot.

Sweetmeats appear to have been plentiful in the colonies from early days. Ships in the "Indian trade" brought to the colonies abundance of sugar, molasses, chocolate, ginger, and other dried fruits. These were apparently far more common here than in England. Candied eringo root, candied lemon peel, angelica candy, as well as caraway comfits and sugared coriander seed and dried ginger were advertised for sale in Boston and show

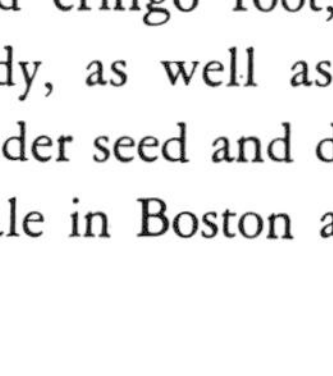

Sugar loaf and cutters, late 18th–early 19th century (The Newark Museum. Photograph by Alfred Tamarin)

the taste of the day. In 1731 a notice in the *Boston News Letter* listed meat jellies for the sick, and homemade preserves, jellies, and syrups, as well as those ancient sweets, macaroons, marchpanes, and crisp almonds. These last do not appear to be the glazed and burnt almonds of the confectioner and may have been salted almonds. Raisins were brought into all the colonial ports in vast amounts and were regarded by children as a great dainty.

Each large city seems to have had some special confectioner or baker who was renowned for special cakes. Boston had Meer's cakes. New York children probably had the greatest variety of cookies, crullers, and various small cakes, as these were distinctly Dutch, and the Dutch vrouws excelled in cake-making.

Strings of rock candy came from China but were rivaled by a distinctly native sweet—maple sugar. Equally American appear to us those Salem sweets, namely, Black Jacks and Salem Gibraltars. Base imitations appeared elsewhere but never equaled the original delights in Salem. Children who were fortunate enough to live in coast towns reaped the sweet fruits of their fathers' foreign ventures. The ship that brought eighty boxes of sugar candy also fetched a hundred boxes of rhubarb and ten of senna.

All the spices used in the household were ground at home, in spice mortars and spice mills. These were of various sizes, including the pepper mills, which were set on the table at mealtimes,

Silver sugar box, by Daniel Greenough, about 1715 (The Metropolitan Museum of Art, Rogers Fund, 1946)

and the tiny ornamental graters which were carried in the pocket.

The entire food of a household could be produced on a farm. But farm food was not varied, for articles of luxury had to be imported. The products of tropical countries, such as sugar, molasses, tea, coffee, spices, found poor substitutes in home food products. Dried pumpkin was a poor sweetening instead of molasses; maple sugar and honey were not esteemed as was sugar; tea was ill replaced by raspberry leaves, loosestrife, hardhack, goldenrod, dittany, blackberry leaves, yeopon, sage, and a score of other herbs; coffee was better than parched rye and chestnuts; spices could not be compensated for or remotely imitated by any substitutes.

So though there was ample quality of food, the quality, save in the town, was not such as English housewives had been accustomed to; there were many deprivations in their kitchens which tried them sorely. The better cooks they were, the more trying were the limitations.

As years passed on and great wealth came to individuals, the tables of the opulent, especially in the Middle colonies, rivaled the luxury of English and French houses of wealth. It is surprising to read about a dinner in New York in 1787, at which fifteen kinds of wine were served besides cider, beer, and porter.

John Adams probably lived as well as any New

Englander of similar position and means. A Sunday dinner at his house was thus described by a visitor: the first course was a pudding of Indian meal, molasses, and butter; then came a course of veal and bacon, neck of mutton, and vegetables.

The Dutch were great beer drinkers and quickly established breweries at Albany and New York. But before the century had ended New Englanders had abandoned the constant drinking of ale and beer for cider. Cider was very cheap; but a few shillings a barrel. It was supplied in large amounts to students at college, and even very little children drank it. President John Adams was an early and earnest wisher for temperance reform, but to the end of his life he drank a large tankard of hard cider every morning when he first got up. It was free in every farmhouse to all travelers and tramps.

A cider mill was usually built on a hillside so the building could be one story high in front and two in the back. Thus cars could easily unload the apples on the upper level and take away the barrels of cider on the lower. Standing below on the lower floor you could see two upright wooden cylinders, set a little way apart, with knobs, or nuts as they were called, on one cylinder which fitted loosely into holes on the other. The cylinders worked in opposite directions and drew in and crushed the apples poured down between them. The nuts and holes frequently clogged with the pomace. Then the mill was stopped and a boy scraped out with a stick or hook the crushed apples. A horse walking in a small circle moved a lever which turned the motor wheel. It was slow work; it took three hours to grind a cartload of apples; but the machinery was efficient and simple. The pomace fell into a large shallow vat or tank, and if it could lie in the vat overnight it was a benefit. Then the pomace was put in a press. This was simple in construction. At the bottom was a platform grooved in channels; a sheaf of clean straw was spread on the platform, and with wooden shovels the pomace was spread thick over it. Then a layer of straw was laid at right angles with the first, and more pomace, and so on till the form was about three feet high; the top board was put on as a cover; the screw turned and blocks pressed down, usually with a long wooden hand lever, very slowly at first, then harder, until the mass was solid and every drop of juice had trickled into the channels of the platform and thence to the pan below.

Perry was made from pears, as cider is from apples, and peachy from peaches. Metheglin and mead, drinks of the old Druids in England, were made from honey, yeast, and water and were popular everywhere. In Virginia whole plantations of the honey locust furnished locust beans for making metheglin. From persimmons, elderberries, juniper berries, pumpkins, corn stalks, hickory nuts, sassafras bark, birch bark, and many other leaves, roots, and barks, various light drinks were made.

Many other stronger and more intoxicating liquors were made in large quantities, among them enormous amounts of rum, which was called often "kill devil." The making of rum aided and almost supported the slave trade in this country. The poor Negroes were bought on the coast of Africa by New England sea captains and merchants and paid for with barrels of New England rum. These slaves were then carried on slave ships to the West Indies and sold at a large profit to planters and slave dealers for a cargo of molasses. This was brought to New England, distilled into rum, and sent off to Africa. Thus the circle of molasses, rum, and slaves was completed. Many slaves were also landed in New England, but there was no crop there that needed Negroes to raise it. So slavery never was as common in New England as in the South, where the tropical tobacco and rice fields needed Negro labor. But New England's share in promoting Negro slavery in America was just as great as was Virginia's.

Besides all the rum that was sent to Africa, much was drunk by Americans at home. At weddings, funerals, christenings, at all public meetings and private feasts, New England rum was ever present.

For many years the colonists had no tea, chocolate, or coffee to drink; for those were not in use in England when America was settled. In 1690 two dealers were licensed to sell tea "in publique" in Boston. Green and bohea teas were sold at the Boston apothecaries in 1712.

Many queer mistakes were made through ignorance of its proper use. Many colonists put the tea into water, boiled it for a time, threw the liquid away, and ate the tea leaves. In Salem they did not find the leaves very attractive, so they put butter and salt on them.

In 1670 a Boston woman was licensed to sell coffee and chocolate, and soon coffeehouses were established there. Some did not know how to cook coffee any more than tea, but boiled the whole coffee beans in water, ate them, and drank the liquid; and naturally this was not very good either to eat or drink.

At the time of the Stamp Act, when patriotic Americans threw the tea into Boston harbor, Americans were just as great tea drinkers as the English. Coffee-drinking, first acquired in the Revolution, has also descended from generation to generation, and we now drink more coffee than tea. This is one of the differences in our daily life caused by the Revolution.

Many home-grown substitutes were used in Revolutionary times for tea: ribwort was a favorite one; strawberry and currant leaves, sage, thoroughwort, and "Liberty Tea," made from the four-leaved loosestrife. "Hyperion tea" was raspberry leaves, and was said by good patriots to be "very delicate and most excellent."

Chapter VI

Babyhood

In the first years of colonial life in this strange new world, it was hard for grown folk to live and just as hard to rear children.

In the Southern colonies the planters found a climate and enforced modes of life widely varying from home life in England. It took several generations to accustom infants to thrive under those conditions. The first years of life at Plym-

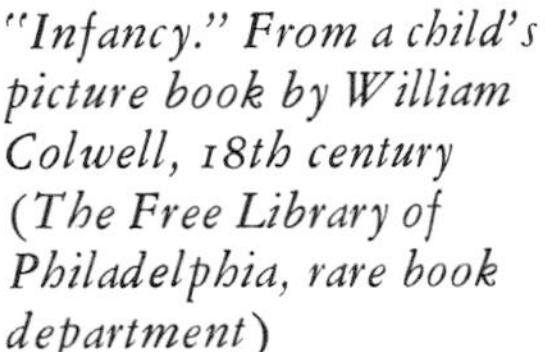

"Infancy." From a child's picture book by William Colwell, 18th century (The Free Library of Philadelphia, rare book department)

outh are the records of a bitter struggle, not for comfort but for existence. Summers wore on in weary work in which the children had to join; and winter came, and death. Yet amid all the want and cold little children were born and welcomed with affection.

From the moment when the baby opened his eyes on the bleak world around him, he had a Spartan struggle for life. All had to be baptized within a few days of birth, and baptized in the meetinghouse. Fortunate, indeed, was the child of midsummer. We can imagine the January babe carried through the narrow streets or lanes to the freezing meetinghouse, which had grown damper and deadlier with every wintry blast, there to be christened, when sometimes the ice had to be broken in the christening bowl.

The mortality among infants was appalling. Putrid fevers, epidemic influenzas, malignant sore throats, "bladders in the windpipe," raging smallpox, carried off hundreds of the children who survived baptism. The laws of sanitation were absolutely disregarded—because unknown; there was no drainage—nor was it deemed necessary; disinfection was feebly desired—but the scanty sprinkling of vinegar was the only expression of that desire; isolation of contagious diseases was proclaimed—but the measures were futile.

In the seventeenth century the science of medicine had not wholly cut asunder from astrology and necromancy, and the trusting Christian still believed in some occult influences, chiefly planetary, which governed not only his crops but his health and life. Hence the entries of births in the Bible usually gave the hour and minute, as well as the day, month, and year. Thus could be accurately calculated what favoring or mischief-bearing planets were in ascendancy at the time of the child's birth; what influences he would have to encounter in life.

The belief that meteorological and astrological conditions affected medicines was strong in all minds. The best physicians gravely noted the condition of the moon when gathering herbs and simples and concocting medicines, and certain drugs were held to be powerless at certain times of the year, owing to planetary influences.

Baby in red chair. Artist unknown, early 19th century (Abby Aldrich Rockefeller Folk Art Collection, Williamsburg, Virginia)

We cannot wonder that children died when we know the nostrums with which they were dosed. There were quack medicines which held sway for a century—among them, a valuable property, *Daffy's Elixir.* These patented—or rather secret—medicines had a formidable rival in snail water, which was used as a tonic and also a lotion.

Venice treacle was a nasty and popular compound, traditionally invented by Nero's physician. It was made of vipers, white wine, opium, "spices from both the Indies," licorice, red roses, tops of germander and St.-John's-wort, and some twenty other herbs, juice of rough sloes, mixed with honey "triple the weight of all the dry spices." The vipers had to be put, "twelve of 'em," into white wine alone. Rubila, made chiefly of antimony and nitre, was frequently dispensed.

Children were grievously afflicted with rickets, though curiously enough it was a new disease. Snails furnished many doses for the rickets.

Various native berries had restorative and preventive properties when strung as a necklace. Uglier decorations were strings of fawn's teeth or wolf's fangs, a sure promoter of easy teething. In spite of these varied charms and doses, children died in vast numbers while teething.

Even so, the average number of children in the family was large, which is always true in a pioneer settlement in a new country. A cheerful home life was insured by these large families when they lived. Sir William Phips was one of twenty-six children, all with the same mother. Green, the Boston printer, had thirty children. Another printer, Benjamin Franklin, was one of a family of seventeen. To the farmer, especially the frontiersman, every child in the home was an extra producer.

Parents searched for names of deep significance, for names appropriate to conditions, for those of profound influence—presumably on the child's life. Glory to God and zealous ambition for the child's future were equally influential in deciding selection.

Abigail, meaning father's joy, was frequently given, and Hannah, meaning grace. Zurishaddai, the Almighty is my rock, was bestowed on more than one boy, as were Comfort, Deliverance,

Temperance, Peace, Hope, Patience, Charity, Faith, Love, Submit, Endurance, Silence, Joy, Rejoice, Hoped for, and similar names indicative of a trait of character. Some children of Roger Clap were named Experience, Waitstill, Preserved, Hopestill, Wait, Thanks, Desire, Unite, and Supply. An early settler of old Narragansett had sixteen children. Their names were Parvis, Picus, Piersus, Prisemus, Polybius, Lois, Lettice, Avis, Anstice, Eunice, Mary, John, Elizabeth, Ruth, Freelove. All lived to be threescore and ten, one to be a hundred and two years old.

The Frenchman Misson, in his *Travels in England,* says, "At the birth of their children they (visitors) drink a glass of wine and eat a bit of a certain cake, which is seldom made but upon these occasions." Anna Green Winslow, a Boston schoolgirl, tells of making what she calls "a setting up visit" to a relative who had a baby about four weeks old. She wore her best and most formal attire and says, "It cost me a pistareen to Nurse Eaton for two cakes which I took care to eat before I paid for them." There certainly was a custom of giving money, clothing, or petty trinkets to the nurse at such visits.

A pincushion was for many years a highly conventional gift to a mother with a young babe. *Poor Robin's Almanack* for the year 1676 says:

> "Pincushions and such other knacks
> A childbed woman always lacks."

One given to a Boston baby, while his new home

was in state of siege, bore the inscription, "Welcome little Stranger, tho the Port is closed." These words were formed by the heads of pins.

The seventeenth century baby slept in a cradle. Nothing could be prettier than the old cradles that have survived successive years of use with many generations of babies. In Pilgrim Hall still may be seen the quaint and finely wrought wicker cradle of Peregrine White, the first child born in Plymouth. This cradle is of Dutch manufacture and is one of the few authentic articles still surviving that came over on the *Mayflower*. It was brought over by William White, whose widow married Governor Edward Winslow. A similar wicker cradle may be seen at the Essex Institute in Salem, together with a heavy wooden cradle in which many members of the Townes family of Topsfield, Massachusetts, were rocked to sleep two centuries ago. A graceful variant of the swinging cradle is the Indian basket hung at either end from a wooden standard or frame. In this strong basket, fashioned by an Indian mother, many a child has been swung and sung to sleep. A still more picturesque cradle was made of birch bark.

In these cradles the colonial baby slept, warmly wrapped in a homespun blanket or pressed quilt. Of these wraps, of the thinner sort, may be named the thin, close-woven, homespun "flannel sheet," spun of the whitest wool into a fine twisted worsted, and woven with a close sley into an even web. The baby's initials were often marked on these sheets and fortunate was the child who had the light, warm wrappings.

A finer coverlet, the christening blanket, was usually made of silk, richly embroidered, sometimes with a text of Scripture. These were often lace bordered or edged with a narrow home-woven silk fringe.

A go-cart or standing-stool was a favorite instrument to teach a child to walk. A standing-stool in which babies stood and toddled is a rather crude frame of wood with a ledge or narrow table for toys.

There is evidence that Locke's *Thoughts on Education,* published in England in 1690, found many readers and ardent followers in the new world. The book is in many old-time library lists

Peregrine White cradle, 1620 (The Pilgrim Society, Plymouth, Massachusetts)

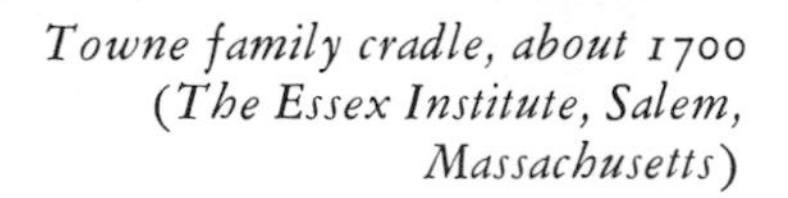

Towne family cradle, about 1700 (The Essex Institute, Salem, Massachusetts)

in New England and among the scant volumes of those who had but a single bookshelf or book box. The notions of the English philosopher appealed to American parents.

One of Locke's instructions was the advice to wash the child's feet daily in cold water and "to have his shoes so thin that they might leak and let in water." Josiah Quincy was the suffering subject of some of this instruction. When only three years old he was taken from his warm bed in winter as well as summer (and this in eastern Massachusetts), carried downstairs to a cellar kitchen and dipped three times in a tub of cold water fresh from the pump. He was also brought up with utter indifference to wet feet. He said that in his boyhood he sat more than half the time with his feet wet and cold, but with no ill results.

Locke also strongly counseled learning dancing, swimming, and playing in the open air. In his diet "flesh should be forborn as long as the boy is

Child's play pen, early 19th century (Old Sturbridge Village)

in coats, or at least till he is two or three years old"; for breakfast and supper he advises milk, milk-pottage, water-gruel, flummery, and similar "spoon-meat," or brown bread with cheese. If the boy called for victuals between meals, he should have dry bread. His only extra drink should be small-beer, which should be warm, and seldom he should taste wine or strong drink. Locke would not have children eat melons, peaches, plums, or grapes, while berries and ripe pears and apples, the latter especially after October, he deems healthful. The bed should be hard, of quilts rather than of feathers. Under these rigid rules were reared many of our Revolutionary heroes and statesmen.

The adoption of Locke's ideas about the use of cold water, or indeed of any frequent bathing, was perhaps the most radical innovation in modes of living. The English never bathed, in our sense of the word, a complete immersion, nor, I suppose, did our Puritan, Cavalier, or Quaker ancestors. The *Youth's Behavior,* an old-time book of etiquette, lays down an assertion that it is a point of wholesomeness to wash one's face and hands as soon as one is up and dressed, and "to comb one's head in time and season, yet not too curiously." Bathing the person in unaccustomed spots was a ticklish proceeding—a water ordeal, to be gravely considered.

Child's high chair, late 17th century (The Metropolitan Museum of Art, Gift of Mrs. Russell Sage, 1909)

Chapter VII

Childhood

The laws of courtesy had much influence upon the development of the character of the colonial child. Everything in the community was made to tend to the preservation of relations of civility; this is plainly shown by the laws. Law suits were common for slander, scandalmongering, name calling, lying, etc. Astonishingly petty seem many of the charges, even the calling of degrading nick-

Mrs. Samuel Mifflin and her granddaughter, Rebecca Mifflin Frances, portrait by Charles Willson Peale (1741–1827), detail
(The Metropolitan Museum of Art, Egleston Fund, 1922)

names, making of wry faces, jeering, and "finger-sticking" were fined and punished. But all this rigidity tended to a preservation of peace. The child who saw a man fined for lying, who beheld another set in the stocks for calling his neighbor ill names, or repeating scandalous assertions, grew up with a definite knowledge of the wickedness and danger of lying and a wholesome regard for the proprieties of life. These sentiments may not have made him a better man, but they certainly made him a more endurable one.

The child of colonial days had little knowledge of the world at large. He probably never had seen a map of the world, and if he had, he didn't understand it. There was no foreign news in the present

From a child's picture book by William Colwell, 18th century (The Free Library of Philadelphia, rare book department)

sense. Of special English events he might occasionally learn, months after they had happened, but never any details nor any ordinary happenings. European information was of the scantiest and rarest kind; knowledge of the result of a war or a vast disaster, like the Lisbon earthquake, might come. From the other great continents came nothing.

Nor was his knowledge of his own land extended. There was nothing to interest him in the newsletter, even if he read it. He cared nothing for the other colonies, he knew little of other towns. If he lived in a seaport, he doubtless heard from the sailors on the wharves tales of adventure and romantic interest, and he heard from his elders details of trade, both of foreign and native ports.

The boy, therefore, grew up with his life revolving in a small circle; the girl's was still smaller. This had its advantages and its serious disadvantages. It developed an extraordinarily noble and pure type of neighborliness, but it did not foster a general broad love of humanity.

Among early printed English books are many containing rules of courtesy and behavior. It certainly conveys an idea of the demeanor of children of colonial days to read what was enjoined upon them in a little book of etiquette which was apparently widely circulated and doubtless carefully read. The little book teaches good listening:

"When any speak to thee, stand up. Say not I have heard it before. Never endeavour to help him out if he tell it not right. Snigger not; never question the Truth of it."

The child is enjoined minutely as to his behavior at school: to take off his hat at entering, and bow to the teacher, to rise up and bow at the entrance of any stranger, to "bawl not in speaking," to "walk not cheek by jole," but fall respectfully behind and always "give the Wall to Superiors."

The young student's passage from his home to his school should be as decorous as his demeanor at either terminus:

"Run not Hastily in the Street, nor go too Slowly. Wag not to and fro, nor use any Antick Postures either of thy Head, Hands, Feet or Body. Throw not aught on the Street, as Dirt or

Stones. If thou meetest the scholars of any other School jeer not nor affront them, but show them love and respect and quietly let them pass along."

This book of manners was reprinted in 1787. An earlier edition, called *The School of Manners,* had been published in London in 1701. The directions in these books of etiquette are copied from a famous book entitled *Youths' Behaviour, or Decency in Conversation Amongst Men,* a book unsurpassed in the seventeenth century as an epitome of contemporary manners and held in such esteem that it ran through eleven editions in less than forty years after its first appearance.

The *Youths' Behaviour* contained many rules and instructions worded from still older books on courtesy, such as *The Babees Book* and *The Boke of Nurture.*

The constant reading of these books and the persistent reprinting of their formal rules of behavior may have tended to conserve the old-fashioned deportment of children.

A certain regard for formality prevailed even in very humble households.

Unmarried women and girls, if deemed worthy of any title at all, were not termed Miss but Mrs. "Miss" was not exactly a term of reproach, but it was not one of respect. It denoted childishness, flippancy, lack of character, and was not applied in public to children of dignified families.

It was certainly natural that children should be affected by the regard for etiquette, the distinctions of social position which they saw heeded all around them, and in all departments of life. No man could enlist in the Massachusetts Cavalry unless he had a certain amount of property. Even boys in college had their names placed in the catalogues, not by classes, years, scholarship, or alphabetical order, but by the dignity and wealth of their family and social position; and a college boy at Harvard had to give the baluster side of the staircase to anyone who was his social superior. Of course the careful "seating of the meeting" was simply an evidence of this regard for rank and station.

(9)

17. Bite not thy bread, but break it, but not with ſlovenly Fingers, nor with the ſame wherewith thou takeſt up thy meat,

18 Dip not thy Meat in the Sawce.

19. Take not ſalt with a greazy Kniſe.

20 Spit not, cough not, nor blow thy Noſe at Table if it may be avoided; but if there be neceſſity, do it aſide, and without much noiſe.

21. Lean not thy Elbow on the Table, or on the back of thy Chair.

22. Stuff not thy mouth ſo as to fill thy Cheeks; be content with ſmaller Mouthfuls.

23. Blow not thy Meat, but with Patience wait till it be cool.

24. Sup not Broth at the Table, but eat it with a Spoon.

From The School of Manners, *1701*

De Peyster girl, about 1730, detail. Artist unknown (The New-York Historical Society)

Though children were certainly subdued and silent in the presence of older folk, they did not always pose either as models of decorum or propriety in their relations with each other. They were still boys and girls, not machine-like models of perfection. They were turbulent in church, and boys in colonial days robbed orchards, played ball in the streets, tore down gates, frightened horses, and threw stones with much vim and violence.

In a little book called *The Village School,* we read of their beating and kicking each other, and that there was one bleeding nose. Worse yet, when the girls went forth to gather "daisies and butter-flowers," the ungallant boys kicked the girls "to make them pipe."

It was inevitable that New England parents,

Colonel Benjamin Tallmadge with his son, detail of portrait by Ralph Earl, 1790 (The Litchfield Historical Society)

with their fairly passionate zeal for the education of their children, should in many cases overstimulate and force the infant minds in their charge. It seems somewhat anomalous with the almost universal distrust and hindrance of female education that one of the most precocious flowers of Puritanism should have been a girl, the "pious and ingenious Mrs. Jane Turell," who was born in Boston in 1708. Before her second year was finished she could speak distinctly, knew her letters, and "could relate many stories out of the Scriptures to the satisfaction and pleasure of the most judicious." When she was three years old she could recite the greater part of the *Assembly's Catechism,* many of the psalms, many lines of poetry, and read distinctly; at the age of four she "asked many astonishing questions about divine mysteries." As her father was president of Harvard College, it may be inferred she had an extended reading course.

In many families of extreme Puritanical thought, the children developed at an early age a comprehension of religious matters which would seem abnormal today, but was natural then.

It is told of Timothy Dwight, President of Yale College, that he learned the alphabet at a single lesson and could read the Bible before he was four years old and taught it to his comrades. At the age of six he was sent to the grammar school and importuned his father to let him study Latin. Being denied, he studied through the Latin grammar twice without a teacher, borrowing a book of an older boy. He could have been prepared for college when but eight years old, had not the grammar school luckily discontinued and left him without a teacher.

The curriculum at Harvard in olden times bore little resemblance to that of today. Sciences were unknown and the requirements in mathematics were meager. Still a boy needed even then to be clever to know enough Greek and Latin to enter at eleven.

In 1799 there was graduated from Rhode Island College (now Brown University) a boy named John Pitman, who was barely fourteen.

There is no evidence that very early marriages, that is, marriages of children and very young lads and girls, which were far from rare in England during the first years of our colonial life, ever were permitted in the new world. But many child marriages were not abolished in America because maturity or majority was established at a greater age. Before the Revolution boys reached man's estate at sixteen years of age, became taxpayers, and served in the militia. Early unions were controlled by restrictive laws, such as the one enacted in Massachusetts in 1646 that no female orphan during her minority should be given in marriage by anyone except with the approbation of the majority of the selectmen of the town in which she resided. Another privilege of the girl orphan was that at fourteen she could choose her own guardian. Thus were children protected in the new world and their rights conserved.

Chapter VIII

Education of Boys and Girls

An education for children in colonial times was warmly desired. "Child," said one noble New England mother of the olden days, "if God make thee a good Christian and a good scholar, 'tis all they mother ever asked for thee."

Not only did parents strive for the education of their children, but the colonies assisted by commanding the building and maintaining of a school

Harvard College in about 1725 (The New York Public Library, Stokes Collection)

in each town where there was a sufficient number of families and scholars. Rhode Island was the only New England colony that did not compel the building of schoolhouses and the education of children.

So determined was Massachusetts to have schools that in 1636, only six years after the settlement of Boston, the General Court, which was composed of representatives from every settlement in the Bay Colony, and which was the same as our House of Representatives today, gave over half the annual income of the entire colony to establish the school which two years later became Harvard College.

In Virginia schoolhouses were few for over a

century. Governor Berkeley, an obstinate and narrow-minded Englishman, wrote home to England in 1670, "I thank God there are in Virginia no free schools nor printing, and I hope we shall not have, for learning hath brought disobedience and heresy into the world." Some Virginia gentlemen did not agree with him, however, and gave money to try to establish free schools for poor children. A far greater hindrance to the establishment of schools than the governor's stupid opposition was the fact that there was no town or village life in Virginia. The houses and plantations were scattered; previous to the year 1700 Jamestown was the only Virginia town, and it was but a petty settlement.

Occasionally, as years passed on, there might be found in Virginia, the Carolinas, and Georgia what was called an old-field school, the uniting of a few neighbors to hire a teacher, too often a poor one; like the "hedge-teachers" of Europe, for a short term of teaching, in a shabby building placed on an old exhausted tobacco field.

In one of these old-field schools George Washington obtained most of his education. A daily ride on horseback for a year to a similar school ten miles away, and for another year a row morning and night even in roughest weather across the river to a Fredericksburg teacher, ended his school career when he was thirteen. But he had then made a big pile of neatly written manuscript school books, and he had acquired a passionate longing to be educated, which accompanied him through life.

New England was controlled, both in public and private life, by the Puritan ministers, who felt, as one of them said, that "unless school and college flourish, church and state cannot live." By a law of Massachusetts, passed in 1647, it was ordered that every town of fifty families should provide a school where children could be taught to read and write, while every town of one hundred householders was required to have a grammar school. In the Connecticut Code of Laws of 1650 were the same orders. These schools were public, but were not free; they were supported at the expense of the parents.

In 1644 the town of Salem ordered "that a note be published the next lecture day, that such as have children to be kept at school, would bring in their names, and what they will give for a whole year; and also that if any poor body hath children or a child to be put to school, and not able to pay for their schooling, that the town will pay it by a rate." Lists of children were made out in towns, and if the parents were well-to-do, they had to pay whether their children attended school or not.

Land was sometimes set aside to partly support the school. It was called the "school-meadows," or "school-fields," and was let out for an income to help to pay the teacher. This was a grant made on the same principle that grants were made to physicians, tanners, and other useful persons. At a later date lotteries were a favorite method of raising money for schools.

It was not until about the time of the Revolution that the modern signification of the word "free"—a school paid for entirely by general town taxes—could be applied to the public schools of most Massachusetts towns, and when the schools of Boston were made free, that community stood alone for its liberality not only in America, but in the world.

The pay was given in any of the inconvenient exchanges which had to pass as money at that time—in wampum, beaver skins, Indian corn, wheat, peas, beans, or any country product known as "truck." It is told of a Salem school that one scholar was always seated at the windows to study and also to hail passers-by and endeavor to sell to them the accumulation of corn, vegetables, etc., which had been given in payment to the teacher.

The logs for the great fireplace were furnished by the parents or guardians of the scholars as a part of the pay for schooling, and an important part it was in the Northern colonies, in the bitter winter, in the poorly built schoolhouses. Some schoolmasters, indignant at the carelessness of parents who failed to send the expected load of wood early in the winter, banished the unfortunate child of the tardy parent to the coldest corner of the schoolroom.

In Pennsylvania the Quakers thought knowledge of the "three R's" was enough. They distinctly disapproved of any extended scholarship, as it fostered undue pride and provoked idleness. Among the Germans there were a few schools of low grade. It was said by these German settlers that schooling made boys lazy and dissatisfied on

Old stone schoolhouse, built 1782–1784 (The Newark Museum. Photograph by Alfred Tamarin)

the farms and that religion would suffer by too much learning.

Scotland furnished the best and largest number of schoolmasters to the colonies.

One contract for the teacher at the Dutch settlement of Flatbush, Long Island, in 1682, is very full in detail, and we learn much of the old-time school from it. A bell was rung to call the scholars together at eight o'clock in the morning, the school closed for a recess at eleven, opened again at one, closed at four. All sessions began and closed with prayer. On Wednesday and Saturdays the children were taught the questions and answers in the catechism and the common prayers. The master was paid (usually in wheat or corn) for "a speller or reader" three guilders a quarter, for "a writer" four guilders. He had many other duties to perform besides teaching the children. He rang the church bell on Sunday, read the Bible at service in church, and led in the singing; sometimes he read the sermon. He provided water for baptisms, bread and wine for communion, and in fact performed all the duties now done by a sexton, including sweeping out the church. He delivered invitations to funerals and carried messages. Sometimes he dug the graves, and often he visited and comforted the sick.

Full descriptions exist of the first country schoolhouses in Pennsylvania and New York. They were universally made of logs. Some had a rough puncheon floor, others a dirt floor that readily ground into dust two or three inches thick, which unruly pupils would purposely stir up in clouds to annoy the masters and disturb the school. The bark roof was a little higher at one side that the rain might drain off. Usually the teacher sat in the middle of the room, and pegs were thrust between the logs around the walls, three or four feet from the ground. Boards were laid on these pegs; at these rude desks sat the older scholars with their backs to the teacher. Younger scholars sat on blocks or benches of logs. Many schoolhouses did not have glass set in the small windows but newspapers or white papers greased with lard were fastened in the rude sashes, or in holes cut in the wall, and let in a dim light. At one end, or in the middle, a "cat and clay" chimney furnished a fireplace. When the first rough log cabin was replaced by a better schoolhouse the hexagonal shape, so beloved in those states for meeting-houses, was chosen, and occasionally built in stone.

The furnishing of the schoolrooms was meager; there were no blackboards, no maps, seldom was there a pair of globes. Faber's pencils were made as early as 1761. Lead pencils were advertised for sale in New York in 1786 with india rubbers, and as early as 1740 they were offered among booksellers' wares in Boston for threepence apiece, both black and red lead.

Still lead pencils were not in common use even in city schools. The manuscript arithmetics or "sum-books" were done in ink. Many a country boy grew to manhood without ever seeing a lead pencil. Copy books were made of foolscap paper carefully sewed into book shape and were ruled by hand. For this children used lead plummets instead of pencils. These plummets were made of lead melted and cast in wooden molds cut out by the ever ready jackknife and were then tied by a hempen string to the ruler. They were usually shaped like a tomahawk and carefully whittled and trimmed to a sharp edge. Slightly varied shapes were a carpenter's or a woodcutter's ax; also there were cannon, battledores, and cylinders.

Paper was scarce and too highly prized for children to waste. It was a great burden even to ministers to get what paper they needed for their sermons and they frequently acquired microscopic handwriting for economy's sake. To the forest the scholars turned for the ever plentiful birch bark, which formed a substitute to cipher on instead of paper. Among the thrifty Scotch-Irish settlers in New Hampshire and the planters in Maine, sets of arithmetic rules were copied by each child on birch bark and made a substantial textbook.

Noah Webster says distinctly in a letter written about the schools of his childhood that "before the Revolution and for some years after no slates were used in common schools." Yet there is a reference to them in America in a schoolboy's letter:

"TO MR. CORNELIUS TEN BROECK
att Albany.

"Stamford, the 13th Day of October, 1752.

"HONORED FETHAR,

"These fiew Lines comes to let you know that I am in a good State of Health and I hope this may find you also. I have found all the things in my trunk but I must have a pare of Schuse. And mama please to send me some Ches Nutts and some Wall Nutts; you please to send me a Slate, and som pensals, and please to send me some smok befe, and for bringing my trunk 3/9, and for a pare of Schuse 9 shillings. You please to send me a pare of indin's Schuse. You please to send me som dride corn. My Duty to Father and Mother and Sister and to all frinds.

"I am your Dutyfull Son,
"JOHN TEN BROECK.

"Father forgot to send me my Schuse."

The first slates were frameless and had a hole pierced at one side on which a pencil could be hung, or by which they could be suspended around the neck. A good education could generally be obtained only in the schools in larger towns, or in the households of learned men. The New England ministers almost universally eked out their meager incomes by taking young lads into their homes to educate. Children went, if possible, to the house of a kinsman.

While the education of the sons of the planters

Voorleezer's House, built 1695 (furniture, reproduction) (The Staten Island Historical Society. Photograph by Alfred Tamarin)

in all the colonies was bravely provided and supported, the daughters fared but poorly. The education of a girl in book learning was deemed of much less importance than her instruction in household duties. Small arrangement was made in any school for her presence, nor was it thought desirable that she should have any varied knowledge. That she should read and write was certainly satisfactory, and cipher a little, but many girls got on very well without the ciphering, and many, alas! without the reading and writing.

Occasionally an intelligent father would carefully teach his daughters.

Conditions remained the same throughout the century. The wife of President John Adams, born in 1744, the daughter of a New England minister of good family and social position, doubtless had as good an education as any girl of her birth and station. She wrote in 1817:

"My early education did not partake of the abundant opportunities which the present days offer, and which even our common country schools now afford. I never was sent to any school. I was always sick. Female education, in the best families, went no further than writing and arithmetic; in some few and rare instances music and dancing."

On another occasion she said that female education had been everywhere neglected and female learning ridiculed, and she speaks of the trifling, narrow, contracted education of American women.

Girls in the other colonies fared no better than New England damsels. The instruction given to girls of Dutch and English parentage in New York was certainly very meager. Mrs. Anne Grant wrote an interesting account of her childhood in Albany, New York, in a book called *Memoir of an American Lady*. The date was the first half of the eighteenth century. She said:

"It was at that time very difficult to procure the means of instruction in those districts; female education was in consequence conducted on a very limited scale; girls learned needlework (in which they were indeed both skillful and ingenious), from their mothers and aunts; they were taught, too, at that period to read, in Dutch, the Bible, and a few Calvinistic tracts of the devotional kind. But in the infancy of the settlement few girls read English; when they did they were thought accomplished; they generally spoke it, however imperfectly, and a few were taught writing."

We seldom find any recognition of girls as pupils in the early public schools. Sometimes it is evident that they were admitted at hours not devoted to the teaching of boys. For instance, in May 1767, a school was advertised in Providence for teaching writing and arithmetic to "young ladies." But the girls had to go from six to half-past seven in the morning, and half-past four to six in the afternoon. The price for this most inconvenient and ill-timed schooling was two dollars a quarter. It is pathetic to read of a learning-hungry little maid in Hatfield, Massachusetts, who would slip away from her spinning and knitting and sit on the schoolhouse steps to listen with eager envy to the boys as they recited within. When it became popular to have girls attend public schools, an old farmer on a country school committee gave these matter-of-fact objections to the innovation. "In winter it's too far for girls to walk; in summer they ought to stay at home to help in the kitchen."

The first school for girls only, where they were taught in branches not learned in the lower schools, was started in 1780 in Middletown, Connecticut, by a graduate of Yale College named William Woodbridge. Boston girls owed much to a famous teacher, Caleb Bingham, who came to that city in 1784 and advertised to open a school where girls could be taught writing, arithmetic, reading, spelling, and English grammar. His school was eagerly welcomed, and it prospered.

There were always dame-schools, which were attended by small boys and girls. The pay of women teachers who taught the dame-schools was meager in the extreme. The town of Woburn, Massachusetts, reached the lowest ebb of salary. In 1641 a highly respected widow, one Mrs. Walker, kept a school in a room of her own house. The town agreed to pay her ten shillings for the first year, but after deducting seven shillings for taxes, and various small amounts for produce, etc., she received finally from the town *one shilling and three pence* for her pedagogical work.

There were always in the large cities small classes where favored girls could be taught the rudiments of an education, and there were many

Ivory busk, early 19th century (The New-York Historical Society)

private teachers who taught young misses. Boston gentlewomen from very early days had a mode of eking out a limited income by taking little girls and young ladies from country homes, especially from the Southern colonies and the Barbados, to board while they attended these classes and recited to these teachers.

An old woman in Boston was given charge in 1719 of her granddaughter Sarah to care for and guard while she received an education. When Missy arrived from Barbados she was eight years old. She brought with her a maid. The grandmother wrote back cheerfully to the parents that the child was well and brisk, as indeed she was. All the very young gentlemen and young ladies of Boston Brahmin blood paid her visits, and she gave a feast at a child's dancing party with the sweetmeats left over from her sea-store. Her stay in her grandmother's household was surprisingly brief. She left unceremoniously and unbidden with her maid and went to a Mr. Binning's to board. She sent home word to Barbados that her grandmother made her drink water with her meals.

Whether the little girl was taught at home or in a private school, to "sew, floure, write, and dance" were really the chief things she learned, usually the only things, save deportment and elegance of carriage. To attain an erect and dignified bearing growing girls were tortured by sitting in stocks, wearing harnesses, and being strapped to backboards. The packthread stays and stiffened coats of "little Miss Custis" were made still more unyielding by metal and wood busks, the latter made of close-grained heavy wood. These were often carved in various designs or with names and verses, or ornamented with drawings in colored inks, and made a favorite gift.

All these constrainments and accessories contributed to a certain thin-chested though erect appearance, which is notable in the portraits of girls and women painted in the eighteenth century.

The backboard certainly helped to produce an erect and dignified carriage and was assisted by the quick, graceful motions used in wool-spinning. The daughter of the Revolutionary patriot General Nathanael Greene stated to her grandchildren that in her girlhood she sat every day with her feet in stocks, strapped to a backboard. She was until the end of her long life a straight-backed elegant dame. Many of the portraits in this book plainly show the reign of the backboard.

Though a Boston Puritan told proudly of her grandchildren's dancing, this accomplishment had not been quietly promoted in that sober city. In early years both magistrates and ministers had declaimed against it.

In 1684 Increase Mather preached a strong sermon against what he termed "Gynecandrical Dancing or that which is commonly called Mixt or Promiscuous Dancing of Men and Women, be they elder or younger Persons together." He called it the great sin of the Daughters of Zion.

Preaching against dancing was as futile as against wig-wearing. "Horrid Bushes of Vanity" soon decked every head, and gay young feet tripped merrily to the sound of music in every village and town. Dancing could not be repressed, and after a time "Ordination-balls" were given when a new minister was ordained. Dancing was a pleasant accomplishment, and a serious one in good society.

We have much contemporary evidence to show that music, as a formulated study, was rarely taught till after the Revolution. But there never was a time in colonial life when music was not loved and clung to with a sentiment that is difficult to explain, but must not be underrated.

Spinets and harpsichords were brought to wealthy citizens. Copies of old-time music show how very elementary were the performances on these instruments. Listeners were profoundly moved at the sound, but it would seem far from inspiring today.

"The notes of slender harpsichords with tapping, twinkling quills,
Or carrolling to a spinet with its thin, metallic thrills."

Even the "new Clementi with glittering keys" gave but a tinny sound. Girls "raised a tune," however, to these far from resonant accompaniments, and sang their ballads and sentimental ditties unhampered by thoughts of technique and methods and schools. Many of these old musical instruments are still in existence.

By Revolutionary times, girls' boarding schools had sprung into existence in large towns and certainly filled a great want. One New England school, haloed with romance, was kept by Mrs. Susanna Rawson, who was an actress, the daughter of an English officer, and married to a musician. She was also a playwright and wrote one novel of great popularity, *Charlotte Temple.* Eliza Southgate Bowne gives some glimpses of the life at this school in her letters. She was fourteen years when she thus wrote to her father:

"HON FATHER:

"I am again placed at school under the tuition of an amiable lady, so mild, so good, no one can help loving her; she treats all her scholars with such tenderness as would win the affection of the most savage brute. I learn Embroidery and Geography at present, and wish your permission to learn Musick. . . . I have described one of the blessings of creation in Mrs. Rawson, and now I will describe Mrs. Lyman as the reverse: she is the worst woman I ever knew of or that I ever saw, nobody knows what I suffered from the treatment of that woman."

This Mrs. Lyman kept a boarding school at Medford. Eight girls slept in one room, the fare was meager, and the education kept close company with the fare.

The Moravian schools at Bethlehem, Pennsylvania, were widely popular. President John Adams wrote to his daughter of the girls' school that 120 girls lived in one house and slept in one garret in single beds in two long rows. He says, "How should you like to live in such a nunnery?"

Chapter IX

Old-time Discipline

Discipline in colonial days was severe and arbitrary. Parents, teachers, and ministers believed in stern repression and sharp correction—above all, in the rod. They found abundant support for this belief in the Bible, their constant guide.

The chief field of the "breaking and beating down" process was in school. Birch trees were plentiful in America—and whippings too. Schol-

From a child's picture book by William Colwell, 18th century (The Free Library of Philadelphia, rare book department)

ars in New England were not permitted to forget the methods of discipline of "the good old days." Massachusetts schools resounded with strokes of the birch rod. Varied instruments of chastisement were known.

A lybbet was a billet of wood. A cruel inquisitor invented an instrument of torture which he termed a flapper. It was a heavy piece of leather six inches in diameter with a hole in the middle. This was fastened by an edge to a pliable handle. Every stroke on the bare flesh raised a blister the size of the hole in the leather. Equally brutal was the tattling stick, a cat-o'-nine-tails with heavy leather straps. That fierce Boston disciplinarian and patriot Master Lovell whipped with strong birch

From Young Wilfred,
19th century

rods and made one culprit mount the back of another scholar to receive his lashing. He called these whippings trouncings, the good old English word of the Elizabethan dramatists. Another brutal Boston master struck his scholars on the head with a ferule until this was forbidden by the school directors; he then whipped the soles of the scholars' feet, and roared out in an ecstasy of cruelty, "Oh! the Caitiffs! it is good for them."

There was sometimes an aftermath of sorrow, when our stern old grandfathers whipped their children at home for being whipped at school.

Many ingenious punishments were invented. A specially insulting one was to send the pupil out to cut a small branch of a tree. A split was made by the teacher at the severed end of the branch, and the culprit's nose was placed in the cleft end. Then he was forced to stand, painfully pinched, an object of ridicule. A familiar punishment of the dame school was the smart tapping of the child's head with a heavy thimble; this was known as "thimell-pie." Another was to yoke two delinquents together in a yoke made with two bows like an ox yoke. Sometimes a boy and girl were yoked together—a terrible disgrace. "Whispering sticks" were used to preserve quiet in the schoolroom—wooden gags to be tied in the mouth with strings, somewhat as a bit is placed in a horse's mouth.

Children were punished by being seated on a unipod, a stool with but a single leg, upon which it was most tiring to try to balance. They were made to stand on dunce stools and wear dunce caps and heavy leather spectacles; they were labeled with large placards marked with degrading or ridiculous names, such as "Tell-Tale," "Bite-Finger-Baby," "Lying Ananias," "Idle-Boy," and "Pert-Miss-Prat-a-Pace."

One of Miss Hetty Higginson's punishments in her Salem school at the beginning of the nineteenth century was to make a child hold a heavy book, such as a dictionary, by a single leaf. Of course any restless motion would tear the leaf. Her rewards of merit should be also told. She would divide a single strawberry in minute portions among six or more scholars, and she had a "bussee," or good child, who was to be kissed.

Many stories have been told of special punishments invented by special teachers. The schoolmaster at Flatbush was annoyed by the children in his school constantly using Dutch words, as he was employed to teach them English. He gave every day to the first scholar who used a Dutch word a little metal token or medal. This scholar could promptly transfer the token to the next child who spoke a Dutch word, and so on; thus it went from hand to hand through the day. But the unlucky scholar who had the token in his possession at the close of school received a sound whipping.

An amusing method of securing good lessons and good behavior was employed by old Ezekiel Cheever and was thus told by Reverend John Barnard, one of his pupils:

"I was a very naughty boy, much given to play, in so much that Master Cheever openly declared, 'You, Barnard, I know you can do well enough if you will, but you are so full of play you hinder your classmates from getting their lessons, therefore if any of them cannot perform their duty, I shall correct you for it.' One day one of my classmates did not look at his book, and could not say his lesson, though I called upon him once and again to mind his book. Whereupon our master beat me. . . . The boy was pleased with my being corrected and persisted in his neglect for which I was still beaten and that for several days. I thought in justice I ought to correct the boy and compel him to a better temper; therefore after school was done I went to him and told him I had been beaten several times for his neglect and since master would not correct him, I would and then drubbed him heartily."

The famous Lancasterian system—that of monitorial schools—discountenanced the rod, but

Wooden paddle, 17th century (reproduction) (The Staten Island Historical Society. Photograph by Alfred Tamarin)

the forms of punishment were not wholly above criticism. They were the neck-and-hands pillory, familiar up to that date in England and America as a public punishment of criminals, wooden shackles, hanging in a sack, tying the legs together, and labeling with the name of the offense against rules.

I have found nothing to show that Dutch schoolmasters were as severe as those of the English colonies. Dr. Curtius, the first master of the Latin School in New Amsterdam, complained that his hands were tied as some of the parents of his scholars forbade him punishing their children, and that as a result these unruly young Dutchmen "beat each other and tore the clothes from each other's backs." The contract between the Flatbush Church and schoolmaster, dated 1682, specifies that he shall "demean himself patient and friendly towards the children."

The discipline of Master Leslie, a New York teacher of the eighteenth century, is described by Eliza Morton Quincy in her delightful *Memoirs*. The date is about 1782.

"His modes of punishment would astonish children of the present day. One of them was to hold the blocks. They were of two sizes. The large one was a heavy block of wood, with a ring in the centre, by which it was to be held a definite number of minutes, according to the magnitude of the offence. The smaller block was for the younger child. Another punishment was by a number of leathern straps, about an inch wide and a finger long, with which he used to strap the hands of the larger boys."

One German schoolmaster, Samuel Dock, stands out in relief in this desert of ignorance and cruelty. With simplicity and earnestness he wrote in 1750 the story of his successful teaching, as in simplicity and earnestness he had taught in his school at Shippack. His story is as homely as his life:

"How I Receive the Children in School.

"It is done in the following manner. The child is first welcomed by the other scholars, who extend their hands to it. It is then asked by me whether it will learn industriously and be obedient. If it promises me this, I explain to it how it must behave; and if it can say its A. B. C.'s in order, one after the other, and also by way of proof, can point out with the forefinger all the designated letters, it is put into the A-b, Abs. When it gets thus far, its father must give it a penny and its mother must cook for it two eggs, because of its industry; and a similar reward is due to it when it goes further into words; and so forth."

He made them little presents as prizes, drew pictures for them, taught them singing and also musical notation, and he had a plan to have the children teach each other. He had a careful set of rules for their behavior to try to change them from brutish peasants to intelligent citizens. They must be clean; delinquents were not punished with rod, but by having the whole school write and shout out their names with the word "lazy" attached. Letter writing was carefully taught with exercises in writing to various people and to each other. Profanity was punished by wearing a yoke and being told the awful purport of the oaths. He taught spelling and reading with much Bible instruction, but he did not teach the catechism, since he had scholars of many sects and denominations; however, he made them all learn and understand what he called the "honey-flowers of the New Testament."

There is no doubt that the practice of whipping servants was common here, not only children who were bound out, and apprentices and young redemptioners, but grown servants as well. Occasionally the cruel master was fined or punished for a brutal overexercise of his right of punishment. At least one little child died from the hand of his murderous master. In Boston and other towns commissioners were elected who had power to sentence to be whipped, exceeding ten stripes, children and servants who behaved disobediently.

The ROYAL BATTLEDORE: Being the first Introductory Part of the *Circle of the Sciences*, &c. Publish'd by the KING'S AUTHORITY.
LONDON: Printed by *J. Newbery*, in *St. Paul's Church-Yard*, and *B. Collins*, in *Salisbury*. Pr
Also the *Royal Primer*, or second Book for Children, Price 3d. bound, adorn'd with Cuts.

a b c d e f g h i j k l m n
p q r ſ s t u v w x y z.

A B C D E F G H I J K L M
O P Q R S T U V W X Y Z

ſt ſi fi ſſ ff ſl fl ſſi ffi ffl Æ &.

a e i o u y.

ab eb ib ob ub | ba be bi bo b
ac ec ic oc uc | ca ce ci co c
ad ed id od ud | da de di do d

IN the Name of the FA-THER, and o
SON, and of the HOLY GHOST. A-m

I Pray GOD to bleſs my Fa-ther and
ther, Bro-thers and Siſters, and all my
Friends, and my E-ne-mies. *A-men.*

OUR Father which art in H
ven, hal-low-ed be thy Name;
King-dom come; thy Will be don
Earth as it is in Heaven. Give us
Day our daily Bread; and forgive us
Treſ-paſſes, as we for-give them
treſ-paſs a-gainſt us; and lead us no
to Temp-tation, but deliver us
Evil; for thine is the King-dom,
Power and the Glo-ry, for e-ver
e-ver. *A-men.* 1 2 3 4 5 6 7 8 9

Chapter X

School Books

The first book from which the children of the colonists learned their letters and to spell was not really a book at all, in our sense of the word. It was what was called a hornbook. A thin piece of wood, usually about four or five inches long and two inches wide, had placed upon it a sheet of paper a trifle smaller, printed at the top with the alphabet in large and small letters; below were

From The Royal Battledore, *1770–1787*

simple syllables such as ab, eb, ib, ob, etc.; then came the Lord's Prayer. This printed page was covered with a thin sheet of yellowish horn, which was not as transparent as glass, yet permitted the letters to be read through it, and both the paper and the horn were fastened around the edges to the wood by a narrow strip of metal, usually brass, which was tacked down by fine tacks or nails. It was, therefore, a book of a single page. At the two upper corners of the page were crosses, hence to read the hornbook was often called "reading a criss-cross row." At the lower end of the wooden back was usually a little handle which often was pierced with a hole; thus the hornbook

Ivory and silver hornbook (English), 18th century (The Free Library of Philadelphia, rare book department)

could be carried by a string, which could be placed around the neck or hung by the side.

From these shabby little relics and from thousands of their ill-printed but useful kinsfolk, childish lips in America first read aloud the letters, pointed out firmly by a knitting needle in some schooldame's hand. Unthreatened by scientific principles of instruction, the young colonists stoutly shouted their abc's, spelled out their prayer, read in triumphal chorus their criss-cross row.

The knitting needle of the schooldame could be dignified by the pompous name of fescue, a pointer; and something of that nature, a straw, a pin, a quill, a skewer of wood, was always used to direct children's eyes to letter or word.

"Gilt horns" were sold in Philadelphia with Bibles and primers, as we learn from the *Pennsylvania Gazette* of December 4, 1760, and in New York in 1753, so says the *New York Gazette* of

May 14, of that year. Pretty little lesson-toys these must have proved.

The hornbook was called by other names, horn-gig, horn-bat, battledore-book, absey-book, etc.; and in Dutch it was the *a-b-boordje.* They were worked in needlework and written in ink, stamped on tin and carved in wood, as well as printed.

In England, at certain fairs and in Kensington bake shops, gingerbread hornbooks were made and sold.

In New England there were "cookey-moulds," which were of heavy wood incised with the alphabet. They were of ancient Dutch manufacture and had been used for making "koeckje" hornbooks.

The printed cardboard battledore was a successor of the hornbook. This was often printed on a double fold of stiff card with a third fold or flap lapping over like an old pocketbook. These battledores were issued in such vast numbers that it is futile to attempt even to allude to the myriad of publishers. A form of the hornbook was seen in the wooden "reading-boards" that were used in Erasmus Hall, the famous old academy built in 1786 in Flatbush, Long Island. These "reading-boards" are tablets of wood, fifteen inches long, covered on either side with time-yellowed paper printed in large letters with some simple reading lesson. The old-fashioned long "s"—*ſ*—in the type proves their age. Through a pierced hole a loop of string suspended these boards before a class of little scholars, who doubtless all read in chorus. They were certainly used in Dutch schools in the seventeenth century, as the illustrations of old Dutch books prove.

A prymer, or primer, was specifically and ecclesiastically before and after the Reformation in England a book of private devotions. As authorized by the Church and written or printed partially or wholly in the vernacular, it contained devotions for the hours, the Creed, Lord's Prayer, Ten Commandments, some psalms and certain instructions as to the elements of Christian knowledge. These little books often opened with the criss-cross row or alphabet arranged hornbook fashion, hence the term primer naturally came to be applied to all elementary books for children's use. A, B, C, the Middle English name for the alphabet in the forms apsey, abce, absie, etc., was also given to what we now call a primer.

The book which succeeded the hornbook in general use was the *New England Primer.* It was the most universally studied schoolbook that has ever been used in America. It was *the* schoolbook of America and was frequently printed and much used. More than three million copies of this *New England Primer* were printed. These were studied by many more millions of schoolchildren. It was so religious in all its teachings and suggestions that it has been fitly called the "Little Bible of New England."

It is a poorly printed little book about five inches long and three wide, of about eighty pages. It contains the alphabet, and a short table of easy syllables, such as a-b ab, e-b, eb, and words up to those of six syllables. This was called a syllabarium. There were twelve five-syllable words; of these five were *abomination, edification, humiliation, mortification,* and *purification*. There were a morning and evening prayer for children, and a grace to be said before meat. Then followed a set of little rhymes which have become known everywhere. Each letter of the alphabet is illustrated with a blurred little picture. Of these, two-thirds represent Biblical incidents. They begin

"In Adam's fall
We sinned all."

and end with Z

"Zaccheus he
Did climb a tree
His Lord to see."

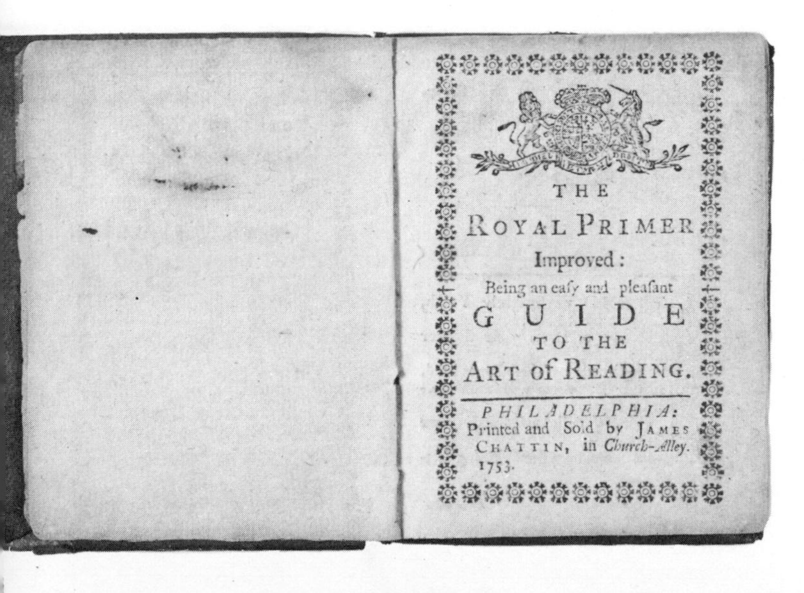
THE
ROYAL PRIMER
Improved:
Being an easy and pleasant
GUIDE
TO THE
ART of READING.

PHILADELPHIA:
Printed and Sold by JAMES
CHATTIN, in *Church-Alley.*
1753.

From the first American edition of The Royal Primer, *1753 (The Free Library of Philadelphia, rare book department)*

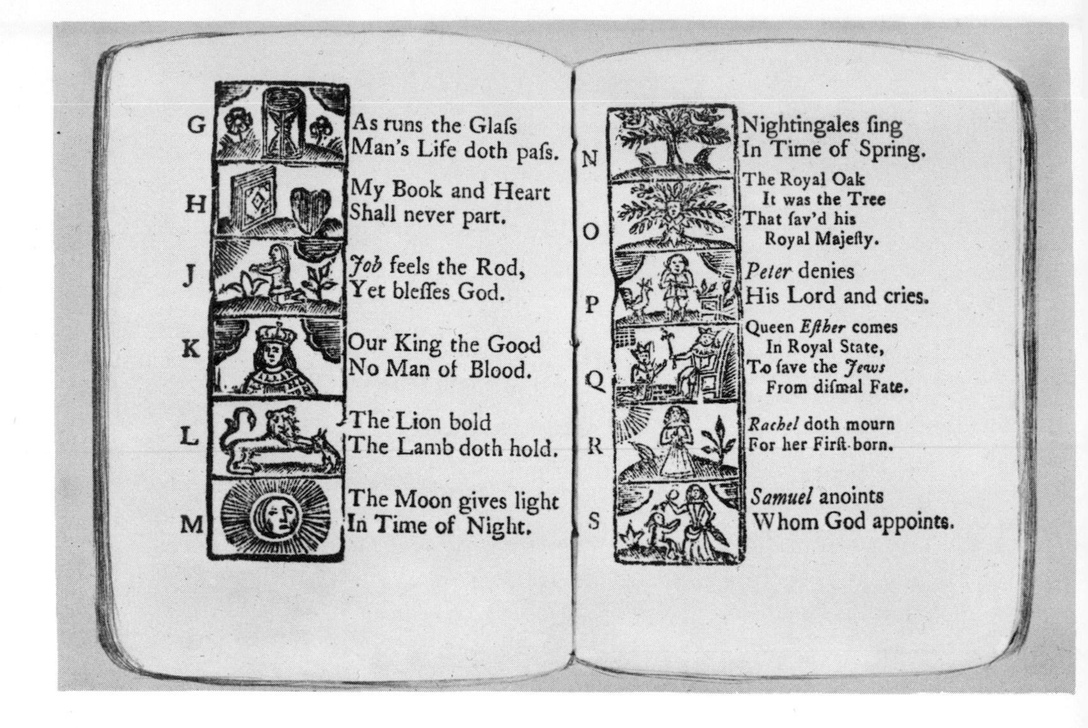

G As runs the Glaſs
Man's Life doth paſs.

H My Book and Heart
Shall never part.

J *Job* feels the Rod,
Yet bleſſes God.

K Our King the Good
No Man of Blood.

L The Lion bold
The Lamb doth hold.

M The Moon gives light
In Time of Night.

N Nightingales ſing
In Time of Spring.

O The Royal Oak
It was the Tree
That ſav'd his
Royal Majeſty.

P *Peter* denies
His Lord and cries.

Q Queen *Eſther* comes
In Royal State,
To ſave the *Jews*
From diſmal Fate.

R *Rachel* doth mourn
For her Firſt-born.

S *Samuel* anoints
Whom God appoints.

From New England Primer, *1769* (*The Free Library of Philadelphia, rare book department*)

In the early days of the primer, all the colonies were true to the English king, and the rhyme for the letter K reads

"King Charles the Good
No man of blood."

But by Revolutionary years the verse for K was changed to

"Queens and Kings
Are Gaudy Things."

Later verses tell the praise of George Washington. Then comes a series of Bible questions and answers; then an "alphabet of lessons for youth," consisting of verses of the Bible beginning successively with A, B, C, and so on. X was a difficult initial letter, and had to be contented with "Xhort one another daily, etc." After the Lord's Prayer and Apostles' Creed appeared sometimes a list of names for men and women, to teach children to spell their own names. The largest and most interesting picture was that of the burning at the stake of John Rogers, and after this a six-page set of pious rhymes which the martyr left at his death for his family of small children.

After the year 1750, a few very short stories were added to its pages and were probably all the children's stories that many of the scholars of that day ever saw. It is interesting to see that the little prayer so well known today, beginning "Now I lay me down to sleep," is usually found in the *New England Primer* of dates later than the year 1737. The *Shorter Catechism* was, perhaps, the most important part of this primer. It was so called in contrast to the catechism in use in England called *The Careful Father and Pious Child,* which had 1200 questions with answers. The *Shorter Catechism* had but 107 questions, though some of the answers were long. Usually another catechism was found in the primer, called *Spiritual Milk for Babes.* It was written by the Boston minister John Cotton and it had but 87 questions with short answers. Sometimes a *Dialogue between Christ, Youth, and the Devil* was added.

The *Shorter Catechism* was the special delight of all New Englanders. Cotton Mather begged writing masters to set sentences from it to be copied by their pupils, and he advised mothers to "continually drop something of the Catechism on their children, as Honey from the Rock." Learning the catechism was enforced by law in New England, and the deacons and ministers visited and examined families to see that the law was obeyed.

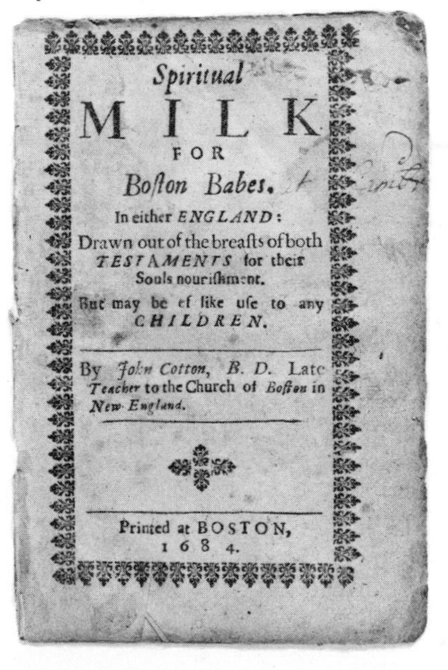

Spiritual

MILK

FOR

Boſton Babes.

In either *ENGLAND*:

Drawn out of the breaſts of both *TESTAMENTS* for their Souls nouriſhment.

But may be of like uſe to any *CHILDREN.*

By *John Cotton, B. D.* Late *Teacher* to the Church of *Boſton* in *New-England.*

Printed at BOSTON, 1684.

Title page from Spiritual Milk for Boston Babes, *1684 (The Free Library of Philadelphia, rare book department)*

When any scholar could advance beyond hornbook and primer he was ready for grammar. This was not English grammar, but Latin, and the boy usually began to study it long before he had any book. A bulky and wretched grammar called Lilly's was most popular in England.

Ezekiel Cheever, the old Boston schoolmaster who taught for over seventy years, also wrote a Latin grammar, *Cheever's Accidence,* which had unvarying popularity for over a century.

Josiah Quincy, later in life the president of Harvard College, wrote an account of his dismal school life at Andover. He entered the school when he was six years old, and on the form by his side sat a man of thirty. Both began *Cheever's Accidence* and committed to memory pages of a book which the younger child certainly could not understand, and no advance was permitted till the first book was conquered. He studied through the book twenty times before mastering it. The hours of study were long—eight hours a day—and this upon lessons absolutely meaningless.

The custom in Boston was to study through the grammar three times before any application to parsing.

The first English grammar used in Boston public schools was *The Young Lady's Accidence, or a Short and Easy Introduction to English Grammar, design'd principally for the use of Young Learners, more especially for those of the Fair Sex, though Proper for Either.* It is said that 100,000 copies of it were sold. It was a very little grammar about four or five inches long and two or three wide and had only fifty-seven pages, but it was a very good little grammar when compared with its fellows, being simple and clearly worded.

The fashion of the day was to set everything in rhyme as an aid to memory, and even so unpoetical a subject as English grammar did not escape the rhyming writer. In the *Grammar of the English Tongue,* a large and formidable book in fine type, all the rules and lists of exceptions and definitions were in verse. A single specimen, the definition of a letter, will show the best style of composition, which, when it struggled with moods and tenses, was absolutely meaningless.

"A Letter is an uncompounded Sound
Of which there no Division can be Found,
Those Sounds to Certain Characters we fix,
Which in the English Tongue are Twenty-Six."

The spelling of that day was wildly varied. *Dilworth's Speller* was one of the earliest used, and the spelling in it differed much from that of the *British Instructor.* A third edition of *The Child's New Spelling Book* was published in 1744. Famous English lesson books known among common folk as "Readamadeasies," and book traders as "Reading Easies"—really Reading made easy—belied their name. Some had alphabets on two pages because "One Alphabet is commonly worn out before the Scholar is perfect in his Letters." It is interesting to find "Poor Richard's" sayings in these English books, but it is natural, too, when we consider Franklin's popularity abroad, and know that broadsides printed with his pithy and worldly-wise maxims were found hanging on the wall of many an English cottage.

Not until the days of Noah Webster and his famous Spelling Book and Dictionary was there any decided uniformity of spelling. In the same letter, men of high education would spell the same word several different ways.

The teaching of spelling in many schools was peculiar. The master gave out the word, with a blow of his strap on the desk as a signal for all to start together, and the whole class spelled out the word in syllables in chorus. The teacher's ear was so trained and acute that he at once detected any misspelling. If this happened, he demanded the name of the scholar who made the mistake. If there was any hesitancy or refusal in acknowledgment, he kept the whole class until, by repeated trials of long words, accuracy was obtained. The roar of the many voices of the large school, all pitched in different keys, could be heard on summer days for a long distance. In many country schools the scholars not only spelled aloud but studied all their lessons aloud, and the teacher was quick to detect any lowering of the volume of sound and would reprove any child who was studying silently. Sometimes the combined roar of voices became offensive to the neighbors of the school, and restraining votes were passed at town meetings.

The colonial school and schoolmaster took a

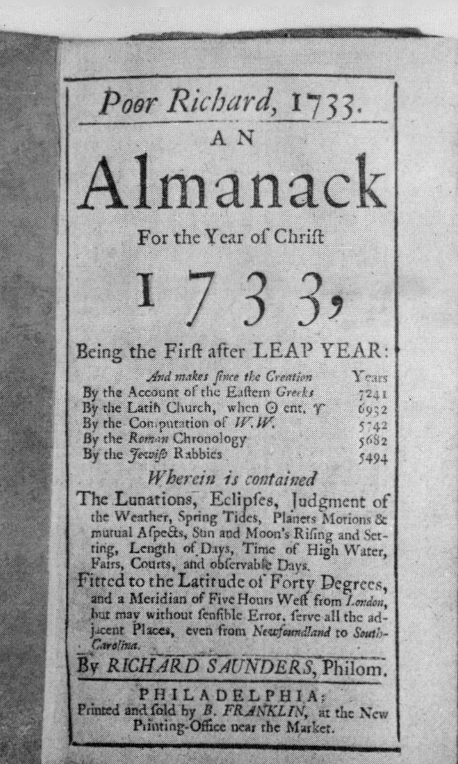

Poor Richard, 1733.

AN

Almanack

For the Year of Chriſt

1733,

Being the Firſt after LEAP YEAR:

And makes ſince the Creation	Years
By the Account of the Eaſtern *Greeks*	7241
By the Latin Church, when ☉ ent. ♈	6932
By the Computation of *W.W.*	5742
By the *Roman* Chronology	5682
By the *Jewiſh* Rabbies	5494

Wherein is contained

The Lunations, Eclipſes, Judgment of the Weather, Spring Tides, Planets Motions & mutual Aſpects, Sun and Moon's Riſing and Setting, Length of Days, Time of High Water, Fairs, Courts, and obſervable Days.

Fitted to the Latitude of Forty Degrees, and a Meridian of Five Hours Weſt from *London*, but may without ſenſible Error, ſerve all the adjacent Places, even from *Newfoundland* to *South-Carolina*.

By *RICHARD SAUNDERS*, Philom.

PHILADELPHIA:
Printed and ſold by *B. FRANKLIN*, at the New Printing-Office near the Market.

From Poor Richard's Almanac, *1733* (*The Free Library of Philadelphia, rare book department*)

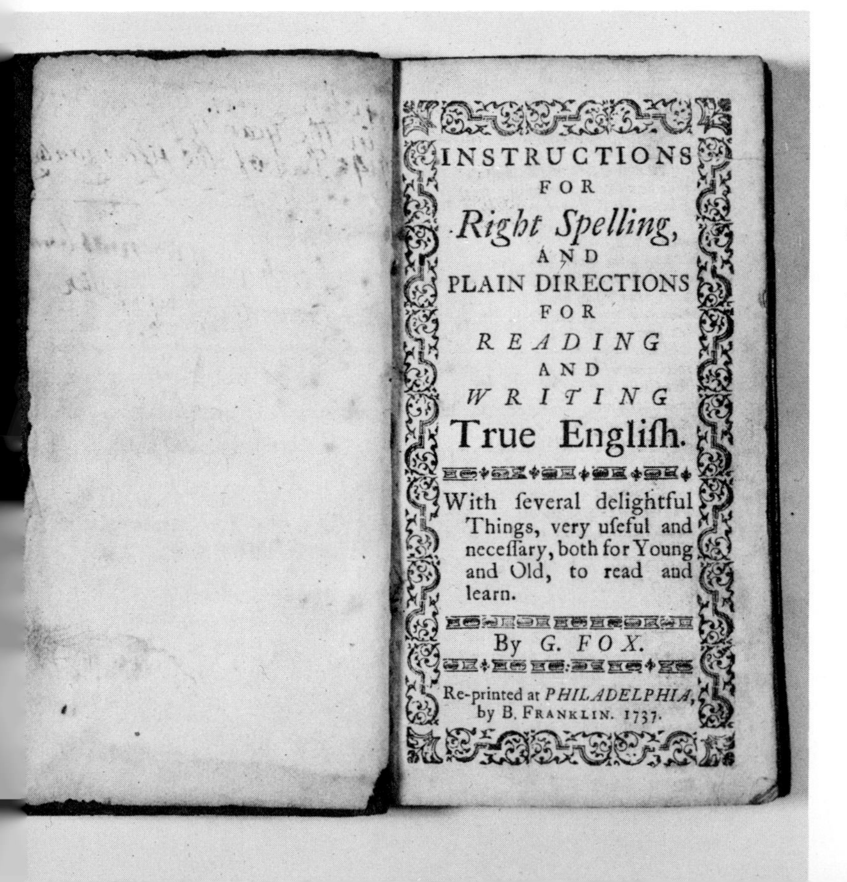

INSTRUCTIONS

FOR

Right Spelling,

AND

PLAIN DIRECTIONS

FOR

READING

AND

WRITING

True Engliſh.

With ſeveral delightful Things, very uſeful and neceſſary, both for Young and Old, to read and learn.

By G. FOX.

Re-printed at *PHILADELPHIA*, by B. FRANKLIN. 1737.

From speller printed by Franklin, 1737 (*The Free Library of Philadelphia, rare book department*) firm stand on "cyphering." "The Bible and figgers is all I want my boys to know," said an old farmer. Arithmetic was usually taught without textbooks. Teachers had manuscript "sum books," from which they gave out rules and problems in arithmetic to their scholars. Too often these sums were copied by the pupil without any explanation of the process being offered or rendered by the master.

Sometimes a zealous teacher would write out tables of measures and a few blind rules for his scholars. This amateur arithmetic would be copied and recopied until it was punctuated with mistakes.

Many scholars never saw a printed arithmetic, and when the master had one for circulation it was scarcely more helpful than the sum book. An edition of *Cocker's Arithmetick* was published in Philadelphia in 1779.

The age that would rhyme a grammar would rhyme an arithmetic. Thomas Hylles published one in 1620, *The Arte of Vulgar Arithmiteke,* written in dialogue with the rules and theorems in verse. This is an example of his poesy:

"THE PARTITION OF A SHILLING INTO HIS ALIQUOT PARTES.

"A farthing first finds forty-eight
A Halfpeny hopes for twentiefoure
Three farthings seeks out 16 streight
A peny puls a dozen lower
Dicke dandiprat drewe 8 out deade
Twopence took 6 and went his way

Tom trip a goe with 4 is fled
But Goodman grote on 3 doth stay
A testerne only 2 doth take
Moe parts a Shilling cannot make."

In 1633 Nicholas Hunt added to his rules and tables an "Arithmetike-Rithmeticall or the Handmaid's Song of Numbers," which rhymes are simply unspeakable.

After the Revolution, in new and zealous America, textbooks by American authors outsold English books. The blue-backed spelling book of Noah Webster drove Perry and Dilworth from the field. Bingham and Webster took advantage of the need of suitable school books and divided the field between them. Webster's Spelling Book outstripped Bingham's *Child's Companion,* but Bing-

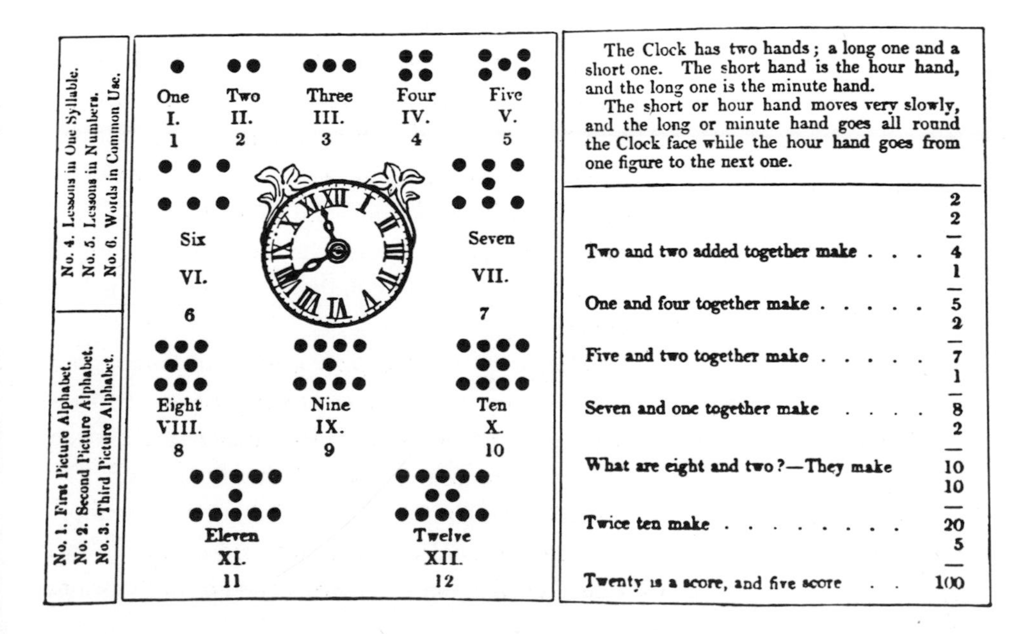
No. 4. Lessons in One Syllable.
No. 5. Lessons in Numbers.
No. 6. Words in Common Use.

No. 1. First Picture Alphabet.
No. 2. Second Picture Alphabet.
No. 3. Third Picture Alphabet.

One I. 1 — Two II. 2 — Three III. 3 — Four IV. 4 — Five V. 5

Six VI. 6 — Seven VII. 7

Eight VIII. 8 — Nine IX. 9 — Ten X. 10

Eleven XI. 11 — Twelve XII. 12

The Clock has two hands; a long one and a short one. The short hand is the hour hand, and the long one is the minute hand.

The short or hour hand moves very slowly, and the long or minute hand goes all round the Clock face while the hour hand goes from one figure to the next one.

	2
	2
Two and two added together make . . .	4
	1
One and four together make	5
	2
Five and two together make	7
	1
Seven and one together make	8
	2
What are eight and two?—They make	10
	10
Twice ten make	20
	5
Twenty is a score, and five score . .	100

From battledore,
Lessons in Numbers

hams's Readers, such as *The American Preceptor* and *The Columbian Orator,* held their ground against Webster's. Not one of Bingham's books proved a failure. *The Columbian Orator* contained seven extracts from speeches of Pitt in opposition to the measures of George III ; it had speeches by Fox and Sheridan, part of the address of President Carnot at the establishment of the French Republic, and the famous speech of Colonel Barré on the Stamp Act.

Nicholas Pike of Newburyport, Massachusetts, wrote an arithmetic that routed the English books. It had 363 barren rules and not a single explanation of one of them. Many of them would now be wholly unintelligible to scholars.

The tables of measures were longer than ours today. In measuring liquids were used the terms anchors, tuns, butts, tierces, kilderkins, firkins, puncheons, etc. In dry measure were pottles, strikes, cooms, quarters, weys, lasts. Examples in currency were in pounds, shillings, and pence, and doubtless helped to retain the use of these terms in daily trade long after dollars had been coined in America.

Wingate's Arithmetic, printed in 1620, was used for over a century in Massachusetts. "Pythagoras his Table," is, of course, our multiplication table. Then comes the "Rule of Three," the "double Golden Rule," the "Rule of Fellowship," the "Rule of False," etc., etc., ending with "Pastimes, a collection of pleasant and polite Questions to exercise all the parts of Vulgar Arithmetick." Here is one:

"This Problem is usually propounded in this manner, viz. fifteen *Christians* and fifteen *Turks* being at Sea in one and the same Ship in a terrible Storm, & the Pilot declaring a necessity of casting the one half of those Persons into the Sea, that the rest might be saved; they all agreed that the

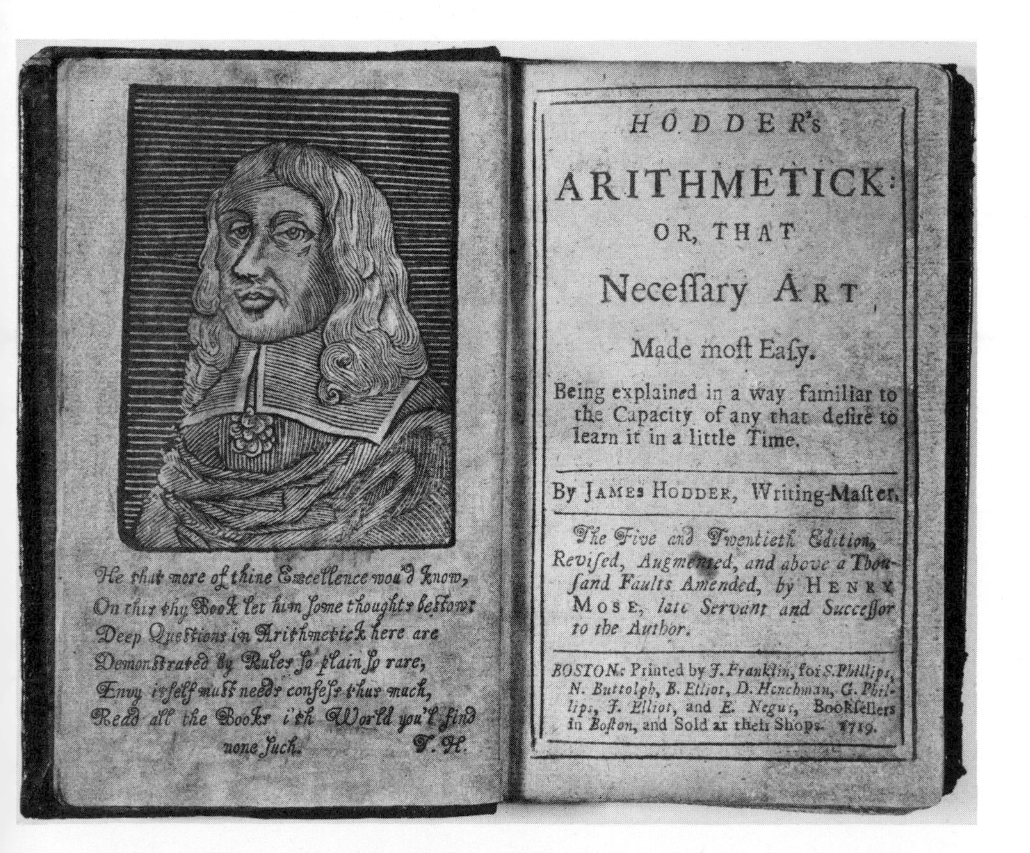

He that more of thine Excellence wou'd know,
On this thy Book let him ſome thoughts beſtow:
Deep Queſtions in Arithmetick here are
Demonſtrated by Rules ſo plain ſo rare,
Envy it ſelf muſt needs confeſs thus much,
Read all the Books i'th World you'l find
none ſuch. T. H.

HODDER's

ARITHMETICK:

OR, THAT

Neceſſary ART

Made moſt Eaſy.

Being explained in a way familiar to the Capacity of any that deſire to learn it in a little Time.

By JAMES HODDER, Writing-Maſter.

The Five and Twentieth Edition, Reviſed, Augmented, and above a Thouſand Faults Amended, by HENRY MOSE, *late Servant and Succeſſor to the Author.*

BOSTON: Printed by *J. Franklin*, for *S. Phillips, N. Buttolph, B. Elliot, D. Henchman, G. Phillips, J. Elliot*, and *E. Negus*, Bookſellers in *Boſton*, and Sold at their Shops. 1719.

From the first American edition of Hodder's Arithmetick, *1719 (The Free Library of Philadelphia, rare book department)*

persons to be cast away should be set out by lot after this manner, viz. the thirty persons should be placed in a round form like a *Ring,* and then beginning to count at one of the Passengers, and proceeding circularly, every ninth person should be cast into the Sea, until of the thirty persons there remained only fifteen. The question is, how those thirty persons ought to be placed, that the lot might infallibly fall upon the fifteen *Turks* & not upon any of the fifteen *Christians?* For the more easie remembering of the rule to resolve this question shall presuppose the five vowels, a, e, i, o, u, to signifie five numbers to wit, (a) one, (e) two, (i) three, (o) four, and (u) five; then will the rule it self be briefly comprehended in these two following verses:—

From numbers, aid and art
Never will fame depart.

In which verses you are principally to observe the vowels, with their correspondent numbers before assigned, and then beginning with the *Christians* the vowel *o* (in *from*) signifieth that four *Christians* are to be placed together; next unto them, the vowel *u* (in *num*) signifieth that five *Turks* are to be placed. In like manner *e* (in *bers*) denoteth 2 *Christians, a* (in *aid*) 1 *Turk, i* (in *aid*) 3 *Christians, a* (in *and*) 1 *Turk, a* (in *art*) 1 *Christian, e* (in *ne*) 2 *Turks, e* (in *ver*) 2 *Christians, i* (in *will*) 3 *Turks, a* (in *fame*) 1 *Christian, e* (in *fame*) 2 *Turks, e* (in *de*) 2 *Christians, a* (in *part*) 1 *Turk.*

"The invention of the said Rule and such like, dependeth upon the subsequent demonstration, viz. if the number of persons be thirty, let thirty figures or cyphers be placed circularly or else in a right line as you see:—

oooooooooooooo."

I trust the little children understood this sum, and its explanation, and that the Christians were all saved, and the Turks were all drowned.

Geography was an accomplishment rather than a necessary study and was spoken of as a diversion for a winter's evening. Many objections were made that it took the scholar's attention away from "cyphering." It was not taught in the elementary schools. *Morse's Geography* was not written till after the Revolution. It had a mean little map of the United States, only a few inches square. On it all the land west of the Mississippi River was called Louisiana, and nearly all north of the Ohio River, the Northwestern Territory.

Chapter XI

Writing

Without doubt the chief requisite of a satisfactory teacher in colonial days was that he should be a good teacher of penmanship.

The colonists whose lives ended with the seventeenth century had a characteristic handwriting which retained certain elements of Old English, even of medieval script. It was a handsome and dignified chirography and an impressive one and

John Hancock, detail from portrait by John Singleton Copley (1738-1815) (Courtesy, City of Boston)

was usually easy to read. The writing of the first Pilgrim and Puritan fathers was not overgood.

The first half of the succeeding century did not send forth such good writers, nor did it send forth writers so universally; the proportion of signatures to public documents by cross instead of writing increased. Children at the close of the eighteenth century wrote beautifully rounded, clear, and uniform hands, if we can judge from their copybooks.

Writing-masters were universally honored in every community. A part of the funeral notice of one in Boston, who died in 1769, reads thus:

"Last Friday morning died Mr. Abiah Holbrook in this town. He was looked upon by the best

From The Juvenile Biographer, *1787*
(The Free Library of Philadelphia, rare book department)

Judges as the Greatest Master of the pen we ever had among us, of which he has left a beautiful Demonstration."

This "beautiful demonstration" of his penmanship was a most intricate piece of what was known as fine knotting, or knotwork. It was said to be "written in all the known hands of Great Britain," and was valued at £100. John Hancock had been one of Master Holbrook's pupils and, as we know from the fine bold signature of his own name to the Declaration of Independence, was a very creditable scholar.

This work had occupied every moment of what Abiah Holbrook called his "spare time" for seven years. As he had, in the year 1745, 220 scholars at one time in one school, his spare time must have been very short. He and other writing-masters of the Holbrook family left behind a still nobler demonstration than this knot-work in the handwriting of their scholars—Boston ministers, merchants, statesmen, and patriots—whose elegant penmanship really formed a distinct style and was known as "Boston Style of Writing."

A well-known Boston writing-master was familiarly known as Johnny Tileston. He was born in 1738 and taught till 1823, when he was pensioned off. He was a rough-mannered old fellow, his

PEN.

these command

Rank of Fame shall stand

God makes the PEN his Herald to proclaim
The splended Glories of his Works and Name.

Abiah Holbrook Scripsit 1767.

Writing of Abiah Holbrook, 1767

chief address to the scholars being the term, "You gnurly wretch." His ideal was his own teacher, Master Proctor, and when late in life he saw a scholar wipe his pen on a bit of cloth, he approached the desk, lifted the rag and said, "What's this? Master Proctor had no such thing." Tileston himself always wiped his pens with his little finger and in turn dried his finger on his own white hairs under his wig. An old spelling book has these lines for a "writing-copy":

"X things a penman should have near at hand—
Paper, pomice, pen, ink, knife, horn, rule, plummet, wax, sand."

It will be noted that a penwiper is not upon the list.

In olden times only one kind of pen was used; one cut from a goose quill with the feathers left on the handle. The selection and manufacture of these goose-quill pens was a matter of considerable care in the beginning and of constant watchfulness and "mending" till the pen was worn out. One of the indispensable qualities of a colonial schoolmaster was that he was a good pen-maker and pen-mender. It often took the master and usher two hours to make the pens for the school. Boys studied arithmetic at eleven years of age but were not allowed to make pens in school till they were twelve years old.

Ink was not bought in convenient liquid form as

at present. Each family, each person, had to be an ink manufacturer. The favorite method of ink-making was through the dissolving of ink powder. Liquid ink was but seldom seen for sale. In remote districts of Vermont, Maine, and Massachusetts, homemade ink, feeble and pale, was made by steeping the bark of swamp maple in water, boiling the decoction till thick, and diluting it with copperas. Each child brought to school an ink bottle or ink horn filled with the varying fluid of domestic manufacture.

There are no remains of olden times that put us more closely in touch with the men, women, and children who moved and lived in these shadowy days than do the letters they wrote.

Manuscripts known under the various titles of the *Mather Papers,* the *Cotton Papers,* the *Torrey Papers,* etc., are delightful to see and to read, for the ink is still clear and black, the paper firm and good, the letters well formed, and the text breathes a spirit of kindness, affection, and loving thoughtfulness that speaks of the beauty of Puritan home life. Some of the letters are written by Puritan women, and these letters are uniformly well spelled, well written, and intelligent. Perhaps only intelligent women were taught to write. These letters are on fine Dutch paper; there was no English writing paper till the time of William and Mary. They are carefully folded with due regard to the etiquette of letter folding and plainly and neatly addressed. The letters are very tender and gentle, sometimes written to children.

We cannot but wonder at the precision and ele-

Writing master's initial

gance of the letter writing of our forbears when we know the "painful" precepts of parents in regard to their children's penmanship and composition. In the letters written by a plain New England farmer, in the years 1749 and on to his son Elijah, while the latter was in Princeton College, is shown the respect felt for a good handwriting. Nearly every letter had some such sentences as these:

"I would intreet you to endeavour daily to Improve yourself in writting and spelling; they are very ornimentall to a scholar and the want of them is an execeeding great Blemish."

"I desire you would observe in your Wrighting to make proper Distances between words; don't blend your words together use your utmost endeavours to spell well; consult all Rules likely to help you; Such words as require it allways begin with a capitoll Letter, it will much Grace your wrighting."

He urges him to study the spelling rules laid down in the *Youth's Instructor in the English Tounge* and tells him not to follow his (the father's) writing for an example as he has "but common English learning." He reproves, admonishes, and finally says Elijah's sisters will prove better scholars than he, if he does not have a care, which was a bitter taunt.

A father in Maryland wrote to his little daughter some very intelligent advice, of which these lines are a portion:

"In letter writing as in conversation it will be found that those who substitute the design of dis-

Thomas Mumford V, by William Johnston, (1732-1772) (The Brooklyn Museum, Dick S. Ramsay and Carl H. De Silver Funds)

tinguishing themselves for that of giving pleasure to those whom they address must ever fail. Having decided upon what is proper to be said accustom yourself to express it in the best possible manner. Always use the words that most exactly correspond with the ideas you mean to express. There are fewer synonymous words in our language than is generally supposed, as you will find in looking over your Dictionary. It has been remembered upon as a great excellence of Gen'l Washington's writings that no one could substitute a single word which could so well express his meaning. I have heard (whether it be true or not I cannot say) that for seven years of his life he never wrote without having his Dictionary before him."

Children (and grown people too) had a very

reprehensible habit of scribbling in their books. Of course each owner wrote his name with more or less elegance and accompanying flourishes, according to his capacity. Some very valuable autographs have by this means been preserved. They also wrote various rhymes and sentiments.

This rhyme is frequently seen:

> "Steal not this Book for if You Do
> The Devil will be after You."

THE
Penman's Advice

To Young Gentlemen.

Ye British Youths, our Age's Hope & Care,
You whom the next may polish, or impair;
Learn by the Pen those Talents to insure,
That fix ev'n Fortune, & from Want secure;
You with a dash in time may drain a Mine,
And deal the Fate of Empires in a Line;
For Ease and Wealth, for Honour & Delight,
Your Hand's yr. Warrant, if you well can Write.
True ease in Writing comes from Art, not Chance,
As those move easiest, who have learn'd to Dance.

To Young Ladies.

Ye springing Fair, whom gentle Minds incline,
To all that's curious, innocent, and fine!
With Admiration in your Works are read,
The various Textures of the twining Thread.
Then let the Fingers, whose unrivall'd Skill,
Exalts the Needle, grace the Noble Quill.
An artless Scrawl ye blushing Scribler shames,
All shou'd be Fair that Beauteous Woman frames.
Strive to excell, with Ease the Pen will move;
And pretty Lines add Charms to infant Love.

Samuel Vaux scrip.
1734.
No. VII

From The Universal Penman, *London, 1743* *(Old Sturbridge Village)*

Occasionally a child's book had a valentine sentiment, or a riddle, or a drawing of hearts and darts; crude pictures of Indians and horses are many.

Grown folk had in colonial days a habit of keeping diaries and making notes in interleaved almanacs. They are chiefly devoted to weather reports and moral and religious reflections, both original and in the form of sermon and lecture notes. Such records were tiresome, but not, however, to those of Puritan faith. There were but few old-time diaries which were not composed on those lines. The chief exception is that historical treasure house, Judge Sewall's diary, which shows plainly, also, the deep religious feeling of its author. Another of more restricted interest, but of value, is that of Dr. Parkman, the Westborough minister. Governor Winthrop's *History* has much of the diary element in it. Naturally, the diaries of children copied in quality and wording those of their elders. A unique exception in these youthful records is the journal of a year or two of the life of a Boston schoolgirl, Anna Green Winslow, which is a story of her life, not of her thoughts.

One Mary Osgood Sumner, sister of Mrs. Holmes (an aunt of Oliver Wendell Holmes), left behind her sermon notes and a "Monitor," or diary, which had what she called a black list of her childish wrong-doings, omissions of duty, etc., while the white list showed the duties she performed. Though she was evidently absolutely conscientious these are the only entries on the "Black Leaf":

"July 8. I left my staise on the bed.
" 9. Misplaced Sister's sash.
" 10. Spoke in haste to my little Sister, spilt the cream on the floor in the closet.
" 12. I left Sister Cynthia's frock on the bed.
" 16. I left the brush on the chair; was not diligent in learning at school.
" 17. I left my fan on the bed.
" 19. I got vexed because Sister was a-going to cut my frock.
" 22. Part of this day I did not improve my time well.
" 30. I was careless and lost my needle.
Aug. 5. I spilt some coffee on the table."

Not a very heinous list.

Here are entries from the good page of her little "Monitor":

WHITE LEAF.

"July 8. I went and said my Catechism to-day. Came home and wrote down the questions and answers, then dressed and went to the dance, endeavoured to behave myself decent.
" 11. I improved my time before breakfast; after breakfast made some biscuits and did all my work before the sun was down.
" 12. I went to meeting and paid good attention to the sermon, came home and wrote down as much of it as I could remember.

" 17. I did everything before breakfast; endeavored to improve in school; went to the funeral in the afternoon, attended to what was said, came home and wrote down as much as I could remember.

" 25. A part of this day I parsed and endeavored to do well and a part of it I made some tarts and did some work and wrote a letter.

" 27. I did everything this morning same as usual, went to school and endeavored to be diligent; came home and washed the butter and assisted in getting coffee.

" 28. I endeavored to be diligent to-day in my learning, went from school to sit up with the sick, nursed her as well as I could.

" 30. I was pretty diligent at my work to-day and made a pudding for dinner.

Aug. 1. I got some peaches for to stew after I was done washing up the things and got my work and was midlin Diligent."

This record of this monotonous young life proves the simplicity of the daily round of a child's life at that time. The pages prove with equal force the domination of the Puritan temperament, a nervous desire and intent to be good, industrious, attentive, and helpful.

John Quincy Adams, when eleven years old,

determined to write a Journal, and he thus lucidly and sensibly explains his intentions to his mother:

"HONOURED MAMMA: My Papa enjoins it upon me to keep a journal, or diary of the Events that happen to me, and of objects I see, and of Characters that I converse with from day to day; and altho' I am convinced of the utility, importance, & necessity of this Exercise, yet I have not patience & perseverance enough to do it so Constantly as I ought. My Pappa, who takes a great deal of Pains to put me in the right way, has also advised me to Preserve copies of all my letters, and has given me a Convenient Blank Book for this end; and altho' I shall have the mortification a few years hence to read a great deal of my Childish nonsense, yet I shall have the Pleasure and advantage of Remarking the several steps by which I shall have advanced in taste judgment and knowledge. . . . My father has given me hopes of a Pencil & Pencil Book in which I can make notes upon the spot to be transferred afterwards to my Diary, and my letters, this will give me great pleasure, both because it will be a sure means of improvement to myself & make me to be more entertaining to you.

"I am my ever honoured and revered Mamma your Dutiful & Affectionate Son.

"JOHN QUINCY ADAMS."

The family of President Adams preserved a vast number of family papers, but this was not among them. When John Quincy Adams was about seven years old, his father was away from home as a delegate to a Congress in Philadelphia which sought to secure unity of action among the rebellious colonies. His patriotic mother taught her boy in their retreat at Braintree to repeat daily each morning, with the Lord's Prayer, Collins' inspiring ode beginning, "How sleep the brave who sink to rest." Later in life Adams wrote to a Quaker friend:

"For the space of twelve months my mother with her infant children dwelt, liable every hour of the day and of the night to be butchered in cold blood, or taken and carried into Boston as hostages. My mother lived in unintermitted danger of being consumed with them all in a conflagration kindled by a torch in the same hands which on the seventeenth of June (1775) lighted the fires of Charlestown. I saw with my own eyes those fires, and heard Britannia's thunders in the Battle of Bunker Hill, and witnessed the tears of my mother and mingled them with my own."

The mother took her boy by the hand and mounted a height near their home and showed him the distant signs of battle. Thus she fixed an impression of a war for liberty on his young memory. Two years later, to relieve her anxious and tedious waiting for intelligence from her husband, the boy became '"post rider" for her between Braintree and Boston, which towns were eleven miles apart—not a light or easy task for the nine-year-old boy with the unsettled roads and unsettled times. The spirit of patriotism which filled the mind of all grown folk was everywhere reflected in the minds of the children.

Besides journal keeping, folks of that day had a useful custom of keeping a commonplace book; that is, they wrote out in a blank book memorable sentences or words which attracted their attention or admiration in the various books they read, or made abstracts or notes of the same. This writing out of aphorisms, statements, etc., not only fixed them in the memory, but kept them where the memory, if faulty, could easily be assisted. It also served as practice in penmanship.

People invented methods of keeping commonplace books and gave rules and instructions in commonplacing. The matter read by many children is clearly indicated by their commonplace books. One entry shows evidence of light reading. It is of riddles which are headed "GUESSES"; they appear in *Mother Goose's Melodies*. The answers are written in a most transparent juvenile shorthand. Thus the answer, "Well," is indicated by the figures 23, 5, 12, 12, referring to the position of the letters in the alphabet.

The usual entries are of a religious character; extracts from sermons, answers from the catechism, verses of hymns, accompany stilted religious aspirations and appeals. In them a painful familiarity with and partiality for quotations bearing on hell and the devil show the religious teaching of the times.

Chapter XII

Story and Picture Books

There seem to have been absolutely no books for the special delight of young men and maids in the first years in the New World, no romances or tales of adventure; or were there any in England.

A chap-book, a cheap, ill-printed edition of Æsop's *Fables,* was read in New England, but there is nothing to indicate that these fables were

THE
ONDERFUL LIFE.
AND
RPRIZING ADVENTURES
OF THE RENOWNED HERO,
OBINSON CRUSOE:
Who lived TWENTY-EIGHT YEARS
ON AN
NINHABITED ISLAND,
Which he afterwards colonifed.

NEW-YORK:
by HUGH GAINE, at his Book-Store in
ver-Square, where may be had a great Variety
tle Books for *Young Mafters* and *Miffes.*
M,DCC,LXXIV.

From Robinson Crusoe, *New York, 1774 (The Free Library of Philadelphia, rare book department*)

specially printed or bought for children, or that children were familiar with them.

Though no great books were written for children during all these years, three of the great books of the world, written with deep purpose, for grown readers, were calmly appropriated by children with a promptness that would seem to prove the truth of the assertion that children are the most unerring critics of a story. These books were *Pilgrim's Progress,* first published in 1688; *Robinson Crusoe,* in 1714; and *Gulliver's Travels,* in 1726. The religious, political, and satirical purposes of these books have been wholly obscured by their warm adoption as stories.

The history of children's storybooks in both England and America begins with the life of John Newbery, the English publisher, who settled in London in 1744. Newbery was the first English bookseller who made any extended attempt to publish books especially for children's reading. The text of these books was written by himself and by various English authors, among them no less a genius than Oliver Goldsmith. Newbery's books were promptly exported to America, where they were doubtless as eagerly welcomed as in England. The meager advertisements of colonial newspapers contain his lists. During Newbery's active career as a publisher—and activity was his distinguishing characteristic—he published over two hundred books for children. One of the earliest was announced in 1744 as "a pretty little pocket book." It contained the story of Jack the Giant Killer.

An amusing, albeit thrifty, intermezzo of all children's books was the publisher's persistent advertisement of his other juvenile literary wares. If a generous godfather is introduced, he is at once importuned to buy another of good Mr. Newbery the printer's books. When Tommy Truelove is to have his reward of virtue and industry, he implores that it may be a little book sold at the Book Shop over against Aldermary Churchyard, Bow Lane. If a kind mama sets out to "learn Jenny June to read," she does it with one of Marshall's "Universal Battledores, so beloved of young masters and misses." The old-time reader was never permitted to forget for over a page that the good, kind, thoughtful gentleman who printed this book had plenty of others to sell.

Other books were sold "with a Ball and Pincushion, the use of which will infallibly make Tommy a good boy, and Polly a good girl." The juvenile characters in the books are always turning aside to read or buy some one of Mr. Newbery's little books, or pulling one of Mr. Newbery's "nice gilded library" out of their pockets, or taking Dr. James' Fever Powder, which was also one of Mr. Newbery's popular specialties.

The Revolutionary patriot and printer Isaiah Thomas was a bright, stirring man of quick wit and active intelligence in all things. He brought out just after the Revolution many little books for children. Nearly all are wholesale reprints of various English books for children, chiefly those of John Newbery.

Isaiah Thomas lived in Worcester, printed these books there, and founded there the American Antiquarian Society. In the library of the society now in that city may be seen copies of nearly all these children's books which he reprinted; and a collection of pretty, quaint little volumes they are.

It is the universal decision of the special students of juvenile literature that Goldsmith wrote *Goody Two Shoes*. Washington Irving thought the title page plainly "bore the stamp of the sly and playful humour" of the author of the *Vicar of Wakefield*. It reads thus:

THE
HISTORY
OF
Little Goody Two-Shoes;
Otherwise called,
Mrs. Margery Two-Shoes.
WITH
The Means by which she acquired her Learning and Wisdom, and in Consequence thereof her Estate.
Set forth at large for the Benefit of those,
Who from a State of Rags and Care,
And having Shoes but half a Pair,
Their Fortune and their Fame would fix,
And gallop in a Coach and Six.
See the Original Manuscript in the *Vatican* at *Rome,* and the Cuts by *Michael Angelo;* illustrated with the Comments of our great modern Critics.

NEW-YORK:
Printed by H. GAINE, at the Bible and Crown, in Hanover-Square. 1775.

From The History of Little Goody Two-Shoes (*The Free Library of Philadelphia, rare book department*)

"The History of Little Goody Two Shoes, otherwise called Mrs. Margery Two Shoes, with the means by which she acquired her Learning and Wisdom, and in consequence thereof, her Estate; set forth at large for the Benefit of those

"Who from a state of Rags and Care
And having Shoes but half a pair,
Their fortune and their fame would fix
And gallop in a Coach and Six."

The first Worcester edition of *Goody Two Shoes* was printed in 1787, with some alterations suited to time and place.

It will doubtless be a surprise to many that *Tommy Trip's History of Beasts and Birds,* etc., was written by Goldsmith. This little book opens with an account of Tommy and his dog Jowler, who serves Tommy for a horse:

"When Tommy has a mind to ride, he pulls a little bridle out of his pocket, whips it upon honest Jowler, and away he gallops tantwivy. As he rides through the town he frequently stops at the doors to know how the good children do within, and if they are good and learn their books, he then leaves an apple, an orange or a plumb-cake at the door, and away he gallops again tantwivy tantwivy."

As a specimen of Tommy's literary skill he gives the lines beginning

"Three children sliding on the ice
Upon a summer's day," etc.

The descriptions of animals are such as would be expected from the author of *Animated Nature,* an amusing medley of truth and tradition.

The name Tommy Trip seems to have been deemed a taking one in juvenile literature and is found in many books for children, both in the titles and as the name of the ascribed author. *A New Lottery Book by Tommy Trip* was used in the manner explained thus:

"As soon as the child can speak let him stick a pin through the page by the side of the letter you wish to teach him. Turn the page every time and explain the letter by which means the child's mind will be so fixed upon the letter that he will get a perfect idea of it, and will not be liable to mistake it for any other. Then show him the picture opposite the letter and make him read the name of."

Old-time joke books called *Guess Books* were deemed proper reading for children, such as *Joe Miller's* and *Merry Tales of the Wise Men of Gotham;* very stale and dull were the jests. The *Puzzling Cap* was a popular one, also *The Sphinx or Allegorical Lozenges.* Others were *Guess Again,* and one entitled *Food for the Mind,* which bore these lines on the title page:

"Who Riddles Tells and Many Tales,
O'er Nutbrown Cakes and Mugs of Ale."
—HOMER.

Nurse Truelove was a popular character in these books, and a popular story was *Nurse True*

Love's New Year Gift, designed as a present to every little Boy who would become a great Man, and ride upon a fine Horse, and to every little Girl who would become a fine Woman and ride in a Governour's Coach; But Turn over the Leaf and see More of the Matter. This was originally an English book, one of Newbery's.

The Brother's Gift, or the Naughty Girl Reformed of which the third Worcester edition was printed in 1791 bore these lines as a motto:

"Ye Misses, Shun the Coxcomb of the Mall,
The Masquerade, the Rout, the Midnight Ball;
In lieu of these more useful arts pursue,
And as you're fair, be wise and virtuous too."

Though useful arts were inculcated by this book, the reward of virtue to the reformed girl was a fine new pair of stays.

Another of Newbery's beloved books was *The History of Tommy Careless, or the Misfortunes of a Week.* On Monday Tommy fell in the water, spoiled his coat, and was sent to bed. On Tuesday he lost his kite and ended the day in bed. On Wednesday he fell from the apple tree and again was put in bed. Thursday the maid gave him two old pewter spoons; he made some dump-molds, and in casting his dumps scalded his fingers, and as ever was put in retirement. On Friday he killed the canary bird—and to bed again. On Saturday he managed to incite Dobbin to kick the house dog and kill him; then he caught his own fingers in a trap, and ended the week in bed as he began it.

When we think of the vast number of these books, it seems strange that so few have survived. The penny books were too valueless to be saved. It has been the fate, however, of most children's books to be destroyed by children. With coarse, time-browned paper, poor type, and torn, worn leaves, they are not very attractive.

In these books is found an entirely different code from that inculcated by modern books or taught by earlier books. The first books for children simply exhorted goodness, giving no reasons, but commanding obedience and virtue. The books of the Puritan epoch taught children to be good for fear of hell. The succeeding school instructed them to be good because it was profitable. All the advice is frankly politic; much is of a mercenary mold. Children are instructed to do right, not because they should, but because they will benefit thereby—and profit is given the most worldly guise, such as riding in a coach, having a purse full of gold, wearing silks and satins, or becoming Lord Mayor. Punishment, the abhorrence of parents, and evil results fall upon children not so fiercely for lying, stealing, treachery, or cruelty as they do for soiling their clothes, falling into the water, tumbling off walls, breaking windows or china, and a score of other actions which are the result of carelessness, clumsiness, or indifference, rather than of viciousness.

It was the constant effort of the artists, authors, and teachers of olden times to imbue youth with the notion that no harm could possibly come to the good—unless early death could be counted an evil. Children were taught that virtue and each good action was ever, immediately, and conspicuously rewarded. The pictures repeated and emphasized the didactic teachings, and morality, industry, and good intentions were made to triumph over things animate and inanimate. That the old illustrations were a delight to children cannot be doubted; they were so easily comprehended. The bad boys of the story always bore a miserable countenance and figure, and the good boys were smugly prosperous. The prim girls are shown the beloved of all, and the tomboys equally the misery and embarrassment.

There was one book which children loved, that every little child loves today—*Mother Goose's Melodies,* the popular name for a collection of nursery rhymes printed for John Newbery about 1760. About 1785 Isaiah Thomas issued at Worcester, Massachusetts, an edition of *Mother Goose's Melodies* with the songs from Shakespeare, and certainly this must have been an oasis in the desert of dull books for New England children.

Included in these melodies are the verses "Three children sliding on the ice," which we know were written by Goldsmith. Here is an example of one of the melodies and its note:

"Trip upon Trenchers
Dance upon Dishes
My mother sent me for some Barm, some Barm.
She bade me tread Lightly

And leave again Quickly,
For fear the Young Men should do me some Harm.
Yet! don't you see?
What naughty tricks they put upon me!
They broke my Pitcher
And spilt my Water
And huffed my Mother
And chid her Daughter,
And kiss'd my Sister instead of me.

"What a Succession of Misfortunes befell this poor Girl? But the last Circumstance was the most affecting and might have proved fatal."
—WINSLOW'S *View of Britain.*

According to the notion of humor of the day, the notion of Goldsmith, or some other book-hack-wag, these notes were all ascribed as quotations from some profound author. Thus after the rhymes, "See-saw, Margery Daw," etc., is the sober comment, "It is a mean and Scandalous Practice in an author to put Notes to a Thing that deserves no Notice. Grotius." After the "Three Wise Men of Gotham," which ends with the lines

"If the bowl had been stronger
My tale had been longer,"

is the sentemtious note "It's long enough. Never lament the Loss of what is not worth having. Boyle."

From Cobwebs to Catch Flies, *first published 1783*

A very priggish little book was entitled *Cobwebs to Catch Flies*. The tone of its text may be shown in the dialogue about "The Toss About." The brothers who attended a country fair had been forbidden by their mother to ride in the Merry-go-round. Dear Ned wished to try the fun. Dear James said with propriety, "Dear Ned, I am sure our mamma would object to our riding in this Toss-about." Ned answered, "Dear James, did you ever hear her name the Toss-about?" "No, dear Ned, but I am certain that if she had known of it she would have given us the same caution as she did about the Merry-go-round." Ned paused a moment, then said, "How happy am I to have an elder brother who is so prudent." Whereupon James replied, "I am no less happy that you are so willing to be advised," etc.

A distinctly American book for children was printed in Philadelphia in 1793, a *History of the Revolution*. It was in Biblical phraseology. This sort of writing had been made popular by Franklin in his famous *Parable against Persecution,* which he wrote, committed to memory, and pretended to read as the last chapter in Genesis.

Exceeding plainness and even coarseness of speech was presented in the pages of these old-time storybooks. It was simply the speech of the times shown in the plays, tales, and essays of the day and reflected to some degree even in the literature for children. As an example of what was deemed wit may be given a portion of the prologue to "Who Killed Cock Robin." The book is entitled *Death and Burial of Cock Robin.*

"We were all enjoying ourselves very agreeably after dinner, when on a sudden, Sir Peter's Lady gave so loud a sneeze as threw the whole company into disorder. Master Danvers instead of cracking a nut gave his fingers a tolerable squeeze in the nut-crackers. Miss Friendly who had carried with intent to put a fine cherry in her mouth missed the mark and bit her finger. Sir Peter himself, who was filling a glass of wine, spilled the bottle on the table. Miss Comely and Miss Danvers who were talking with each other with their heads very close to each other very politely knocked them together to see which was the hardest. I myself had twelve of my ten toes handsomely trod on by one of the young ladies jumping off a chair in a fright. But this is not all, no nor half what I was an eye witness of; for just at the time her Ladyship sneezed, I was busy contemplating the beauty and song of Miss Prudence's Cock Robin that was singing and as noisy as a grig when my Lady sneezed which so frightened him he fell to the bottom of the Cage as dead as a Stone."

A widely read little book was somewhat pompously entitled *The Looking Glass for the Mind.* It was chiefly translated from that much-admired work, *L'Ami des Enfans.* Those terse and entertaining tales of Berquin had perennial youth in their English form and were reprinted often.

In the *Boston Gazette and Country Journal,* January 20, 1772, the Boston booksellers Cox and Berry gave this notice of their wares:

"The following Little Books for the Instruction and Amusement of all good Boys and Girls:—

The Brother Gift or the Naughty Girl Reformed.
The Sister Gift or the Naughty Boy Reformed.
Hobby Horse or Christian Companion.
Robin Good-Fellow, a Fairy Tale.
Puzzling Cap, a Collection of Riddles.
The Cries of London as exhibited in the Streets.
Royal Guide or Early Instruction in Reading English.
Mr. Winlove's Collection of Moral Tales.
History of Tom Jones abridg'd.
" " Joseph Andrews "
" " Pamela "
" " Grandison "
" " Clarissa " "

It may be seen by the last-named books on this list that another series of books for children were abridgments of *Tom Jones, Joseph Andrews, Pamela,* and other great novels of the day. The childish reader is notified that if he likes the little books, his good friend Mr. Thomas has the larger books for sale.

Little Anna Green Winslow speaks occasionally in her diary of storybooks. She had for a New-Year's gift the "History of Joseph Andrews abbreviated in guilt and flowered covers." She read the *Pilgrim's Progress,* the *Mother's Gift, Gulliver's Travels, The Puzzling Cap, The French Orators,* and *Gaffer Two Shoes*—this may have been our own Goody, not Gaffer.

These books were cheap enough, but a penny apiece, some of them, others sixpence. It is doubtful whether they were ever sold in America in vast numbers. Children lent them to each other. Anna Green Winslow borrowed them, and letters of her day show other children doing likewise. It was a day of book lending, for circulating libraries were slow of formation. The minister's library was often the largest one in each town, and he lent his precious books to his flock. In the sparse advertisements of colonial newspapers are many advertisements of book owners who have lent books, forgotten to whom, and wish them returned. The only way country children had of reading many books was by borrowing.

Chapter XIII

Games, Pastimes, and Toys

It is interesting to note the persistent survival of games which are seldom learned from printed rules but are simply told from child to child from year to year. Hopscotch is still played as our ancestors played "Scotch-hoppers" in their day.

The variants of tag are played just as they were played when Boston and New York streets were lanes and cowpaths. The pretty game, "I catch

From The Juvenile Biographer, *1787* (*The Free Library of Philadelphia, rare book department*)

you without green," mentioned by Rabelais, is well known in the Carolinas, whither it was carried by French Huguenot immigrants, who retained many of their home customs. Stone tag and wood tag took the place in America of the tag on iron of Queen Elizabeth's day. Squat tag and cross tag have their times and seasons, and in Philadelphia tell tag was also played. Pickadill is a winter sport, a tag played in the snow. Another tag game known as poison, or stone-poison, is where the player is tagged if he steps off stones.

A truly historic game taught by children to each other is what is called cat's cradle or cratch cradle. One player stretches a length of looped cords over the extended fingers of both hands in a symmetri-

From A Little Pretty Pocketbook, *1787* (*The Free Library of Philadelphia, rare book department*)

cal form. The second player inserts the fingers and removes the cord without dropping the loops in a way to produce another figure. These various figures had childish titles.

In a quaint little book called *The Pretty Little Pocket Book,* published in America in Revolutionary times, is a list of boys' games with dingy pictures showing how the games were played. The names given were chuck-farthing, kite-flying, dancing round May-pole, marbles, hoop and hide, thread the needle, fishing, blindman's buff, shuttlecock, king am I, peg-farthing, knock out and span, hop, skip, and jump, boys and girls come out to play, I sent a letter to my love, cricket, stool-ball, base-ball, trap-ball, swimming, tip-cat, train-banding, fives, leap-frog, bird-nesting, hop-hat, shooting, hop-scotch, squares, riding, rosemary tree. The descriptions of the games are given in rhyme and to each attached a moral lesson in verse. Some of the verses read thus:

"CHUCK-FARTHING

"As you value your Pence
  At the Hole take your Aim.
Chuck all safely in,
  And You'll win the Game.

"MORAL.

"Chuck-Farthing like Trade,
Requires great Care.
The more you observe
The better you'll fare."

A few of the games are today unknown, or little known. For instance, the game called in the book "Pitch and Hussel":

"Poise your hand fairly,
Pitch plumb your Slat.
Then shake for all Heads
Turn down the Hat."

The game called "All the birds of the air," reads

"Here various boys stand round and soon
Does each some favorite bird assume;
And if the Slave once hits his name,
He's then made free and crowns the game."

A list and description of many of the historic singing games and rounds of American children would include: "Here we go round the mulberry bush," "Here come three Lords out of Spain," "On the green carpet here we stand," "I've come to see Miss 'Ginia Jones," "Little Sally Waters, sitting in the sun," "Green gravel, green gravel, the grass is so green," "Old Uncle John is very sick, what shall we send him?" "Oats, pease,

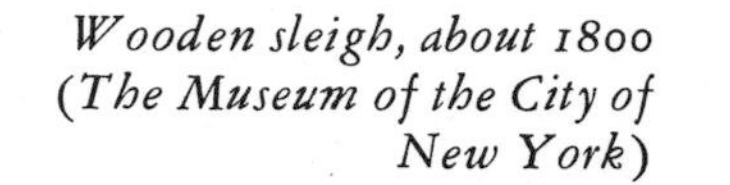

Wooden sleigh, about 1800 (The Museum of the City of New York)

beans and barley grows," "When I was a shoemaker," "Here I brew, Here I bake, Here I make my Wedding Cake," "The needle's eye that doth supply," "Soldier Brown will you marry, marry me?" "O dear Doctor don't you cry," "There's a rose in the garden for you, young man," "Ring around a rosy," "Go round and round the valley," "Quaker, Quaker, How art thee?" "I put my right foot in," "My master sent me to you, sir," "London Bridge is falling down."

Some of these rhymes were founded on certain lines of ballads, but without any printed words or music everyone knew them well, and the music was the same that was always used.

The Dutch settlers had many games. They were very fond of bowling on the grass. A well-known street in New York, Bowling Green, shows the popularity of the game and where it was played. They played "tick-tack," a complicated sort of backgammon; and trock, on a table somewhat like a billiard table. In it an ivory ball was struck under wire wickets with a cue. Coasting downhill became a most popular sport. Many attempts were made to control and stop the coasters. At one time the Albany constables were ordered to take the "small or great slees" in which "boys and girls ryde down the hills," and break them in pieces. At another time the boy had to forfeit his hat if he were caught coasting on Sunday. The sleds were low with a rope in front and were started and guided by a sharp stick.

There is a Massachusetts law of the year 1633 against "common coasters, unprofitable fowlers and tobacco-takers"—three classes of detrimentals. At first coasting meant loafing along the shore, then idling in general, then sliding downhill for fun. In New England they used a double runner, a long narrow board platform on two sleds or two sets of runners.

"Sports of the Innyards" languished in New England. Innkeepers were ordered not to permit the playing of "Dice, Cards, Tables, Quoits, Loggats, Bowls, Ninepins, or any other Unlawful Game in house, yard, Garden or backside." Slide-groat was also forbidden. Shovel-board was almost the only game that was tolerated. This game was perhaps the most popular of old-time domestic pastimes and was akin to slide-groat.

Cockfighting was popular in the Southern colonies and New York. There are prohibitions against it in the rules of William and Mary College. Cockfights were often held on Shrove Tuesday. The cruel Dutch sport of riding for the goose was riding at full speed to catch a swinging greased goose.

Playing cards were fiercely hated and their sale prohibited in Puritan communities, but games of cards could not be "beaten down." Grown folk had a love of card-playing and gaming. But young children did not indulge much in card-playing in any of the colonies.

William Bradford, then governor of the colony at Plymouth, thus grimly records in his now famous Log-book, the first Christmas Day in that settlement:

"The day called Christmas Day ye Gov[r] cal'd them out to worke (as was used) but ye moste of this new company excused themselves, and saide y[t] went against their consciences to work on y[t] Day. So ye Gov[r] tould them that if they made it mater of conscience, he would spare them till they were better informed. So he led away ye rest and left them; but when they came home at noon from their work he found them in ye street at play openly, some pitching ye bar, and some at stoolball and such like sports. So he went to them and took away their implements and tould them it was against his conscience that they should play and others work."

The American Indians were found playing a game of football like that of their white brothers. The Indians' game was described thus:

"There was that day a great game of Foot-ball to be played. There was another Town played against 'em as is sometimes common in England; but they played with their bare feet, which I thought very odd; but it was upon a broad sandy Shoar free from Stones which made it the more easie. Neither were they so apt to trip up one another's heels and quarrel as I have seen 'em in England."

A record of old-time sports would be incomplete without reference to the laws of sport times.

Children cannot explain them, nor is their any leader who establishes them. It is not a matter of reason; it is instinct. A Swiss writer says that boys' games there belong chiefly to the first third of the year, always return in the same order, and "without the individual child being able to say who had given the sign, and made the beginning." From Maine to Georgia the first time is marble time. Then comes tops. The saying is, "Top time's gone, kite time's come, April Fool's Day will soon be here." Ballplaying in Boston had as its time the first Thursday in April. Whistle-making would naturally come at a time when whistle wood was in good condition. All the boys in all the towns perch on stilts closely and in unison. There is much sentiment in the thought that for years, almost for centuries, thousands of boys in every community have had the same games at the same time, and the recital almost reaches the dignity of history.

Playthings for children in colonial time were few in number, save the various ones they manufactured for themselves. They played more games and had fewer toys than modern children. In 1712, on the list of rich goods brought into Boston by a privateersman and sold there were "Boxes of Toys." In 1743 the *Boston News Letter* advertised "Dutch and English Toys for Children," and Boston had a flourishing toy shop at that date. Other towns did not, as we know from many shipping orders.

The Toy Shop or Sentimental Preceptor, one

Queen Anne Doll (English), 18th century (The Metropolitan Museum of Art, Gift of Mrs. Screven Lorillard, 1953)

of Newbery's books, gives a list of toys which the young English scholar sought. They are a looking-glass, a "spying glass," a "fluted dog," a pocket book, a mask, a drum, a doll, a watch, a pair of scales. Few of these articles named would really be termed toys. Some of the games already alluded to, such as top spinning, hoop rolling, and the various games of ball, required toys to carry them on.

The first childish girl emigrants to this solemn new world had something in the semblance of a doll, though far removed from the radiant doll creatures of this day; little puppets, crude and shapeless, yet ever beloved symbols of maternity, have been known to children in all countries and all ages. Dolls were called puppets in olden times, and babies. The circulation of dressed dolls as fashion transmitters was a universal custom. Dolls were sent from house to house, from town to town, from country to country, and even to a new continent.

These babies for fashion models came to be

made in large numbers for the use of milliners. As the finest ones came from the Netherlands, they were called "Flanders babies." To the busy fingers of Dutch children, English and American children owed many toys besides these dolls. It was a rhymed reproach to the latter that

"What the children of Holland take pleasure in making,
The children of England take pleasure in breaking."

Fashions changed, and the modish raiment grew antiquated and despised, but still the "Flanders babies" had a cherished old age. They were graduated from milliners' boxes and mantua-makers' show rooms to nurseries and playrooms.

Doll (English), 1790 or later (The New-York Historical Society)

The best dolls in England were originally sold at Bartholomew Fair and were known as "Bartholomew babies." In *Poor Robin's Almanack,* 1695, is a reference to a "Bartholomew baby trickt up with ribbons and knots"; and they were known at the time of the landing of the Pilgrims.

Skillful jackknives could manufacture homemade dolls' furniture. Birch bark was especially adaptable to such uses. The wicker cradles and "chaises" of babies were copied in miniature for dolls. Tin toys were scarce, for tin was not much used for domestic utensils. The eternal desire of a child for something suggestive of a horse found satisfaction in homemade hobby horses. When American ships wandered over the world in the India trade, they brought home to American chil-

Rocking horse, 18th century (The New-York Historical Society)

dren strange coaches and chariots of gay colors and strange woods. These were often comical copies of European shapes, sometimes astonishingly crude, but ample for the ever active imagination of a child to clothe with beautiful outlines.

The word "jack" as a common noun and in compound words has been held to be a general term applied to any contrivance which does the work of a boy or servant, or a simple appliance which is subjected to common usage. In French the name Jacques was a term for a young man of menial condition. The term "country jake" is of kindred sense. Jack lord, jack meddler, jackanapes, Jack Tar, smoke-jack, jack-o'-lantern, black-jack, jack-rabbit, the term jack applied to the knave in playing cards, and the expressions jack-at-a-pinch, jack in office, jack in bedlam, jack in a box, jack of all trades, and many others show the derivative meaning. Hence jackknife may mean a boy's knife. In English dialect the word was jack-lag-knife, also jack-a-legs, in Scotch, jock-te-leg—these by a somewhat fanciful derivation said to be from Jacques de Liege, the celebrated cutler.

The boy's stock of toys was largely supplied by his own jackknife: elder pop guns, chestnut and willow whistles, windmills, water wheels, box traps, figure-4 traps. Toy weapons have varied little since the beginning of the Christian era. Clubs, slings, bows and arrows, air guns, are as old as the year One. Ere these were used as toys, they had been formidable weapons. They were weapons still, for some years of colonial life. In 1645 the court of Massachusetts ordered that all boys from ten to sixteen years old should be exercised with bows and arrows.

Wooden skates shod with iron runners were invented in the Low Countries. Dutch children in New Netherlands all skated. Advertisements of men's and boys' skates and of "Best Holland skates of different sizes" show a constant demand and use. The first skates that William Livingstone had on the frozen Hudson were made of beef bones, as were those of medieval children. In Massachusetts and Connecticut skating was among

Toy kitchen, late 18th century (The Metropolitan Museum of Art, the Sylmaris Collection, Gift of George Coe Graves, 1930)

Ice skates, about 1800
(The Staten Island Historical Society. Photograph by Alfred Tamarin)

the many Dutch ways and doings practiced by English folk in the new world. The Plymouth Pilgrims brought these Dutch customs to the new world through their long and intimate sojourn in Holland. The New Haven and Connecticut Valley settlers learned them through their constant trade and intercourse with their neighbors, the Dutch of Manhattan, but the Massachusetts Bay settlers of Boston and Salem had known these Dutch ways longer—they brought them from England across seas, from the counties of Essex and Suffolk, where the Dutch had gone years before and married with the English.

Toy cupboard, about 1800
(The Brooklyn Museum. Photograph by Alfred Tamarin)

It was not until October 1771 that a pleasure-filled item appeared—"Boys' Marbles." In *The Pretty Little Pocket Book* are these lines:

"MARBLES

"Knuckle down to your Taw.
Aim well, shoot away.
Keep out of the Ring,
You'll soon learn to Play.

"MORAL

"Time rolls like a Marble,
And drives every State.
Then improve each Moment,
Before its too late."

Boys played with them precisely as boys do now. The poet Cowper in his *Tirocinium* says of the games of his school life:

"The little ones unbutton'd, glowing hot
Playing our games and on the very spot
As happy as we once, to kneel and draw
The chalky ring, and knuckle down at taw."

From A Little Pretty Pocketbook, *1787* (*The Free Library of Philadelphia, rare book department*)

The terms used were taws, vent, back-licks, rounces, dubs, alleys, and alley-taws, agates, bull's-eyes, and commoneys.

Jackstones was an old English game known in Locke's day as dibstones. Other names for the game were chuckstones, chuckie-stones, and clinches. The game is the same as was played two centuries ago; it was a girl's game then.

Battledores and shuttles were advertised for sale in Boston in 1761, but they are far older than that. Many portraits of children show battledores, as that of Thomas Aston Coffin. All books of children's games speak of them. It was, in fact, a popular game and deemed a properly elegant exercise for decorous young misses to indulge in.

Chapter XIV

Girls' and Boys' Occupations

A multitude of household occupations kept the hands of boys and girls from idleness. Some notion of the qualification of a housekeeper in colonial days may be obtained from this advertisement in the *Pennsylvania Packet* of September 23, 1780:

"Wanted at a Seat about half a day's journey from Philadelphia, on which are good improve-

Pieced quilt, 1812
(The New-York Historical Society)

ments and domestics, A single Woman of unsullied Reputation, an affable, cheerful, active and amiable Disposition; cleanly, industrious, perfectly qualified to direct and manage the female Concerns of country business, as raising small stock, dairying, marketing, combing, carding, spinning, knitting, sewing, pickling, preserving, etc., and occasionally to instruct two young Ladies in those Branches of Oeconomy, who, with their father, compose the Family. Such a person will be treated with respect and esteem, and meet with every encouragement due to such a character."

One day's entries in a diary written by a young girl named Abigail Foote, of Colchester, Connecticut, in 1775, included—dressmaking, mending, carding, cheese-making, hatcheling, pleating, ironing, spooling, milking, spinning and dyeing thread, broom-making and scouring the pewter.

She tells also of washing, cooking, knitting, weeding the garden, picking geese, etc., and of many visits to her friends. She dipped candles in the spring and made soap in the autumn. This latter was a trying and burdensome domestic duty, but the soft soap was important for home use.

In preparation for making soft soap all the refuse grease from cooking, butchering, etc., was stored through the winter, as well as woodashes from the great fireplaces. The first operation was to make the lye, to "set the leach." Many families owned a strongly made leach barrel; others made a sort of barrel from a section of bark of the white birch. This barrel was placed on bricks or set at a slight angle on a circular groove in a wood or stone base, then filled with ashes; water was poured in till the lye trickled or leached out through an outlet cut in the groove into a small wooden tub or bucket. The water and ashes were frequently replenished as they wasted, and the lye accumulated in a large tub or kettle. If the lye was not strong enough, it was poured over fresh ashes.

The grease and lye were then boiled together in a great pot over a fire out of doors. It took about six bushels of ashes and twenty-four pounds of grease to make a barrel of soap. The soft soap made by this process seemed like a clean jelly, and showed no trace of the repulsive grease that helped to form it. A hard soap also was made with the tallow of the bayberry and was deemed especially desirable for toilet use. But little hard soap was purchased, even in city homes.

The soap was always carefully stirred one way. The Pennsylvania Dutch used a sassafras stick to stir it. A good smart worker could make a barrel of soap in a day and have time to sit and rest in the afternoon and talk her luck over, before getting supper.

This soft soap was used in the great monthly washings which, for a century after the settlement of the colonies, seem to have been the custom. The household wash was allowed to accumulate, and the washing was done once a month, or in some households once in three months.

Another duty of the women of the old-time household was the picking of domestic geese. Geese were raised for their feathers more than as food. In some towns every family had a flock, and their clanking was heard all day and sometimes all night. In midwinter they were kept in barnyards, but the rest of the year they spent the night in the street.

Goose-picking was cruel work. Three or four times a year the feathers were stripped from the live birds. A stocking was pulled over the bird's head to keep it from biting. Sometimes the head was thrust into a goose basket. The pickers had to wear old clothes and tie covers over the hair, as the down flew everywhere. Goose quills were used for pens. Among the Dutch, geese were raised everywhere, for featherbeds were, if possible, more desired by the Dutch than the English.

When the beautiful and intricate straw bonnets of Italian braid, Genoese, Leghorn, and others, were brought here, they were too costly for many to purchase, and many attempts, especially by countrybred girls, were made to plait at home straw braids to imitate these envied bonnets. Many towns claim the first American straw bonnet; in fact, the attempts were almost simultaneous. A Connecticut girl, Miss Sophia Woodhouse, was given a prize for "leghorn hats" that she had plaited, and she took out a patent in 1821 for a new material for bonnets—the stalks, above the upper joint, of spear grass and redtop grass. The wife of President John Quincy Adams wore one of these bonnets, to the great pride of her husband.

When the bonnet was braided and sewed into shape, it had to be bleached, for it was the dark natural straw.

The feminine love of color, the longing for decoration, as well as pride in skill of needlecraft, found riotous expansion in quilt-piecing. A thrifty economy, too, a desire to use up all the fragments and bits of stuffs which were necessarily cut out in the shaping, chiefly of women's and children's garments, helped to make the patchwork a satisfaction. The amount of labor, of careful fitting, neat piecing, and elaborate quilting, the thousands of stitches that went into one of these patchwork quilts, are today almost painful to regard. Women reveled in intricate and difficult patchwork; they eagerly exchanged patterns with one another; they talked over the designs, and admired pretty bits of calico, and pondered what combinations to make with zest. There was one satisfactory condition in the work, and that was the quality of the cottons and linens of which the patchwork was made. A piece of "chaney," "patch," or "copper-plate" of colonial times will be as fresh today as when woven. Real India chintzes and palampours are found in these quilts, beautiful and artistic stuffs, and the firm, unyielding, high-priced "real" French calicoes.

A sense of the idealization of quilt-piecing is given also by the quaint descriptive names applied to the various patterns. Of those the "Rising Sun," "Log Cabin," and "Job's Trouble" are perhaps the most familiar. "To set a Job's Trouble" was to cut out an exact hexagon for a pattern (preferably from tin, otherwise from firm cardboard); to cut out from this many hexagons in stiff brown paper or letter paper. These were covered with the bits of calico with the edges turned under. The sides were then sewed carefully together over and over, till a firm expanse permitted the removal of the papers.

The name of the pattern seldom gave an expression of its character. "Dove in the Window," "Rob Peter to Pay Paul," "Blue Brigade," "Fan-mill," "Crow's Foot," "Chinese Puzzle," "Fly-wheel," "Love-knot," "Sugar-bowl," are simply whims of fancy. Floral names, such as "Dutch

Tulip," "Sunflower," "Rose of Sharon," "Bluebells," "World's Rose," might suggest a love of flowers.

When the patchwork was completed, it was laid flatly on the lining (often another expanse of patchwork), with layers of wool or cotton wadding between, and the edges were basted all around. Four bars of wood, about ten feet long, "the quiltin'-frame," were placed at the four edges, the quilt was sewed to them with stout thread, the bars crossed and tied firmly at corners, and the whole raised on chairs or tables to a convenient height. Thus around the outstretched quilt a dozen quilters could sit running the whole together with fanciful set designs of stitching. When about a foot on either side was wholly quilted, it was rolled upon its bar, and the work went on. Sometimes several quilts were set up. A quilting bee in Narragansett in 1752 lasted for ten days. A Job's Trouble, made of hexagon pieces, could be neatly done by little children, but more complicated designs required more "judgement," and the age of a little daughter might be accurately guessed by her patchwork. The quilt-making was the work of older folk. It required long arms, larger hands, greater strength.

In early days calicoes were not common, but everyone had woolen garments and pieces, and the quilts made of these were of grateful warmth in bleak New England. All kinds of commonplace garments and remnants of decayed gentility were pressed into service in these quilts: portions of the moth-eaten and discarded uniforms of militiamen, worn-out flannel sheets dyed with some brilliant home-dye, old coat and cloak linings, well-worn petticoats.

These woolen quilts had a thin wadding and were usually very closely quilted, so they were quite flat. They were called "pressed quilts."

As much ingenuity was exercised in the design of the quilting as in the pattern of the patchwork, and the marking for the quilt design was exceedingly tedious, since, of course, no drawings could be used. A quilt might be marked by chalking strings which were stretched tightly across at the desired intervals and held up and snapped smartly down on the quilt, leaving a faint chalky line to guide the eye and needle. Another simple design was to quilt in rounds, using a saucer or plate to form a perfect circle.

One of the most elaborate quilts was of silk containing portions of a wedding dress. When Washington came to Newport, this splendid quilt was sent to grace the bed upon which the hero slept.

A form of decorative work in which many women took great delight and became astonishingly skillful was what was known as "Papyrotamia." It was simply the cutting out of stiff paper of various decorative and ornamental designs with scissors. At the time of the Revolution it was evidently deemed a very high accomplishment, and the best pieces of work were carefully cherished, mounted on black paper, framed and glazed, and

Cut-out silhouette, 19th century (The Brooklyn Museum. Photograph by Alfred Tamarin)

given to friends or bequeathed by will. Valentines in exceedingly delicate and appropriate patterns, wreaths and baskets of varied flowers, marine views, religious symbols, landscapes, all were accomplished. Coats of arms and escutcheons cut in black paper and mounted on white were highly prized. Portrait silhouettes were cut with the aid of a machine which marked and reduced mechanically a sharp shadow cast by the sitter's profile through candlelight on a sheet of white paper.

The *Memoirs* of the missionaries David and John Brainerd show that boys were kept as busy as girls in colonial times. A boy's life on a Connecticut farm is thus described:

"The boy was taught that laziness was the worst form of original sin. Hence he must rise early and make himself useful before he went to school, must be diligent there in study, and promptly home to do "chores" at evening. His whole time out of school must be filled up with some service, such as bringing in fuel for the day, cutting potatoes for the sheep, feeding the swine, watering the horses, picking the berries, gathering the vegetables, spooling the yarn. He was expected never to be reluctant and not often tired."

The sawing and chopping of wood was a never diminishing incubus. This outdoor work on wood was continued within doors in the series of articles fashioned for farm and domestic use by the boy's jackknife and the few heavy carpenter's tools at his command; some gave to the farm boy the rare pennies of his spending money. The making of birch splinter brooms was the best paying work. For these the boy got six cents apiece. The splitting of shoe pegs was another. Setting card teeth was for many years the universal income furnished for New England children. Gathering nuts was a scantily paid-for harvest; tying onions a less pleasing one, and chiefly followed in the Connecticut Valley. The crop of wild cherries known as choke-cherries was one of the most lucrative of the boy's resources. They were much desired for making cherry-rum or cherry-bounce and would fetch readily a dollar a bushel. A good-sized tree would yield about six bushels. J. T. Buckingham tells of his first spending money being ninepence received from a brush-maker for hog bristles saved from slaughtered swine.

The care of silkworms was also held to be a specially suitable work for children. It was said two boys, "if their hands be not sleeping in their pockets," could care for six ounces of seed from hatching till within fourteen days of spinning, when "three or four more helps, women and children being as proper as men," had to assist in

feeding, cleansing, airing, drying, and perfuming them.

Mulberry trees were planted everywhere and kept low like a hedge so children could pick the leaves. All the books of instruction of the day reiterate that a child ten years of age could easily gather seventy-five pounds of mulberry leaves a day and make great wages.

In earliest colonial days boys took part in a joyful outing, a public custom known as perambulating, or beating the bounds. The memory of boundaries and division lines, of commons, pub-

lic highways, etc., was kept fresh in the minds of the inhabitants by an old-time Aryan custom—the walking around them once a year, noting lines of boundary, and impressing these on the notice and memory of young people. To induce English boys to accompany these perambulations, it was customary to distribute some little gratuity. This was usually a willow wand, tied at the end with a bunch of points, which were bits of string about eight inches long, consisting of strands of cotton or woolen yarn braided or twisted together, ended by a tag of a bit of metal or wood. These

From a view of the city of New York in 1792
(The New York Public Library, Stokes Collection)

points were used to tie the hose to the knees of the breeches, the waistband of the breeches to the jacket, etc.

"Beating the bounds" was a specially important duty in the colonies where land surveys were imperfect, land grants irregular, and the boundaries of each man's farm or plantation at first very uncertain. In Virginia this beating the bounds was called "processioning." Landmarks were renewed that were becoming obliterated; blazes on a tree would be somewhat grown over—they were deeply recut; piles of great stones containing a certain number for designation were sometimes scattered—the original number would be restored. Special trees would be found fallen or cut down; new marking trees would be planted, usually pear trees, as they were long lived. Disputed boundaries were decided upon and announced to all the persons present, some of whom at the next "processioning" would be living and be able to testify as to the correct line. This processioning took place between Easter and Whitsuntide, that lovely season of the year in Virginia, and must have proved a pleasant reunion of neighbors, a May party. In New England this was called "perambulating the bounds," and the surveyors who took charge were called "perambulators" or "boundsgoers."

By the seashore whole communities turned to the teaming ocean for the means of life. Every fishing vessel that left the towns of Cape Ann and Cape Cod carried, with its crew of grown men, a boy of ten or twelve to learn "the art and mystery" of fishing.

Tabling and cutting broom corn (Old Sturbridge Village)

Boys born in seashore towns often became sailors. Romance, sentiment, mystery, deviltry, haloed the sailor. He was ever welcome to the public and ever a source of interest whether in tarry working garb, or gay shore togs of flapping trousers, crimson sash, eelskin and cutlasses.

Can it be wondered that New England boys, stirred in their quiet round of life by gay comets and tales of adventure, have had a passion in their veins for "the magic and the mystery of the sea," that they have eagerly gone before the mast rounded the Horn, and come home master seamen when in their teens.

In the northern New England states, heavily wooded with yellow birch, every boy knew how to make Indian brooms from birch trees, and every household in country or town had them. There was a constant demand in Boston for them, and sometimes country stores had several hundred brooms at a time.

Girls could whittle as well as boys and often exchanged the birch brooms they made for a bit of ribbon or lace.

Wooden broom, 18th century, (reproduction) (The Newark Museum. Photograph by Alfred Tamarin)

A simpler and less durable broom was made of full-foliaged hemlock branches tied tightly together and wound around with hempen twine.

A systematic plan of raising broom corn for the manufacture of brooms was not developed until 1798, when Levi Dickenson, a Yankee farmer of Hadley, Massachusetts, planted half an acre.

Mr. Dickenson at first scraped the seed from the brush with a knife, then used a kind of hoe, then a coarse comb like a ripple comb. He tied each broom by hand with the help of a servant. Much of this work could be done by little girls, who soon gave great help in broom manufacture, though the final sewing (when the needle was pressed through with a leather "palm" such as sailors use) had to be done by the strong hands of grown women and men. By 1810 seventy thousand brooms were made in his county.

It was emphatically a wooden age in colonial days. Plows were of wood, and harrows; cart wheels were often wholly of wood without tires, though sometimes iron plates called strakes held the felloes together, being fastened to them by long clinch pins. The dish turner and cooper were artisans of importance in those days; piggins, noggins, runlets, kneelers, firkins, buckets, churns, dye tubs, cowles, powdering tubs, were made with little or no metal.

The boy's jackknife was a possession so highly desired, so closely treasured in those days when boys had so few belongings, that it is pathetic to read of many a farm lad's struggles and long hours

Gourd dish, mid 19th century, (reproduction) (The Staten Island Historical Society. Photograph by Alfred Tamarin)

of weary work to obtain a good knife. Barlow knives were the most highly prized for certainly sixty years, and had a vast popularity for over a century. A few battered old soldiers of this vast army of Barlow jackknives still linger. These Yankee jackknives were, said Daniel Webster, the direct forerunners of the cotton gin and thousands of noble American inventions; the New England boy's whittling was his alphabet of mechanics.

In this connection, let us note the skillful adaptation of natural materials and shapes for domestic and farm use. The farmer and his wife both turned to nature for shapes readily adaptable into the implements and utensils of everyday life. When we read of the first Boston settlers that "the dainty Indian maize was eat with clam-shells out of wooden trays," we learn of a primitive spoon, a clam shell set in a split stick. Large flat clam shells were used as skimming shells in the dairy to skim cream from the milk. Gourd shells made good bowls, skimmers, dippers, and bottles; pumpkin shells, good seed and grain holders. Turkey wings made an ever-ready hearth brush. In the forests were many "crooked sticks" that were more useful than any straight ones could be, when the mower wanted a new snathe or snead, as he called it, for his scythe.

Sled runners were made from saplings bent at the root. The best thills for a cart were those naturally shaped by growth, as were the curved pieces of wood, called the hames, in the harness of a draft horse; also portions of ox yokes. The gambrels used in slaughtering times, hay hooks, long-handled pothooks for brick ovens, could all be cut ready-shaped.

The smaller underbrush and saplings had many uses for sled and cart stakes, and whip stocks. Sections of birch bark could be bottomed and served for baskets, or for potash cans, while capital feed boxes could be made in the same way of sections cut from a hollow hemlock. Elm rind and portions of brown ash butts were natural materials for chair seats and baskets, as were flags for doormats. Forked branches made geese and hog yokes.

In the shaping of heavy and large vessels such as salt mortars, pig troughs, maple-sap troughs, the jackknife was abandoned and the methods of the Indians adopted. These vessels were burned and scraped out of a single log. Wooden bread troughs were also made from a single piece of wood. These were oblong, trencher-shaped bowls about eighteen inches long. Across the trough ran lengthwise a stick or rod on which rested the sieve, searse, or temse when flour was sifted into the trough.

Sometimes the mold for an oxbow was dug out of a log of wood. Oftener a plank of wood was cut into the desired shape as a frame or mold and fastened to a heavy backboard. The oxbow was steamed, placed in the bow mold, pinned in, and then carefully seasoned.

The boys whittled cheese ladders, cheese hoops,

Wood carving of Noah's Ark, late 18th century (The New-York Historical Society)

and red-cherry butter paddles for their mothers' dairies; also many parts of cheese presses and churns. They made box traps and "figure 4" traps of various sizes for catching animals.

Many farm implements other than those already named were made, and many portions of tools and implements. Among them were shovels, swingling knives, sled neaps, stanchions, handles for spades and bill hooks, rake stales, fork stales, flails.

The making of flails was an important and useful work. Many were broken and worn out during a great threshing. Both parts, the staff or handle, and the swingle or swiple, were carefully shaped from well-chosen wood, to be joined together later by an eelskin or leather strap.

Wood for ax helves was carefully chosen, sawed, split, and whittled into shape. These were then scraped smooth with broken glass.

A little money might be earned by cutting heel-pegs for shoemakers. These were made of a maple trunk sawed across the grain, making the circular board thin enough—a half inch or so—for the correct length of the pegs. The end was then marked in parallel lines, then grooved across at

Burl-bowl, mid 19th century (The Staten Island Historical Society. Photograph by Alfred Tamarin)

right angles, then split as marked into pegs with knife and mallet.

When the boys had learned to use a few other tools besides their jackknives, as they quickly did, they could get sawed staves from the sawmills and make up shooks of staves bound with hoops of red oak for molasses hogsheads. These would be shipped to the West Indies and form an important link in the profitable rum and slave round of traffic that bound Africa, New England, and the West Indies so closely together in those days. A constant occupation for men and boys was making rived or shaved shingles. They were split with a beetle and wedge. A smart workman could by fast work make a thousand a day.

In the sawing of blocks there would always be some too knotty or gnarled to split into shingles. They formed in many a pioneer's home and in many a pioneer schoolhouse good solid seats for children and even grown people to sit on. And even in pioneer meetinghouses these blocks could sometimes be seen.

Other fittings for the house were whittled out. Long heavy, wooden hinges were cut from hornbeam for cupboard and closet doors; even shed doors were hung on wooden hinges as were house doors in the earliest colonial days. Door latches were made of wood, also oblong buttons to fasten chamber and cupboard doors.

New England housekeepers prized the smooth, close-grained bowls which the Indians made from the veined and mottled knots of maple.

A token of affection and skill from a whittler was a carved busk, which was the broad and strong strip of wood placed in corsets or stays to help to form and preserve the long-waisted, stiff figure then fashionable. One carved busk bears initials and an appropriately sentimental design of arrows and hearts.

On the rim of spinning wheels, on shuttles, swifts, and on niddy-noddys or hand reels was lettering by the hands of rustic lovers. A finely carved legend on a hand reel reads:

> "POLLY GREENE, HER REEL.
> Count your threads right
> If you reel in the night
> When I am far away.
> June, 1777."

Perhaps some Revolutionary soldier gave this as a parting gift to his sweetheart on the eve of battle.

On his powder horn the rustic carver bestowed his best and daintiest work. Emblem both of war and of sport, it seemed worthy of being shaped into the highest expression of his artistic longing. Maps, plans, legends, verses, portraits, landscapes, family history, crests, dates of births, marriages, and deaths, lists of battles, patriotic and religious sentiments, all may be found on powder horns. They have in many cases proved valuable historical records and have sometimes been the only records of events.

Chapter XV

Needlecraft and Decorative Arts

In 1716 Mr. Brownell, the Boston schoolmaster, advertised that at his school young women and children could be taught "all sorts of fine works as Featherworks, Filigree, and Painting on Glass, Embroidering a new way, Turkeywork for Handkerchiefs two new Ways, fine new fashion Purses, flourishing and Plain work." The perishable nature of the material would prevent the

Embroidered mourning piece, 18th century (The Metropolitan Museum of Art, Rogers Fund, 1941)

preservation of many specimens of featherwork, but very pretty flowers for headdresses and bonnets were made of minute feathers or portions of feathers pasted on a firm foundation in many collected shapes.

Young girls in the families of gentlefolk paid much attention to the making of coats of arms. Those painted on glass were the richest in color and the most satisfactory, but embroidered ones were more common. The choicest materials were used, the drawing was carefully executed, and the stitches minute.

Familiar to the descendants of old New England families are the embroidered mourning pieces. On them weeping willows and urns,

Embroidered Saltonstall coat of arms, 18th century (The Museum of Fine Arts, Boston, Gift of Ella Winthrop Saltonstall in Memory of Francis G. Saltonstall)

tombs and mourning figures, names of departed friends with dates of their deaths, and epitaphs were worked with vast skill. They were so much admired and were such delightful home decorations that it is not unusual to find them with empty spaces for names and dates, waiting for someone to die. Funeral pieces and mourning pieces were deemed a very dignified observance of respect and mark of affection.

After the death of Washington, mourning designs appeared in vast numbers. Framed prints of these designs hung on every wall; table china in large numbers and variety bore these funereal emblems, and laudatory and sad mottoes. As other Revolutionary heroes passed away, similar designs appeared in more limited numbers, and the reign of embroidered mourning pieces may be said to have begun at this time. Washington, so to speak, set the fashion.

Religious designs were also eagerly sought for. The Tree of Life was a favorite. A conventional tree was hung at wide intervals with apples, bearing the names of various virtues and estimable traits of humanity, such as Honor, Modesty, Silence, Patience, etc.

There was no limit to the beauty and delicacy of the embroidery of those days. In an old book printed in 1821, a set of rules is given for teaching needlework, and it is doubtless what had been the method for a century. The girls were first shown how to turn a hem on a piece of waste paper, then they proceeded to the various stitches in this order: to hem, to sew and fell a seam, to draw threads and hemstitch, to gather and sew on gathers, to make buttonholes, to sew on buttons, to do herringbone stitch, to darn, to mark, to tuck, whip, and sew on a frill. There is also a long and tedious set of questions and answers like a catechism, explaining the various stitches.

The most universal and best-preserved piece of embroidery done by our foremothers was the sampler. These were known as sampleths, samcloths, saumplers, and sampleres. The titles were all derived from *esampler, examplier.* This piece of needlework was done by every little girl who was carefully brought up. They were worked in various beautiful and difficult stitches in colored silk and wool on a strong, loosely woven canvas.

The sampler "contrived a double debt to pay"

of teaching letters and stitches. It was, in fact, a needlework hornbook, containing the alphabet, a verse indicative of good morals or industry, or a sentence from the Bible, the name and date, and some crude representations of impossible birds, beasts, flowers, trees, or human beings.

In the older samplers little attention is paid to the representation of things in their real colors; a green horse may balance a blue tree. And as flat tints were used there were few effects of light and shade, and no perspective. Distance is indicated by a different color of worsted; thus the green horse will have his off legs worked in red. This is precisely the method used in the Bayeux Tapestry and other antique embroideries.

Sampler verses had their times and seasons and ran through families. They were eagerly copied for young friends, and, in a few cases, were "natural composures," or, as we should say today, "original compositions."

There were certain variants of a popular sampler verse that ran thus:

"This is my Sampler,
Here you see
What care my Mother
Took of me."

Another rhyme was

"Mary Jackson is my name,
America my nation,
Boston is my dwelling place,
And Christ is my salvation."

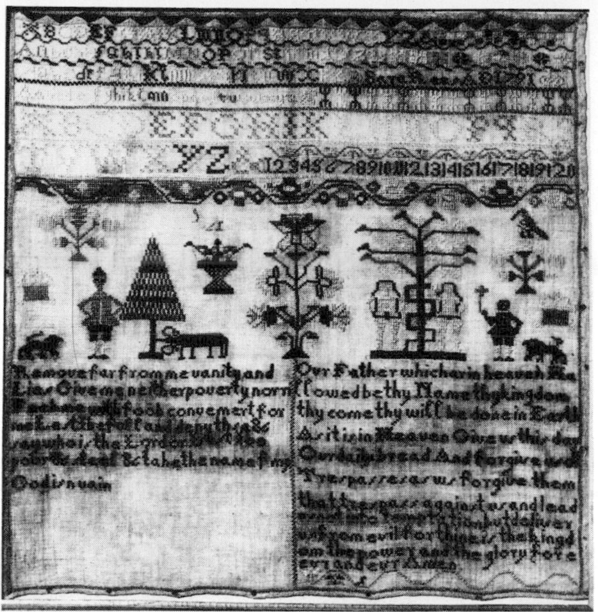

Sampler by Sara Rees, 1791 (The New-York Historical Society)

The doxology, "From all that dwell below the skies," etc., appears on samplers; and these lines:

"Though life is fair
And pleasure young,
And Love on ev'ry
Shepherd's Tongue,
I turn my thoughts
To serious things,
Life is ever on the wing."

Sampler by Lora Standish, 1653 (The Pilgrim Society, Plymouth, Massachusetts)

In English collections, the oblong samplers, long and narrow, are as a rule older than the square samplers; and it is safe to believe the same of American samplers. One of the oldest samplers is in the collection of antique articles now in Pilgrim Hall at Plymouth. It was made by a daughter of the Pilgrims. The verse embroidered on it reads

"Lora Standish is My Name.
Lord Guide my Heart that I may do thy Will,
And fill my Hands with such convenient skill
As will conduce to Virtue void of Shame,
And I will give the Glory to thy Name."

Embroidery of Old South Church, 1756, Boston (The American Antiquarian Society, Worcester, Massachusetts)

Another favorite rhyme was

"When I was young and in my Prime,
You see how well I spent my Time
And by my sampler you may see
What care my Parents took of me."

Strange trees and fruit and birds and beasts, wonderful vines and flowers, were embroidered on these domestic tapestries.

Sometimes pretentious pictures representing events in public or family history were embroidered in crewels on sampler linen. One is a view of the Old South Church, Boston, and with its hooped dames and coach and footman, has a certain value as indicating the costume of the times. It is dated 1756.

In the sixteenth and seventeenth centuries it was high fashion to have mottoes and texts carved or painted on many articles where they would frequently catch the eye. Printed books were then rare possessions, and these mottoes, whether of vanity or piety, took their place. Women dexterous of the needle embroidered mottoes and words on articles of clothing. Whole texts of the Bible are said to have been inscribed on the edges of gowns and petticoats.

Elaborate vines of flowers and other scroll designs were worked on petticoats, often in colored crewels. Silk petticoats were also embroidered and painted by young girls, and are beautiful pieces of work.

Little girls were taught to knit as soon as their hands could hold the needles. Sometimes girls four years of age could knit stockings. Boys had to knit their own suspenders. All the stockings and mittens for the family, and coarse socks and mittens for sale, were made in large numbers. Much fine knitting was done, with many intricate and elaborate stitches. Those known as the "herringbone" and "fox and geese" were great favorites.

An elaborate and much-admired form of knitting was the bead bags and purses which were made with great variety and ingenuity. Beautiful bags were knitted to match wedding gowns. Knitted purses were a favorite token and gift from fair hands to husband or lover. Watch chains

Embroidery frame with stand, 1750–1755 (The Metropolitan Museum of Art, Rogers Fund, 1940)

were more unusual; they were knit in a geometrical design, were about a yard long and about three-eighths of an inch in diameter.

Netting was another decorative handiwork. Netted fringes for edging the coverlets, curtains, testers, and valances of high-post bedsteads were usually made of cotton thread or twine and when tufted or tasseled were a pretty finish. A finer silk or cotton netting was used for trimming sacks and petticoats.

Netted purses and workbags also were made similar to the knitted ones. A homelier and heavier netting of twine was often done at home for small fishing nets.

Embroidery: wool on linen, about 1750 (The Metropolitan Museum of Art, Rogers Fund, 1942)

Previous to the Revolution there was a boardingschool kept in Philadelphia in Second Street near Walnut by a Mrs. Sarah Wilson. She thus advertised:

"Young ladies may be educated in a genteel manner, and pains taken to teach them in regard to their behaviour, on reasonable terms. They may be taught all sorts fine needlework, viz., working on catgut or flowering muslin, sattin stitch, quince stitch, tent stitch, cross-stitch, open work, tambour, embroidering curtains or chairs, writing and cyphering. Likewise waxwork in all its several branches, never as yet particularly taught here; also how to take profiles in wax, to make wax flowers and fruits and pinbaskets." Taking profiles in wax was distinctly artwork, and portraits of Washington and other Revolutionary heroes still exist in wax—a material that could be worked with facility but was very perishable.

Lacemaking was never an industry in the colonies; it was an elegant accomplishment. Pillow lace was made, and the stitches were taught in families of wealth; a guinea a stitch was charged by some teachers. Old lace pillows have been preserved with strips of unfinished lace and hanging bobbins to show the mode—a thread lace much like the fine Swiss handmade laces.

Tambour work on muslin or lace, and a lace made of certain designs darned on net, took the place of pillow lace. Nothing could be more beautiful in execution and design than the rich veils, collars, and caps of this worked net, which remained the mode for many years. Girls sometimes spent years working on a single collar or tucker. In the form of rich veils and collars scores of intricate and beautiful stitches were used, and exquisite articles of wear were manufactured.

Embroidered cotton bag, early 19th century (Old Sturbridge Village)

Chapter XVI

Flax Culture and Spinning

The success of the Americans in the War for Independence was due in no small part to their independence in their own homes. They had little if any outside help to give them every necessity of life. No farmer or his wife need fear any king when on every home farm was found food, drink, medicine, fuel, lighting, clothing, shelter. "Home-made" might be applied to nearly every article in

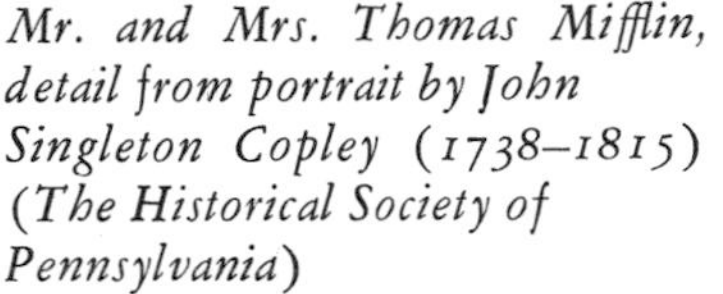

Mr. and Mrs. Thomas Mifflin, detail from portrait by John Singleton Copley (1738–1815) (The Historical Society of Pennsylvania)

the house. In early days every farmer and his sons raised wool and flax; his wife and daughters spun them into thread and yarn, knit these into stockings and mittens, or wove them into linen and cloth, and then made them into clothing. Even in large cities nearly all women spun yarn and thread, all could knit, and many had hand looms to weave cloth at home. These home occupations in the production of clothing have been very happily termed the "homespun industries."

As soon as the colonists had cleared their farms from stones and stumps, they planted a field or "patch" of flax, and usually one of hemp. The seed was sown broadcast like grass seed in May. Flax is a graceful plant with pretty drooping blue flowers; hemp has but a sad-colored blossom.

When the flax plants were three or four inches high, they were weeded by young women or children who had to work barefoot, as the stalks were very tender. If the land had a growth of thistles, the weeders could wear three or four pairs of woolen stockings. The children had to step facing the wind, so if any plants were trodden down the wind would help to blow them back into place. When the flax was ripe, in the last of June or in July, it was pulled up by the roots and laid out carefully to dry for a day or two and turned several times in the sun; this work was called pulling and spreading, and was usually done by men and boys. It then was "rippled." A coarse wooden or heavy iron wire comb with great teeth, called a ripple comb, was fastened on a plank; the stalks of flax were drawn through it with a quick stroke to break off the seed bolls, or "bobs," which fell on a sheet spread to catch them; these were saved for seed for the next crop, or for sale.

Rippling was done in the field. The stalks were then tied in bundles called beats or bates and stacked. They were tied only at the seed end, and the base of the stalks was spread out forming a tent-shaped stack, called a stook. When dry, the stalks were watered to rot the leaves and soften fibers. Hemp was watered without rippling. This was done preferably in running water, as the rotting flax poisoned fish. Stakes were set in the water in the form of a square, called a steep

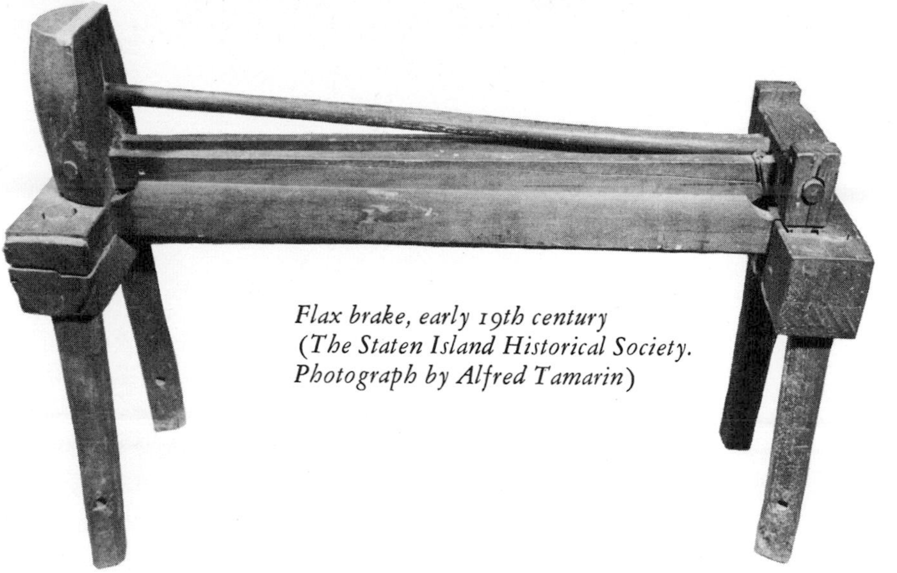

Flax brake, early 19th century (The Staten Island Historical Society. Photograph by Alfred Tamarin)

pool, and the bates of flax or hemp were piled in solidly, each alternate layer at right angles with the one beneath it. A cover of boards and heavy stones was piled on top. In four or five days the bates were taken up and the rotted leaves removed. A slower process, termed dew-retting, was the way chiefly employed in America.

When the flax was cleaned, it was once more dried and tied in bundles. Then came work for strong men, to break it on the ponderous flax brake, to separate the fibers and get out from the center the hard woody "hexe" or "bun." Hemp was also broken.

A flax brake was a heavy log of wood about five feet long, either large enough so the flat top was about three feet from the ground, or set on heavy logs to bring it to that height. A portion of the top was cut down leaving a block at each end, and several long slats were set in lengthwise and held firm at each end with edges up, by being set into the end blocks. Then a similar set of slats, put in a heavy frame, was made with the slats set far enough apart to go into the spaces of the lower slats. The flax was laid on the lower slats, the frame and upper slats placed on it and then pounded down with a heavy wooden mallet weighing many pounds. Sometimes the upper frame of slats, or knives as they were called, was hinged to the big under log at one end and heavily weighted at the other, and thus the blow was given by the fall of the weight, not by the force of the farmer's muscle. The tenacity of the flax can be seen when it would stand this violent beating.

Flax was usually broken twice, once with an open-tooth brake, once with a close or strait brake, that is, one where the long, sharp-edge strips of wood were set close together. Then it was scutched or swingled with a swingling block and knife, to take out any small particles of bark that might adhere. A man could swingle forty pounds of flax a day, but it was hard work. All this had to be done in clear sunny weather when the flax was as dry as tinder.

The clean fibers were then made into bundles called strikes. The strikes were swingled again, and from the refuse called swingle-tree hurds, coarse bagging could be spun and woven. After being thoroughly cleaned the rolls or strikes were sometimes beetled, that is, pounded in a wooden trough with a great pestle-shaped beetle over and over again until soft.

Then came the hackling or hetcheling. The fineness of the flax depended upon the number of hacklings, the fineness of the various hackles or hetchels or combs, and the dexterity of the operator. In the hands of a poor hackler the best of flax would be converted into tow. The flax was slightly wetted, taken hold of at one end of the bunch, and drawn through the hackle teeth toward the hetcheler, and thus fibers were pulled and laid into continuous threads, while the short fibers were combed out. It was dusty, dirty work. The threefold process had to be all done at once; the fibers had to be divided to their fine filaments, the long threads laid in untangled line, and the tow separated and removed. After the first hackle, called a ruffler, six other finer hackles were often used. It was one of the surprises of flax preparation to see how little good fiber would be left after all this hackling, even from a large mass of raw material, but it was equally surprising to see how much linen thread could be made from this small amount of fine flax. The fibers were sorted according to fineness; this was called spreading and drawing. So then after over twenty dexterous manipulations the flax was ready for the wheel, for spinning—the most dexterous process of all—and was wrapped around the spindle.

Seated at the small flax wheel, the spinner placed her foot on the treadle and spun the fiber into a long, even thread. Hung on the wheel was

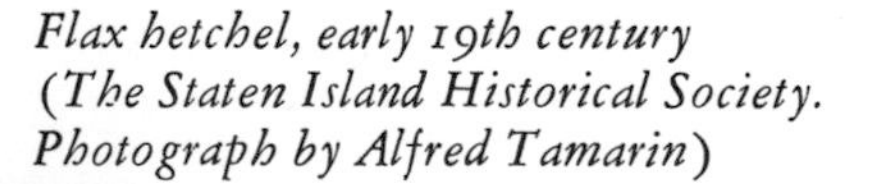

Flax hetchel, early 19th century (The Staten Island Historical Society. Photograph by Alfred Tamarin)

Flax spinning wheel, 1829 (The Newark Museum. Photograph by Alfred Tamarin)

a small bone, wood, or earthenware cup, or a gourd shell, filled with water, in which the spinner moistened her fingers as she held the twisting flax, which by the movement of the wheel was wound on bobbins. When all were filled, the thread was wound off in knots and skeins on a reel. A machine called a clock reel counted the exact number of strands in a knot, usually forty, and ticked when the requisite number had been wound. Then the spinner would stop and tie the knot.

Usually the knots or lays were of forty threads, and twenty lays made a skein or slipping. The number varied, however, with locality. To spin two skeins of linen thread was a good day's work;

for it a spinner was paid eight cents a day and "her keep."

These skeins of thread had to be bleached. They were laid in warm water for four days, the water being frequently changed, and the skeins constantly wrung out. Then they were washed in the brook till the water came from them clear and pure. Then they were bucked, that is, bleached with ashes and hot water, in a bucking tub, over and over again, then laid in clear water for a week, and afterward came a grand seething, rinsing, beating, washing, drying, and winding on bobbins for the loom. Sometimes the bleaching was done with slaked lime or with buttermilk.

One lucrative product of flax should be mentioned—flaxseed. Flax was pulled for spinning when the base of the stalk began to turn yellow, which was usually the first of July. For seed it stood till it was all yellow. The flaxseed was used for making oil. Usually the upper chambers of country stores were filled a foot deep with flaxseed in the autumn, waiting for good sleighing to convey the seed to town.

In New Hampshire in early days, a wheelwright was not a man who made wagon wheels (as such he would have had scant occupation), but one who made spinning wheels. Often he carried them around the country on horseback selling them, thus adding another to the many interesting itineracies of colonial days. Spinning wheels would seem clumsy to carry on horseback, but they were not set up, and several could be compactly carried when taken apart; far more ticklish articles went on packhorses—large barrels, glazed window sashes, etc. Nor would it seem very difficult for a man to carry spinning wheels on horseback, when frequently a woman would jump on horseback in the early morning and with a baby on one arm and a flax wheel tied behind, would ride several miles to a neighbor's to spend the day spinning in cheerful companionship.

Linen was also spun on a hand distaff, called sometimes a rock. It was ordered that children and others tending sheep or cattle in the fields should also "be set to some other employment withal, such as spinning upon the rock, knitting, weaving tape, etc."

Spinning doubtless was an ever-ready refuge in the monotonous life of the early colonist. She soon had plenty of material to work with. Everywhere, even in the earliest days, the culture of flax was encouraged. By 1640 the Court of Massachusetts passed two orders directing the growth of flax, ascertaining what colonists were skillful in breaking, spinning, weaving, ordering that boys and girls be taught to spin, and offering a bounty for linen grown, spun, and woven in the colony. Connecticut passed similar measures. Soon spinning classes were formed, and every family ordered to spin so many pounds of flax a year, or to pay a fine. The industry received a fresh impulse through the immigration of about one hundred Irish families from Londonderry. They settled in New Hampshire on the Merrimac about 1719 and spun and

Clock reel, about 1800
(The Staten Island Historical Society. Photograph by Alfred Tamarin)

wove with far more skill than prevailed among those English settlers who had already become Americans. They established a manufactory according to Irish methods and attempts at a similar establishment were made in Boston.

There was much public excitement over spinning, and prizes were offered for quantity and quality. Women, rich as well as poor, appeared on Boston Common with their wheels, thus making spinning a popular holiday recreation. A brick building was erected as a spinning school costing £15,000, and a tax was placed on carriages and coaches in 1757 to support it. At the fourth anniversary in 1749 of the "Boston Society for promoting Industry and Frugality," three hundred "young spinsters" spun on their wheels on Boston Common. And a pretty sight it must have been:

the fair young girls in the quaint and pretty dress of the times, shown to us in Hogarth's prints, spinning on the green grass under the great trees. At the same time premiums were offered in Pennsylvania for weaving linen and spinning thread. The German colonists in Pennsylvania long before this had been famous flax raisers.

Virginia was earlier even in awakening interest in manufacturing flax than Massachusetts, for wild flax grew there in profusion, ready for gathering. In 1646 two houses were ordered to be erected at Jamestown as spinning schools. These were to be well built and well heated. Each county was to send to these schools two poor childen, seven or eight years old, to be taught carding, spinning, and knitting. Each child was to be supplied by the county authorities on admission to the school with six barrels of Indian corn, a pig, two hens, clothing, shoes, a bed, rug, blanket, two coverlets, a wooden tray, and two pewter dishes or cups. This plan was not wholly carried out. Prizes in tobacco (which was the current money of Virginia in which everything was paid) were given, however, for every pound of flax, every skein of yarn, every yard of linen of Virginia production, and soon flax wheels and spinners were plentiful.

In the revolt of feeling caused by the Stamp Act, there was a constant social pressure to encourage the wearing of goods of American manufacture. As one evidence of this movement the president and first graduating class of Rhode Island College—now Brown University—were clothed in fabrics made in New England. From Massachusetts to South Carolina the women of the colonies banded together in patriotic societies called Daughters of Liberty, agreeing to wear only garments of homespun manufacture, and to drink no tea. In many New England towns they gathered together to spin, each bringing her own wheel.

By Revolutionary times England's General Howe thought "Linen and Woollen Goods much wanted by the Rebels"; hence when he prepared to evacuate Boston he ordered all such goods carried away with him. But he little knew the domestic industrial resources of the Americans. Women were then most proficient in spinning.

In 1789 a social movement was instituted in New England to promote "Oeconomy and Household Industries." "The Rich and Great strive by example to convince the Populace . . . by Growing their own Flax and Wool, having some one in the Family to dress it, and all the Females spin, several weave and bleach the linen." The old spinning matches were revived. Again the ministers preached to the faithful women "Oeconomists," who thus combined religion, patriotism, and industry.

Chapter XVII

Wool Culture and Spinning; Cotton

The art of spinning was an honorable occupation for women, and it was so universal that it furnished a legal title by which an unmarried woman is known to this day. Spinster is the only one of all her various womanly titles that survives; webster, shepster, litster, brewster, and baxter are obsolete. The occupations are also obsolete save those indicated by shepster and baxter—that is, the

Embroidery: silk on satin with painted background, early 19th century (The New-York Historical Society)

cutting out of cloth and baking of bread. Our first colonists showed an intelligent eagerness for wool culture. It was quickly and proudly noted as a proof of rapid and substantial progress that they could carry on any of the steps of the cloth industry. One of the fortunate conditions that tended to the marked success of the Massachusetts Bay Colony was that so many had been "clothiers" or cloth workers in England, or had come from shires in England where wool was raised and cloth made, and hence knew the importance of the industry as well as its practical workings.

It was estimated that the number of sheep in the colony of Massachusetts about 1644 was three thousand. Soon the great wheel was whirring in every New England house. The raising of sheep was encouraged in every way. They were permitted to graze on the commons; it was forbidden to send them from the colony; no sheep under two years old could be killed to sell; if a dog killed a sheep, the dog's owner must hang him and pay double the cost of the sheep. All persons who were not employed in other ways, as single women, girls, and boys, were required to spin. Each family must contain one spinner. These spinners were formed into divisions or "squadrons" of ten persons; each division had a director. There were no drones in this hive; neither the wealth nor the high station of parents excused children from this work. Thus all were leveled to one kind of labor, and by this leveling all were also elevated to independence. When the open expression of revolt came, the homespun industries seemed a firm rock for the foundation of liberty. People joined in agreements to eat no lamb or mutton, that thus sheep might be preserved, and to wear no imported woolen cloth. They gave prizes for spinning and weaving.

Great encouragement was given in Virginia in early days to the raising and manufacture of wool. The Assembly estimated that five children not over thirteen years of age could by their work readily spin and weave enough to keep thirty persons clothed. Six pounds of tobacco was paid to anyone bringing to the county courthouse a yard of homespun woolen cloth, made wholly in his family; twelve pounds of tobacco were offered for reward for a dozen pair of woolen hose knitted

Wool spinning wheel, early 19th century (The Staten Island Historical Society. Photograph by Alfred Tamarin)

at home. Slaves were taught to spin; and wool wheels and wool cards were found by the eighteenth century on every inventory of planters' house furnishings.

The Pennsylvania settlers were early in the encouragement of wool manufacture. Stocking weavers were there certainly as early as 1723, and it is asserted there were knitting machines. In Germantown in 1759, there was great manufacture of stockings.

Among the manufactures of the province of Pennsylvania in 1698 were druggets, serges, and coverlets; among the registered tradesmen were dyers, fullers, comb makers, card makers, weavers, and spinners. The fairs instituted by William Penn for the encouragement of domestic manufactures and trade in general, which were fostered by Franklin and continued till 1775, briskly stimulated wool and flax manufacture.

In 1765 and in 1775 rebellious Philadelphians banded together with promises not to eat or suffer to be eaten in their families any lamb or "meat of the mutton kind"; in this the Philadelphia butchers, patriotic and self-sacrificing, all joined. A wool factory was built and fitted up and an appeal made to the women to save the state. In a month four hundred wool spinners were at work. But the war cut off the supply of raw material, and the manufacture languished. In 1790, after the war, fifteen hundred sets of irons for spinning wheels were sold from one shop, and mechanics everywhere were making looms.

New Yorkers were not behind in industry. In 1705 an English lord wrote that he "had seen serge made upon Long Island that any man might wear; they make very good linen for common use; as for Woollen I think they have brought that to too great perfection."

In the phrase "too great perfection" may be found the key for all the extraordinary and apparently stupid prohibitions and restrictions placed by the mother country on colonial wool manufacture. The growth of the woolen industry in any colony was regarded at once by England with jealous eyes. Wool was the pet industry and principal staple of Great Britain, for until the reign of Henry VIII English garments from head to foot were wholly of wool, even the shoes. Wool was also received in England as currency. Therefore, the Crown, aided by the governors of the provinces, sought to maintain England's monopoly by regulating and reducing the culture of wool in America through prohibiting the exportation to England of any American wool or woolen materials. In 1699 all vessels sailing to England from the colonies were prohibited taking on board any "Wool, Woolfells, Shortlings, Moslings, Wool Flocks, Worsteds, Bays, Bay or Woollen Yarn, Cloath, Serge, Kersey, Says, Frizes, Druggets, Shalloons, etc."; and an arbitrary law was passed prohibiting the transportation of homemade woolens from one American province to another. These laws were never fully observed and never checked the manufacture of wool in this country. Hence our colonies were spared the cruel fate by which England's same policy paralyzed and obliterated in a few years the glorious wool industry of Ireland.

The "all-wool goods a yard wide," which we so easily purchase today, meant to the colonial dame or daughter the work of many weeks and months, from the time when the fleeces were first given to her deft hands. Fleeces had to be opened with care, and have all pitched or tarred locks, daglocks, brands, and feltings cut out. These cuttings were not wasted, but were spun into coarse yarn. The white locks were carefully tossed and separated and tied into net bags with tallies to be dyed. Another homely saying, "dyed in the wool," showed a process of much skill. Blue, in all shades, was the favorite color, and was dyed with indigo. So great was the demand for this dye-stuff that indigo-peddlers traveled over the country selling it.

Madder, cochineal, and dogwood dyed beautiful reds. The bark of red oak or hickory made very pretty shades of brown and yellow. Various flowers growing on the farm could be used for dyes. The flower of the goldenrod, when pressed of its juice, mixed with indigo, and added to alum, made a beautiful green. The juice of the poke-berry boiled with alum made crimson dye, and a violet juice from the petals of the iris, or "flower-de-luce," that blossomed in June meadows, gave a delicate light purple tinge to white wool.

The bark of the sassafras was used for dyeing yellow or orange color, and the flowers and leaves of the balsam also. Fustic and copperas gave yellow dyes. A good black was obtained by boiling woolen cloth with a quantity of the leaves of the common field sorrel, then boiling again with log-wood and copperas.

In the South there were scores of flowers and leaves that could be used for dyes. During the Revolutionary War one enterprising South Carolinian got a guinea a pound for a yellow dye he made from the sweet leaf or horse laurel. Leaves and berries of the gallberry bush made a good black much used by hatters and weavers. The root of the barberry gave wool a beautiful yellow, as did the leaves of the devil's-bit. The petals of Jerusalem artichoke and St. John's wort dyed yellow. Yellow root is a significant name and reveals its use: oak, walnut, or maple bark dyed brown. Often the woven cloth was dyed, not the wool.

The next process was carding. The wool was first greased with rape oil or "melted swine's grease," which had to be thoroughly worked in; about three pounds of grease were put into ten pounds of wool. Wool cards were rectangular pieces of thin board with a simple handle on the

Wool cards, late 18th century (The Newark Museum. Photograph by Alfred Tamarin)

back or at the side; to this board was fastened a smaller rectangle of strong leather, set thick with slightly bent wire teeth, like a coarse brush. The carder took one card with her left hand, and resting it on her knee, drew a tuft of wool across it several times, until a sufficient quantity of fiber had been caught upon the wire teeth. She then drew the second wool card, which had to be warmed, across the first several times, until the fibers were brushed parallel by all these "tummings." Then by a deft and catchy motion the wool was rolled or carded into small fleecy rolls which were then ready for spinning.

Wool combs were shaped like the letter T, with about thirty long steel teeth from ten to eighteen inches long set at right angles with the top of the T. The wool was carefully placed on one comb, and with careful strokes the other comb laid the long staple smooth for hard-twisted spinning. It was tedious and slow work, and a more skillful operation than carding. The combs had to be kept constantly heated, but no machine combing ever equaled hand combing. There was a good deal of waste in this combing, that is, large clumps of tangled wool called noil were combed out. They were not really wasted, we may be sure, by our frugal ancestors, but were spun into coarse yarn.

Wool spinning was truly one of the most flexible and alert series of movements in the world. The spinner stood slightly leaning forward, lightly poised on the ball of the left foot. With her left hand she picked up from the platform of the wheel a long slender roll of the soft carded wool about as large around as the little finger, and deftly wound the end of the fibers on the point of the spindle. She then gave a gentle motion to the wheel with a wooden peg held in her right hand and seized with the left the roll at exactly the right distance from the spindle to allow for one "drawing." Then the hum of the wheel rose to a sound like the echo of wind; she stepped backward quickly, one, two, three steps, holding high the long yarn as it twisted and quivered. Suddenly she glided forward with even, graceful stride and let the yarn wind on the swift spindle. Another pinch of the wood roll, a new turn of the wheel, and *da capo*.

The wooden peg held by the spinner served the purpose of an elongated finger and was called a driver, wheel peg, etc. It was about nine inches long, an inch or so in diameter, and at about an inch from the end was slightly grooved in order that it might surely catch the spoke and thus propel the wheel.

It was a good day's work for a quick, active spinner to spin six skeins of yarn a day. It was estimated that to do that with her quick backward and forward steps she walked over twenty miles.

The yarn might be wound directly upon the wooden spindle as it was spun, or at the end of the spindle might be placed a spool or broach which twisted with the revolving spindle and held the new-spun yarn. This broach was usually simply a stiff roll of paper, a corn cob, or a roll of corn husk. When the ball of yarn was as large as the broach would hold, the spinner placed wooden pegs in certain holes in the spokes of her spinning wheel and tied the end of the yarn to one peg. Then she took off the belt of her wheel and whirred the big wheel swiftly round, thus winding the yarn on the pegs into hanks or clews two yards in circumference, which were afterward tied with a loop of yarn into knots of forty threads; seven of these knots made a skein. The clock reel was used for winding yarn, also a triple reel.

The yarn might be wound from the spindle into skeins in another way—by using a hand reel, an implement which really did exist in every farmhouse (though the dictionaries were ignorant of it, as they were of its universal folk name, niddy-noddy).

Niddy-noddy,
late 18th–early 19th century
(The Newark Museum.
Photograph by Alfred Tamarin)

The three pieces of these niddy-noddys were set together at curious angles. Holding the reel in the left hand, by seizing the central "body" or rod, the yarn was wound from end to end of the reel by an odd, waving, wobbling motion, into knots and skeins of the same size as by the first process described.

Sometimes the woolen yarn was spun twice, especially if a close, hard-twisted thread was desired, to be woven into a stiff, wiry cloth. When there were two, the first spinning was called a roving. The single spinning was usually deemed sufficient to furnish yarn for knitting, where softness and warmth were the desired requisites.

The pride of a good spinster was to spin the finest yarn, and one Mistress Mary Prigge spun a pound of wool into fifty hanks of 84,000 yards;

in all, nearly forty-eight miles. If the yarn was to be knitted, it had to be washed and cleansed.

All these bleaching processes, the wringing out and rinsing in various waters, were far more wearisome then than they would be today, for the water had to be carried laboriously in pails and buckets and drawn with pumps and well sweeps; there were no pipes and conduits. Happy the household that had a running brook near the kitchen door.

Of course all these operations and manipulations usually occupied many weeks and months.

One of the household implements used in wool manufacture, the wool card, deserves a short special history as well as a description. In early days the leather back of the wool card was pierced with an awl by hand; the wire teeth were cut off from a length of wire, were slightly bent, and set and clinched one by one. These cards were laboriously made by many persons at home for their household use. As early as 1667 wire was made in Massachusetts, and its chief use was for wool cards. By Revolutionary times it was realized that the use of wool cards was almost the mainspring of the wool industry, and £100 bounty was offered by Massachusetts for card wire made in the state from iron mined in what they called then the "United American States." In 1784 a machine was invented by an American which would cut and bend thirty-six thousand wire teeth an hour. Another machine pierced the leather backs. This gave a new employment to women and children at home and some spending money. They would get boxes of the bent wire teeth and bundles of the leather backs from the factories and would set the teeth in the backs while sitting around the open fire in the evening. They did this work, too, while visiting—spending an afternoon. It was an unconscious and diverting work like knitting; scholars set wool cards while studying, and schoolmistresses while teaching. This method of manufacture was superseded fifteen years later by a machine invented by Amos Whittemore, which held, cut, and pierced the leather, drew the wire from a reel, cut and bent a looped tooth, set, it, bent it, fastened the leather on the back, and speedily turned out a fully made card. By this time spinning and weaving machinery began to crowd out home work, and the machine-made cards were needed to keep up with the increased demand. At last machines crowded into every department of cloth manufacture. After carding machines were invented in England—great rollers set with card teeth—they were set up in many mills throughout the United States. Families soon sent all their wool to these mills to be carded even when it was spun and woven at home. It was sent rolled up in a homespun sheet or blanket pinned with thorns, and the carded rolls ready for spinning were brought home in the same way, and made a still bigger bundle which was light in weight for its size.

Cotton never formed one of the homespun industries of the colonies; in fact, it was never an article of extended domestic manufacture. A little cotton was always used in early days for stuffing bedquilts, petticoats, soldiers' armor, and similar purposes. East Indian cotton was bought by the pound in small quantities. The seeds were picked out one by one by hand; it was carded on wool cards, and spun into a rather intractable yarn which was used as warp for linsey-woolsey and rag carpets. Even in England no cotton weft, no all-cotton fabrics, were made till after 1760. Sometimes a twisted yarn was made of one thread of cotton and one of wool which was knit into durable stockings. Cotton sewing thread was unknown in England. Pawtucket women named Wilkinson made the first cotton thread on their home spinning wheels in 1792.

Cotton was planted in America, according to one writer in 1621. In a letter in 1786 Thomas Jefferson wrote:

"The four southermost States make a great deal of cotton. Their poor are almost entirely clothed with it in winter and summer. In winter they wear shirts of it and outer clothing of cotton and wool mixed. In summer their shirts are linen, but the outer clothing cotton. The dress of the women is almost entirely of cotton, manufactured by themselves, except the richer class, and even many of these wear a great deal of homespun cotton. It is as well manufactured as the calicoes of Europe."

Still cotton was certainly not a staple of consequence. We were the last to enter the list of cotton-producing countries and we have surpassed them all.

The difficulty of removing the seeds from the staple practically thrust cotton out of common use.

A Yankee schoolmaster, Eli Whitney, set King Cotton on a throne by his invention of the cotton gin in 1792. A man could, by hand picking, clean only about a pound of cotton a day. The cotton gin cleaned as much in a day as had taken the hand picker a year to accomplish. This comparatively simple invention completely revolutionized cloth manufacture in England and America. It also changed general commerce, industrial development, and the social and economic order of things, for it gave new occupations and offered new modes of life to hundreds of thousands of persons. It entirely changed and cheapened our dress and altered rural life both in the North and in the South.

The colonists were constantly trying to find new materials for spinning and also used many makeshifts. In 1704, when a ship was lost that was to bring cloth and wool to Quebec, one of the aristocrats of the French-Canadian colony spun and wove coarse blankets of nettle and linden bark. Similar experiments were made by the English colonists. Coarse thread was spun out of nettle fiber by pioneers in western New York. Deer hair and even cow's hair was collected from the tanners, spun with some wool, and woven into a sort of felted blanket.

Silk grass, a much-vaunted product, was sent back to England on the first ships and was everywhere being experimented with. Coarse wicking was spun from the down of the milkweed—an airy, feathery material.

Chapter XVIII

Hand Weaving

Anyone who passed through a New England village on a week day a century and a half ago or rode up to the door of a Pennsylvania or Virginia house would probably be greeted with a heavy thwack-thwack from within doors, a regular sound which would readily be recognized as proceeding from weaving on a hand loom. Those looms were found in every house of any considerable size.

Hand loom, about 1750
(The Staten Island Historical Society. Photograph by Alfred Tamarin)

Many households had a loom room, usually in an ell part of the house; others used an attic or a shed loft as a weaving room. Every farmer's daughter knew how to weave as well as to spin, yet it was not recognized as wholly woman's work as was spinning, for there was a trade of hand weaving for men. Every town had professional weavers. They took in yarn and thread to weave on their looms at their own homes at so much a yard, wove their own yarn into stuffs to sell, had apprentices to their trade, and also went out working by the day at their neighbors' houses, sometimes carrying their looms many miles with them.

Weavers were a universally popular element of the community. The traveling weaver was, like all other itinerant tradesmen of the day, a welcome newsmonger, and the weaver who took in weaving was often a stationary gossip and gathered inquiring groups in his loom room. Even children loved to go to his door to beg for bits of colored yarn—thrums—which they used in their play and also braided tightly to wear as shoestrings, hair laces, etc.

The hand loom consists of a frame of four square timber posts about seven feet high, connected at top and bottom. From post to post across one end, which may be called the back part of the loom, is the yarn beam, about six inches in diameter. Upon it are wound the warp threads, which stretch in close parallels from it to the cloth beam at the front of the loom. The cloth beam is about ten inches in diameter, and the cloth is wound as the weaving proceeds. The yarn beam was made of close-grained, well-seasoned wood.

The homespun yarn, whether linen or woolen, was left in carefully knotted skeins after being spun and cleaned, bleached or dyed. To prepare if for use on the loom a skein was placed on the swift, a revolving cylindrical frame made of strips of wood arranged so the size can be increased or diminished at pleasure, and thus take on and hold firmly any size skein of yarn. The quill or bobbin was a small reed or quill, pierced from end to end. Both quills for the weft and spools for the warp were wound from the swift. When wound the quill was set in the recess of the shuttle.

When the piece was to be set, a large number of shuttles and spools were filled in advance. The

full spools were then placed in a row one above the other in a spool holder, sometimes called a skarne or scarne.

The laying of the piece, that is the orderly placing of the warp on the warp beam was simple enough to execute. The warping bars, an accessory, not a part of the loom, were two upright bars of wood, each holding a number of wooden pins and held together by crosspieces. Forty full spools were placed in the skarne, one above the other. The free ends of threads from the spools were gathered in the hand and fastened to a pin at the top of the warping bars. The group of threads then were carried from side to side of the bars, passing around a pin on one bar, then around a pin on the opposite bar, to the extreme end; then back again in the same way, the spools revolving on wires and freely playing out the warp threads till a sufficient length of threads was stretched on the bars. Forty warp threads made what was called a bout, or section. From the warping bars these bouts were carefully wound on the warp beam.

Swift, early 19th century (The Newark Museum. Photograph by Alfred Tamarin)

The "warping" and "beaming" finished, the "drawing" or "entering" came next. The end of each warp thread in regular order was "thumbed" or drawn in with a warping needle through the eye or "mail" of the harness, or heddle.

The heddle was a row of twines, cords, or wires, called leashes, which were stretched vertically between two horizontal bars or rods, placed about a foot apart. One rod was suspended by a pulley at the top of the loom, and to the lower rod was hitched the foot treadle. In the middle of each

Shuttles, late 18th–early 19th century (The Newark Museum. Photograph by Alfred Tamarin)

length of twine or wire was the loop or eye, through which a warp thread was passed. In ordinary weaving there were two heddles, each fastened to a foot treadle.

The warp threads next were drawn through the interspaces between two dents or strips of the sley or reed. Two warp threads were drawn in each space.

The sley or reed was composed of a row of short and very thin parallel strips of cane or metal, somewhat like comb teeth, called dents, fixed at both ends closely in two long, strong, parallel bars of wood set two or three or even four inches apart. This reed was placed in a groove on the lower edge of a heavy batten (or lay or lathe). This batten hung by two swords or side bars and swung from an axle or "rocking tree" at the top of the loom. As the heavy batten swung on its axle, the reed forced with a sharp blow every newly placed thread of the weft into its proper place close to the previously woven part of the texture. This was the heavy thwacking sound heard in handweaving.

There were three motions in handweaving. First: by the action of one foot treadle, one harness or heddle holding alternate warp threads was depressed from the level of the entire expanse of warp threads. The separation of the warp threads by this depression of one harness was called a shed.

Room was made by this shed for the shuttle, which, by the second motion, was thrown from one side of the loom to the other by the weaver's hand, and thus went over every alternate thread. By the third motion the batten crowded this weft thread into place. Then the motion of the other foot treadle forced down the other warp threads, which passed through the second set of harnesses; the shuttle was thrown back through this shed, and so on.

Looms and their appurtenances were usually made by local carpenters. The various parts of the looms were in unceasing demand, though apparently they never wore out. The sley was the most delicate part of the mechanism. Spools were turned and marked with the maker's initials. There were choice and inexplicable lines in the shape of a shuttle as there are in a boat's hull. Apple wood and boxwood were the choice for shuttles.

Smaller looms, called tape looms, braid looms, belt looms, garter looms, or "gallus frames," were used for weaving. Narrow bands such as tapes, none-so-pretty's, ribbons, caddises, ferretings, inkles, were woven for garters, points, glove ties, hair laces, shoestrings, belts, hat bands, stay laces, suspenders, etc.

Tape loom, about 1790–1810 (The Newark Museum. Photograph by Alfred Tamarin)

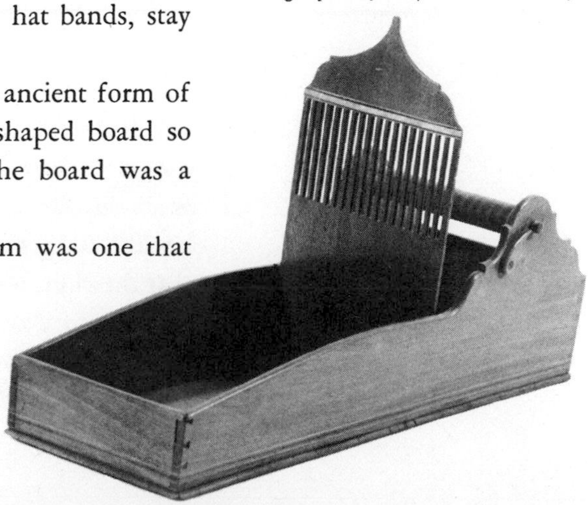

These tape looms were a truly ancient form of appliance. They were a slightly shaped board so cut in slits that the center of the board was a row of narrow slats.

A common form of braid loom was one that

was laid upon a table. A still simpler form was held upright on the lap. It was such light and pretty work that girls carried their tape looms to a neighbor's house for an afternoon's work, just as they did their knitting needles and ball of yarn. A fringe-loom might also be occasionally found, for weaving decorative fringes; these were more common in the Hudson River valley than elsewhere.

Cloth that came from the weaving was not comely to wear till it was fulled under foot or in fulling stocks, washed well in water, scratched and dressed with teazels, dyed and tented, and put in the tailor's hands. If grease had been put on the wool when it was carded, or sizing in the warp for the weaving, it was washed out by good rinsing from the woven cloth. This became now somewhat uneven and irregular in appearance and full of knots and fuzzes which were picked out with hand tweezers by burlers before it was fulled or milled, as it was sometimes called. The fulling stocks were a trough in which an enormous oak hammer was made to pound up and down, while the cloth was kept thoroughly wet with warm soap and water or fullers' earth and water. Naturally this thickened the web much and reduced it in length. It was then teazeled; that is, a nap or rough surface was raised all over it by scratching it with weavers' teazels or thistles.

If the cloth were to be dyed, it was done at this period, and it was then spread on the tenter field and caught on tenter hooks, to shrink and dry.

Linen webs after they were woven had even

more manipulations than woolen stuffs. In spite of all the bleaching of the linen thread, it still was light brown in color, and it had to go through at least forty other processes, of bucking, possing, rinsing, drying, and bleaching on the grass. Sometimes it was stretched out on pegs with loops sewed on the selvage edge. This bleaching was called grassing in America. Often it was thus spread on the grass for weeks and was slightly wetted several times a day; but not too wet, else it would mildew. In all, over forty bleaching operations were employed upon "light linens." Sometimes they were "soured" in buttermilk to make them purely white. Thus at least sixteen months had passed since the flaxseed had been sown. In the winter months the fine, white, strong linen was made into "board cloths" or tablecloths, sheets, pillow cases, aprons, shifts, shirts, petticoats, short gowns, gloves, cut from the spinner's own glove pattern, and a score of articles for household use. These were carefully marked and sometimes embroidered with home-dyed crewels, as were also splendid sets of bed hangings, valances, and testers for four-post bedsteads.

The strong, firm linen woven in many struggling country homes was too valuable and too readily exchangeable and salable to be kept wholly for farm use, especially when there were so few salable articles produced on the farm. It was sold or more frequently exchanged at the village store for any desired commodity, such as calico, salt, sugar, spices, or tea. It readily sold for forty-two cents a yard. Therefore the boys and even the fathers did not always have linen shirts to wear. From the tow that had been hatcheled out from harl, a coarse thread was spun and cloth was woven, which was made chiefly into shirts and smocks and tow "tongs" or "skilts"—loose, flapping summer trousers that ended almost halfway between the knee and the ankle. This tow stuff was never free from prickling spines, and it proved, so tradition states, an absolute instrument of torture to the wearer, until frequent washings had worn it out and thus subdued its knots and spines.

The Scotch-Irish linen weavers who settled in New Hampshire made what was known as striped frocking. It was worn also to a considerable extent in Connecticut and Massachusetts. The warp was strong white cotton or tow thread, the weft of blue and white stripes made by weaving alternately a shuttleful of indigo-dyed homespun yarn and one of white wool or tow. Many boys grew to manhood never wearing, except on Sundays, any kind of coat save a long, loose, shapeless jacket or smock of this striped frocking, known everywhere as a long-short.

Another material which was universal in country districts had a flax or tow warp and a coarser slack-twisted cotton or tow filling. This cloth was dyed and pressed and was called fustian. It was worth a shilling a yard in 1640.

Another coarse cloth made in New England, Pennsylvania, Virginia, and the Carolinas was crocus. The stuff is obsolete and the name is forgotten save in the folk saying which lingers in Virginia—

"as coarse as crocus." Vast quantities of homespun cloth were made on Virginia plantations; thousands of yards were made annually at Mount Vernon.

It is told of Martha Washington that she always carefully dyed all her worn silk gowns and silk scraps to a desired shade, raveled them with care, wound them on bobbins, and had them woven into chair and cushion covers. Sometimes she changed the order of things. To a group of visitors she at one time displayed a dress of red and white striped material of which the white stripes were cotton, and the red, raveled chair covers and silk from the General's worn-out stockings.

Checked linen with bars of red or blue was much used for bedticks, pillow cases, toweling, aprons, and even shirts and summer trousers.

It is impossible to overestimate the durability of homespun materials. Cradle sheets of this thin, closely woven, white worsted stuff are not slimsy like thin flannel, yet are softer than flannel. Years of use with many generations of children have left them firm and white.

The product of these hand looms which lingered longest in country use was the rag carpet, an economical and comely floor covering.

The warp of these carpets was, in olden times, a strong, heavy flaxen thread. The weft or filling was narrow strips of all the clean and varicolored rags that accumulated in a household.

Everything appertaining to the manufacture of

homespun materials could be found in the loom room of an old-time weaver—wheels, skarnes, sleys, warping bars, clock reels, swifts, quilling wheels, vast bales of yarns and thread. There are piles of old and new bed coverlets woven in those fanciful geometric designs which formed a favorite bed covering of our ancestors. These coverlets the weaver calls by the good old English name of hap-harlot. The manuscript pattern book is over 150 years old and has the rules for setting the harnesses. They bear many pretty and odd names, such as "Rosy Walk," "Baltimore Beauty," "Girl's Love," "Queen's Fancy," "Devil's Fancy," "Everybody's Beauty," "Four Snow Balls," "Five Snow Balls," "Bricks and Blocks," "Gardener's Note," "Green Vails," "Rose in Bloom," "Pansies and Roses in the Wilderness," "Flag-Work," "Royal Beauty," "Indian March," "Troy's Beauty," "Primrose and Diamonds," "Crown and Diamonds," "Jay's Fancy," "In Summer and Winter," "Boston Beauty," and "Indian War." One named "Bony Part's March" was very pretty, as was "Orange Peel," and "Orange Trees"; "Dog Tracks" was even checkerwork, "Blazing Star," a herringbone design. "Perry's Victory" and "Lady Washington's Delight" show probably the date of their invention and were handsome designs, while the "Whig Rose from Georgia," which had been given to the weaver by a lady a hundred years old, had proved a poor and ugly thing. "Kapa's Diaper" was a complicated design which took "five harnesses" to make. "Rattlesnake's Trail,"

"Wheels of Fancy," "Chariot Wheels and Church Windows," and "Bachelor's Fancy" were all exceptionally fine designs.

In the summer of 1775, when all the preparations for the Revolution were in a most unsettled and depressing condition, especially the supplies for the Continental army, the Provincial Congress made a demand on the people for 13,000 warm coats to be ready for the soldiers by cold weather. There were no great contractors to supply the cloth and make the garments, but by hundreds of hearthstones throughout the country wool wheels and hand looms were started eagerly at work, and the order was filled by the handiwork of patriotic American women. In the record book of some New England towns may still be found the lists of the coat-makers. In the inside of each coat was sewed the name of the town and the maker. Every soldier volunteering for eight months' service was given one of these homespun, homemade, all-wool coats as a bounty. So highly were these "Bounty Coats" prized, that the heirs of soldiers who were killed at Bunker Hill before receiving their coats were given a sum of money instead. The list of names of soldiers who then enlisted is known to this day as the "Coat Roll," and the names of the women who made the coats might form another roll of honor. The English sneeringly called Washington's army the "Homespuns." It was a truthful nickname, but there was deeper power in the title than the English scoffers knew.

Chapter XIX

Dress of the Colonists

At the time America was settled, rich dress was almost universal in Europe among persons of any wealth or station.

In England extravagance in dress in court circles and grotesqueness in dress among educated folk had become abhorrent to that class of persons who were called Puritans. As an expression of their dislike they wore plainer garments, cut off their

The Gore children, detail of painting by John Singleton Copley (1738–1815) (The Henry Francis du Pont Winterthur Museum)

flowing locks, and soon were called Roundheads. The Massachusetts settlers who were Puritans were determined to discourage extravagance in dress and they attempted to control the fashions in the New World.

In 1634 the Massachusetts General Court passed restricting laws. These laws forbade the purchase of woolen, silk, or linen garments with silver, gold, silk, or thread lace on them. Two years later a narrow binding of lace was permitted on linen garments. The colonists were ordered not to make or buy any slashed clothes except those with one slash in each sleeve and another in the back. Gold or silver girdles, hat bands, belts, ruffs, and beaver hats were forbidden. Liberty was

Lady in 18th century costume (The Brooklyn Museum. Photograph by Alfred Tamarin)

thriftily given, however, to the colonists to wear out any garments they chanced to have except for inordinately slashed apparel, immoderate great sleeves and rails, and long wings, which could not be endured.

In 1639 men's attire was approached and scanned, and "immoderate great breeches" were tabooed; also broad shoulder bands, double ruffles and capes, and silk roses, which were worn on the shoes.

Connecticut called to its aid in repressing extravagant dress the economic power of taxation by ordering that whoever wore gold or silver lace, gold or silver buttons, silk ribbons, silk scarfs, or bone lace worth over three shillings a yard should be taxed as worth £150.

Virginia fussed a little over "excess in cloathes." Only the Council and the heads of Hundreds were permitted to wear gold on their clothes, or to wear silk till they made it—which was intended more to encourage silk-making than to discourage silk-wearing. And it provided that unmarried men should be assessed according to their apparel, and married men according to that of their family. In 1660 Virginia colonists were ordered to import no "silke stuffe in garments or in peeces except for whoods and scarfs, nor silver or gold lace, nor bone lace of silk or threads, nor ribbands wrought with gold or silver in them."

To know how the colonists were dressed, we have to learn from the lists of their clothing which they left by will, still preserved in court records; from the inventories of the garments furnished to each settler who came by contract; from the orders sent back to England for new clothing; from a few crude portraits, and from some articles of ancient clothing which are still preserved.

When Salem was settled the Massachusetts Bay Company furnished to all the men who emigrated and settled that town four pairs of shoes, four pairs of stockings, a pair of Norwich garters, four shirts, two suits of doublet and hose of leather lined with oiled skin, a woolen suit lined with leather, four bands, two handkerchiefs, a green cotton waistcoat, a leather belt, a woolen cap, a black hat, two red knit caps, two pairs of gloves, a mandillion or cloak lined with cotton, and an extra pair of breeches.

George Washington, mezzotint after Stuart by Edward Savage (1761–1817) (The Metropolitan Museum of Art, Bequest of Charles Allen Munn, 1924)

Little boys just as soon as they could walk wore clothes made precisely like their fathers': doublets which were warm double jackets, leather knee breeches, leather belts, knit caps. The outfit for the Virginia planters was not so liberal, for the company was not so wealthy. It was called a "Particular of Apparell." It had only three bands, three pairs of stockings, and three shirts instead of four. The suits were of canvas, frieze, and cloth. The clothing was doubtless lighter, because the climate of Virginia was warmer. They had "a dozen points," which were simply tapes to hold up the clothing and fasten it together. The clothing of the Piscataquay planters varied but little from the others. They had scarlet waistcoats and cassocks of cloth, not of leather.

Through the seventeenth and eighteenth centuries there was a constant succession of rich and gay fashions, for American dress was carefully modeled upon European, especially English modes. Men's wear was as rich as women's. But with all the richness there was no wastefulness. The sister of the rich Boston merchant Peter Faneuil, who built Faneuil Hall, sent her gowns to London to be turned and dyed and her old ribbons and gowns to be sold.

New Yorkers were dressed in gauzes, silks, and laces; even women Quakers in Pennsylvania had to be warned against wearing hoop petticoats, scarlet shoes, and puffed and rolled hair.

Southern dames, especially of Annapolis, Baltimore, and Charleston, were said to have the richest brocades and damasks that could be bought in London. The heroes of the Revolution had a high regard for dress. The patriot John Hancock was seen at noonday wearing a scarlet velvet cap, a blue damask gown lined with velvet, white satin embroidered waistcoat, black satin small-clothes, white silk stockings, and red morocco slippers. George Washington wore the richest silk and velvet suits. His style of dress was described:

"He wore a pea-green coat, white vest, nankeen small clothes, white silk stockings, and pumps fastened with silver buckles which covered at least half the foot from instep to toe. His small clothes were tied at the knees with ribbon of the same colour in double bows, the ends reaching down to the ancles. His hair in front was well loaded with

Miniature portrait of Mrs. Peter De Lancy, about 1780 (The Metropolitan Museum of Art, Fletcher Fund, 1938)

Captain James Gooch, by John Smibert, about 1740 (The Brooklyn Museum, Carl H. De Silver and A. T. White Memorial Funds)

pomatum, frizzled or craped and powdered. Behind, his natural hair was augmented by the addition of a large queue called vulgarly a false tail, which, enrolled in some yards of black ribbon, hung half-way down his back."

Rich laces, silk materials, velvet, and fine cloth of light and gay colors were ordered from Europe. Also ordered were nightgowns of silk and damask. These nightgowns, a sort of dressing gown, were called banyan and became very fashionable.

With the increase of trade with China many Chinese and East Indian goods became fashionable. A few were of silk or linen, but far more of cotton.

Both men and women wore great cloaks or capes known by various names, such as roquelaures, capuchins, pelisses, etc.

When riding, women in the colonies wore, as did Queen Elizabeth, a safeguard, a long over-petticoat to protect the gown from mud and rain. This was sometimes called a foot mantle, also a weather skirt. Women's shoes were of very thin materials, and paper soled. To protect these frail shoes, when walking on the ill-paved streets, various forms of overshoes were worn, known as goloe-shoes, clogs, pattens, etc. Men wore sherry-vallies or spatterdashes to protect their gay breeches.

One fashion which lasted for a century and a half was wig-wearing by men. The first colonists wore their own natural hair. The Cavaliers had long perfumed lovelocks, and though the Puritans had been called Roundheads, their hair waved,

Man's purse, 18th century (The Brooklyn Museum. Photograph by Alfred Tamarin)

Pattens, 18th century (Old Sturbridge Village)

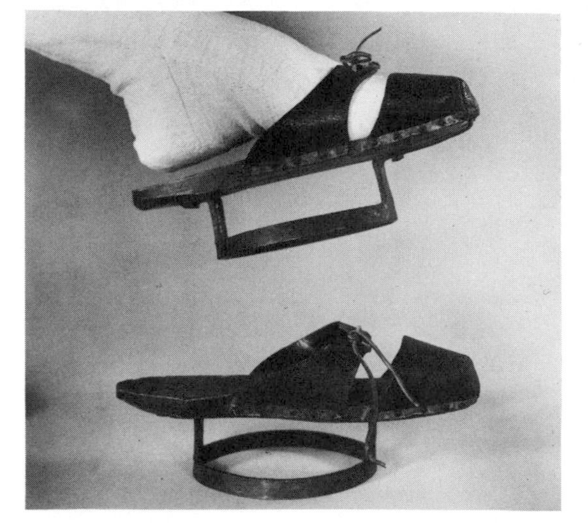

Ladies shoes, 18th century (The Brooklyn Museum. Photograph by Alfred Tamarin)

also, over the band or collar, and often hung over the shoulder. The Quakers, also, wore long locks, as the lovely portrait of William Penn shows. But by 1675 wigs had become common enough to be denounced by the Massachusetts government and to be preached against by many ministers, while other ministers proudly wore them. Wigs were called horrid bushes of vanity and hundreds of other disparaging names, which seemed to make them more popular. They varied from year to year. Sometimes they swelled out at the sides or rose in great puffs, or turned under in heavy rolls, or hung in braids and curls and pigtails. They were made of human hair, of horsehair, goat's hair, calves' and cows' tails, of thread, silk, and mohair. They had scores of silly and meaningless names, such as "grave full-bottom," "giddy feather-top," "long-tail," "fox-tail," "drop-wig," etc. They were bound and braided with pink, green, red, and purple ribbons, sometimes all these colors on one wig. They were very heavy, very hot, and very expensive. The care of them was a great item, often ten pounds a year for a single wig, and some gentlemen owned eight or ten wigs. Even little children wore them. After wigs had become unfashionable, the natural hair was powdered, and was tied in a queue in the back. This was an untidy, troublesome fashion, which ruined the clothes, for the hair was soaked with oil or pomatum to make the powder stick.

Comparatively little jewelry was worn. A

few men had gold or silver sleeve buttons; a few women had bracelets or lockets. Nearly all of any social standing had rings, which were chiefly mourning rings. These gloomy ornaments were given to all the chief mourners at funerals.

Men sometimes wore thumb rings, which seems no queerer than the fact that they carried muffs..

Gloves also were gifts at funerals. At the funeral of the wife of Governor Belcher in 1738 over a thousand pairs were given away. Reverend Andrew Eliot, who was pastor of the North Church in Boston, had 2900 pairs of gloves given him in thirty-two years. Many of these he sold.

The early watches and clocks were clumsy affairs and were owned by very few of the first colonists. Instead, sun dials, set in the street in front of houses, and noon marks on the threshold of the front door or window sill helped to show the hour of the day.

The dress of infants in colonial times was based on linen, a chilling substructure. Thin, low-necked, short-sleeved shirts and even underwear were made of linen. These little linen shirts were daintier than the warmest silk or fine woolen underwear that succeeded them. They were edged with fine narrow thread lace, hemstitched with tiny rows of stitches, and sometimes embroidered by hand. A little shirt and a cap embroidered with the coat of arms of the Lux and Johnson families had the motto, "God bless the Babe."

In the Essex Institute in Salem, Massachusetts, are the baptismal shirt and mittens of the Pilgrim Father William Bradford, second governor of the Plymouth Colony, who was born in 1590. All are of firm, close-woven, homespun linen, but the little mittens have been worn at the ends by active baby hands and are patched with colored "chiney" or calico. A similar colored material frills the sleeves and neck.

It seems infants wore no woolen petticoats; their shirts, petticoats, and gowns were of linen or some cotton stuff like dimity. Warmth of clothing was given by tiny shawls pinned around the shoulders and heavier blankets and quilts and shawls in which baby and petticoats were wholly enveloped.

The baby dresses of olden times are either rather shapeless sacks drawn in at the neck with narrow cotton ferret or linen bobbin, or little straight-waisted gowns of state. All were exquisitely made by hand, and usually of fine stuff. But the babies in pioneer settlements had to share in wearing homespun.

A young boy about ten years old named John Livingstone was sent from New York to school in New England at the latter part of the seventeenth century. An "account of his new linen and clothes" has been preserved, and it gives an excellent idea of the clothing of a son of wealthy people at that time. It reads thus, in the old spelling:

"Eleven new shirts,
4 pair laced sleves,
8 Plane Cravats,
4 Cravats with Lace,
4 Stripte Wastecoats with black buttons,
1 Flowered Wastecoat,
4 New osenbrig britches,
1 Gray hat with a black ribbon,
1 Gray hat with a blew ribbon,
1 Dousin black buttons,
1 Dousin coloured buttons,
3 Pair gold buttons,
3 Pair silver buttons,
2 Pair Fine blew Stockings,
1 Pair Fine red Stockings,
4 White Handkerchiefs,
2 Speckled Handkerchiefs,
5 Pair Gloves,
1 Stuff Coat with black buttons,
1 Cloth Coat,
1 Pair blew plush britches,
1 Pair Serge britches,
2 Combs,
1 Pair new Shooes,
Silk & Thred to mend his Cloathes."

Osenbrig was a heavy, strong linen. This would seem to be a summer outfit and scarcely warm enough for New England winters. Other schoolboys at that date had deerskin breeches.

Leather was much used, especially in the form of tanned buckskin breeches and the deerskin hunters' jackets.

Soon in the larger cities and among wealthy folk a much more elaborate and varied style of dress became fashionable. The dress of little girls in families of wealth was certainly almost as for-

Deborah Hall,
by William Williams, 1766
(The Brooklyn Museum,
Dick S. Ramsay Fund)

mal and elegant as the dress of their mamas, and it was a very hampering and stiff dress. They wore vast hoop petticoats, heavy stays, and high-heeled shoes, made of silk, morocco, or light stuff, which unfitted them for very active exercise. Some children's stays were made of heavy strips of board and steel, tightly wrought with heavy buckram or canvas into an iron frame like an instrument of torture. Staymakers advertised stays, jumps, gazzets, costrells, and caushets (which were doubtless corsets) for ladies and children, "to make them appear strait."

A girl who was twelve years old in 1771 gives a full description of the way her hair was dressed over a high roll, so heavy and hot that it made her head "itch & ach & burn like anything." She tells of the height of her headgear:

"When it first came home, Aunt put it on & my new cap on it; she then took up her apron & measur'd me, & from the roots of my hair on my forehead to the top of my notions, I measur'd above an inch longer than I did downwards from the roots of my hair to the end of my chin."

Girl's complexions were objects of special care. They wore masks of cloth or velvet to protect them from the tanning rays of the sun and long-armed gloves. Little Dolley Payne, who later became the wife of President Madison, went to school wearing "a white linen mask to keep every ray of sunshine from the complexion, a sunbonnet sewed on her head every morning by her careful mother, and long gloves covering the hands and arms."

In the middle of the eighteenth century George Washington sent to England for an outfit for his stepdaughter, Miss Custis, who was four years old. He ordered for her pack-thread stays, stiff coats of silk, masks, caps, bonnets, bibs, ruffles, necklaces, fans, silk and calamanco shoes, and leather pumps. There were also eight pairs of kid mitts and four pairs of gloves. These with the masks show that this little girl's complexion was also well guarded.

The Dutch never attempted or wished to simplify the dress of either men or women. In New York dress was ample, substantial, varied in texture, and variegated in color. It always formed a considerable item in personal property. The children of the Dutch settlers had plentiful and warm and sometimes very rich clothing.

One old Virginia gentleman had two child wards. As befitted young gentlefolk of that day of opulence and extravagance, they had their dress from England. In 1736 when Robert Carter, the younger child, was about nine years old, suits of fine holland, laced, and of red worsted and green German serge came across the seas for him,

Woman's calash, 1780 or later (Old Sturbridge Village)

with laced hats with loops and buttons. When he was twelve years old part of his "winter cloathes" were six pairs of shoes and two of pumps, four pairs of worked hose and four of thread hose, gloves, hats, and shoe buckles. His sister Betty had a truly fashionable wardrobe, and the stiff, restrictive dress of the times was indicated by the items of stays, hoops, masks, and fans.

From a letter describing the dress of two young girls who were boarding in Boston while they were being taught, there is no doubt that very rich dress was desired and possibly required of these young scholar-boarders. One of the girl's wardrobes shows the elegance of dress. She had twelve silk gowns, but word was sent home to Norwich that a recently imported rich fabric was most suitable for her rank and station. In answer to the teacher's request the parents ordered the purchase of this elegant dress.

When cotton fabrics from the Orient became everywhere worn, children's dress, like that of grown folk, was much reduced in elegance as it was in warmth. Hoops disappeared and heavy petticoats also. The soft, flimsy, clinging stuffs, suitable only for summer wear, were not discarded in winter. Boys wore nankeen suits the entire year. Calico and chintz were fashioned into trousers and jackets.

Children must have suffered sadly with the cold in this age of cotton. Girls' dresses were half low-necked and were filled in with a thin tucker. Separate sleeves were tied in at the arm hole, and

William Verstile, attributed to William Johnson, 18th century (The Henry Francis du Pont Winterthur Museum)

often long-armed mitts of nankeen or linen took the place of the sleeves.

Soon after the Revolution, there were definite changes of dress which set in with other republican institutions. At this date there began to be worn a special dress for both boys and girls. Until then, as soon as a boy put on breeches he dressed precisely like his father—in miniature. By tradition Marie Antoinette was the first who had a special dress made for her young son. And sadly was she reviled for dressing her poor little dauphin in jacket and trousers instead of flapped coat, waistcoat, and knee breeches.

Children in America, if gentlefolk, dressed just as children did in England at that date; and boys wore "coats" in England till they were six or seven.

Nothing could show so fully the costume of children in olden times as their portraits. There were few painters of any rank in the community. Many of the pictures have no artist's signature, but as records of costume they are of interest and historical worth.

Jonathon Mountford, by John Singleton Copley (1738–1815) (The Detroit Institute of Arts)

There is a certain sweetness in some of these old-time portraits. They are stiff and flat, have little grace of figure, but the details of costume make them pleasing even if they are not beautiful. John Quincy as an infant was pictured wearing a dress which, with the exception of the neck of the body of the frock, is much like the dress of grown women of that day. The sleeve is the most noticeable feature, with its single slash, double puff drawn in below the elbow and confined with pretty ribbon knots. This sleeve was known as the virago sleeve. John Quincy wore a loosely tied rather shapeless hood and a close cap under his hood.

Robert Gibbs, the rich Boston merchant, another Massachusetts boy contemporary with John Quincy, had his portrait painted when he was four and a half years old. He wears the same stiff cuirass as John Quincy, the same odd truncated shoes of buff leather, and has the same masculine swing of the petticoats. Robert Gibbs wears a more boyish collar, or band, as befits a bigger boy. The long hanging sleeves are an important feature of his dress. Hanging sleeves were so distinctively

Jane Bonner, artist unknown, 1698 (The Connecticut Historical Society)

the dress of a little child that the term had at that time a symbolic significance, implying childishness both of youth and second childhood.

Thomas Aston Coffin, in an exquisite painting by Copley, wears a rich full-skirted satin overdress which brushes the ground. A light-hued satin petticoat front can be seen underneath. The pretty satin sleeves have white undersleeves and wrist ruffles, but the neck is cut very low and round. The child holds two pigeons by a leash, and a feathered hat is by his side.

A demure and quaint portrait is that of Jane Bonner. She was born in 1691, the daughter of Captain John Bonner, of Boston, and was married in 1710 to John Ellery. She was about eight or ten years old when the portrait was painted. The lace of the stomacher and sleeve frills is of the nature of what is now called rose point.

Chapter XX

Religion in the Colonies

The first building used as a church at the Plymouth colony was the fort, and to it the Pilgrim fathers and mothers and children reverently walked on Sunday three in a row, the men fully armed with swords and guns, till they built a meeting-house in 1648. In other New England settlements the first services were held in tents, under trees, or under any shelter. The settler who had a

From The History of Little Goody Two-Shoes, *1787* (*The Free Library of Philadelphia, rare book department*)

roomy house often also had the meeting. The first Boston meetinghouse had mud walls, a thatched roof, and earthen floor. It was used till 1640. Usually the earliest meetinghouses were log houses with clay-filled chinks and roofs thatched with reeds and long grass, like the dwelling houses. At Salem is still preserved one of the early churches. The second and more dignified form of New England meetinghouse was usually a square wooden building with a truncated pyramidal roof, surmounted often with a belfry, which served as a lookout station and held a bell, from which the bell rope hung down to the floor in the center of the church aisle. The old church at Hingham, Massachusetts, still standing and still used, is a

The Old Ship Church, Hingham, Massachusetts (The Society for the Preservation of New England Antiquities)

good specimen of this shape. It was built in 1681 and is known as the "Old Ship," and is a comely and dignified building. As more elegant and costly dwelling houses were built, so were better meetinghouses. The third form with lofty wooden steeple at one end, in the style of architecture invented by Sir Christopher Wren after the great fire of London, multiplied and increased until every town was graced with an example. In all these the main body of the edifice remained as bare, prosaic, and undecorated as were the preceding churches, while all the ambition of both builders and congregation spent itself in the steeple. The Old South Church of Boston is a good example of this school of ecclesiastical architecture, and is a well-known historic building as well.

The earliest meetinghouse had oiled paper in the windows, and when glass came it was not set with putty, but was nailed in. The windows had what were termed "heavy current side-shutters." The outside of the meetinghouse was not "colored," or "stained" as it was then termed, but was left to turn gray and weather stained, and sometimes moss covered with the dampness of the great shadowing hemlock and fir trees which were usually planted around New England churches. The first meetinghouses were often decorated in a very singular and grotesque manner. Rewards were paid by all the early towns for killing wolves, and any person who killed a wolf brought the head to the meetinghouse and nailed it to the outer wall. The fierce grinning heads and splashes of blood made a grim and horrible decoration. All kinds of notices were also nailed to the meetinghouse door where all of the congregation might readily see them—notices of town meetings, of sales of cattle or farms, lists of town officers, prohibitions from selling guns to the Indians, notices of intended marriages, vendues, etc. It was the only meeting place, the only method of advertisement. In front of the church was usually a row of stepping stones or horse blocks, for nearly all came on horseback, and often on the meetinghouse green stood the stocks, pillory, and whipping post.

The first church at Jamestown, Virginia, gathered the congregation by beat of drum. While attendants of the Episcopal, Roman Catholic, and Dutch Reformed churches in the New World were in general being summoned to divine service by the ringing of a bell, New England Puritans were summoned by drum, or horn, or shell. The shell was a great conch shell, and a man was hired to blow it—a mournful sound—at the proper time, which was usually nine o'clock in the morning. In Stockbridge, Massachusetts, the church

Interior of Rocky Hill Meeting House, Amesbury, Massachusetts, built in 1785 (The American Antiquarian Society. Photograph by Richard Merrill)

shell was afterward used for many years as a signal to begin and stop work in the haying field. In Windsor, Connecticut, a man walked up and down on a platform on the top of the meetinghouse and blew a trumpet to summon worshipers. Many churches had a church drummer, who stood on the roof or in the belfry and drummed; a few raised a flag as a summons, or fired a gun.

Within the meetinghouse all was simple enough: raftered walls, puncheon and sanded or earthen floors, rows of benches, a few pews, all of unpainted wood, and a pulpit which was usually a high desk overhung by a heavy sounding board, which was fastened to the roof by a slender metal rod. The pulpit was sometimes called a scaffold. When pews were built they were square with high partition walls and had narrow, uncomfortable seats around three sides. The word was always spelled "pue," and they were sometimes called "pits." A few of the old-time meetinghouses, with high pulpit, square pews, and deacons' seats, still remain in New England.

The seats were carefully and thoughtfully assigned by a church committee called the Seating

Committee, the best seats being given to older persons of wealth and dignity who attended the church. Whittier wrote of this custom:

"In the goodly house of worship, where in order
due and fit,
As by public vote directed, classed and ranked
the people sit."

In the early meetinghouses men and women sat on separate sides. Sometimes a group of young men were permitted to sit in the gallery together. Little girls sat beside their mothers or on footstools at their feet, or sometimes on the gallery stairs; a little cage or frame held Puritan babies in meeting. Boys did not sit with their families but were in groups by themselves, usually on the pulpit and gallery stairs, where they were carefully watched.

The deacons sat in a "Deacons' Pue" just in front of the pulpit; sometimes also there was a "Deaf Pue" in front for those who were hard of hearing. After choirs were established the singers' seats were usually in the gallery. High up under the beams in a loft sat the Negroes and Indians. If any person seated himself in any place which was not assigned to him, he had to pay a fine.

The churches were all unheated. The chill of the damp buildings, never heated from autumn to spring, and closed and dark throughout the week, was hard for everyone to bear. In some of the early log-built meetinghouses, fur bags made of wolf-

Foot stove, about 1800
(The Staten Island Historical Society. Photograph by Alfred Tamarin)

skins were nailed to the seats, and in winter church attendants thrust their feet into them. Dogs, too, were permitted to enter the meetinghouse and lie on their masters' feet. Dog whippers or dog pelters were appointed to control and expel them when they became unruly or unbearable. Women and children usually carried foot stoves, which were little pierced metal boxes that stood on wooden legs and held hot coals. During the noon intermission the half-frozen church attendants went to a neighboring house or tavern or to a noon-house to get warm. A noon-house or "Sabba-day house," as it was often called, was a long low building near the meetinghouse, with horse stalls at one end and a chimney at the other. In it the farmers kept, says one church record, "their duds and horses." A great fire of logs was built there each Sunday, and before its cheerful blaze noonday luncheons of brown bread, doughnuts, or gingerbread were eaten, and foot stoves were filled. Boys and girls were not permitted to indulge in idle talk in those noon-houses, much less to play. Often two or three families built a noon-house together, or the church built a "Society-house," and there the children had a sermon read to them by a deacon during the "nooning"; sometimes the children had to explain aloud the notes they had taken during the sermon in the morning. There was no nearer approach to a Sunday school until the nineteenth century.

The services were not shortened because the churches were uncomfortable. By the side of the pulpit stood a brass-bound hourglass which was turned, but it did not hasten the closing of the sermon. Sermons two or three hours long were customary and prayers from one to two hours in length. When the first church in Woburn was dedicated, the minister preached a sermon nearly five hours long. Many prayers were two hours long. The doors were closed and watched and none could leave even if tired or restless unless with good excuse. The singing of the psalms was tedious and unmusical. Singing was by ear, and very uncertain, the congregation had no notes, and many had no psalm books, and hence no words. So the psalms were "lined" or "deaconed," that is, a line was read by the deacon and then sung by the congregation. Some psalms when lined and sung occupied half an hour, during which the congregation stood. There were but eight or nine tunes in general use and even these were often sung incorrectly. There were no church organs to help keep the singers together, but sometimes pitch pipes were used to set the key. Bass viols, clarionets, and flutes were played upon at a later date in meeting to help the singing. Violins were too associated with dance music to be thought decorous for church music. Still the New England churches clung to and loved their poor confused psalm singing as one of their few delights, and whenever a Puritan, even in road or field, heard the distant sound of a psalm tune he removed his hat and bowed his head in prayer.

Contributions at first were not collected by the

deacons, but the entire congregation, one after another, walked up to the deacons' seat and placed gifts of money, goods, wampum, or promissory notes in a box. When the services were ended, all remained in the pews until the minister and his wife had walked up the aisle and out of the church.

The strict observance of Sunday as a holy day was one of the characteristics of the Puritans. Any profanation of the day was severely punished by fine or whipping. Citizens were forbidden to fish, shoot, sail, row, dance, jump, or ride, save to and from church, or to perform any work on the farm. An infinite number of examples might be given to show how rigidly the laws were enforced. The use of tobacco was forbidden near the meetinghouse. These laws were held to extend from sunset on Saturday to sunset on Sunday, for in the first instructions given to Governor Endicott by the company in England, it was ordered that all in the Massachusetts Bay Colony cease work at three o'clock in the afternoon on Saturday. The Puritans found support of this belief in the Scriptural words, "The evening and the morning were the first day."

The Virginia Cavaliers were strict Church of England men and the first who came to the colony were strict Sunday keepers. Rules were laid down to enforce Sunday observance. Journeys were forbidden, boat lading was prohibited, also all profanation of the day by sports, such as shooting, fishing, game playing, etc. The offender who broke the Sabbath laws had to pay a fine and be set in the stocks. When that sturdy watchdog of

Bruton Parish Church, Colonial Williamsburg, 1711–1715 (Photograph by Stephen M. Toth)

religion and government—Sir Thomas Dale—came over, he declared absence from church should be punishable by death, but this severity never was executed. Every Sunday, half an hour before service time, at the last tolling of the bell, the captain of the watch stationed sentinels, then searched all the house and commanded and forced all (except the sick) to go to church. Then, when all were driven churchward before him, he went with his guards to church himself.

Captain John Smith vividly described the first places of divine worship in Virginia as an awning, an old sail, hung from three or four trees as protection from the sun, with walls of wood railing; seats of unhewed trees and a pulpit, a bar of wood nailed to two neighboring trees.

Later a mud and clay chapel was erected. A timber church sixty feet long took its place, and this was in turn replaced by a brick one whose ruined arches are still standing. The wooden church saw the most pompous ceremony of the day when the governor, De La Warre, or Delaware as we now call it, in full dress, attended by all his councilors and officers and fifty halbert-bearers in scarlet cloaks, filed within its flower-decked walls.

This decoration of flowers was significant of the difference between the church edifices of the Puritans and of the Cavaliers. The churches of the Southern colonies were, as a rule, much more richly furnished. Many were modeled in shape after the old English churches and were built of stone. Many of the churches and the chapels-of-ease stood by the waterside, and to the services came the church attendants in canoes, periaugers, dugouts, etc.

Sometimes the seats were comfortably cushioned, and they were carefully assigned as in the Puritan meetings. In some Virginia churches seats in the galleries were deemed the most dignified. There was a pew for the magistrates, another for the magistrates' ladies; pews for the representatives and church wardens, vestrymen, etc. Persons crowded into pews above their stations, just as in New England, and were promptly displaced. Groups of men built pews together, and there were schoolboys' galleries and pews.

Sunday was not observed with as much rigidity in New Netherland as in New England, but strict rules and laws were made for enforcing quiet during service time. Fishing, gathering berries or nuts, playing in the streets, working, and going on pleasure trips were forbidden. On Long Island shooting of wild fowl, carting of grain, traveling for pleasure, all were punished. In Revolutionary times a cage was set up in City Hall Park in New York in which boys were confined who did not properly regard the Sabbath.

The New Dutch Church, New York, 1731 (The Metropolitan Museum of Art, Photograph by Alfred Tamarin)

Before the Dutch settlers had any churches or domines, as they called their ministers, they had *krankbesoeckers,* or visitors of the sick, who read sermons to an assembled congregation every Sunday. The first church at Albany was much like the Plymouth fort, simply a blockhouse with loopholes through which guns could be fired. The roof was mounted with three cannon. It had a seat for the magistrates and one for the deacons, and a handsome octagonal pulpit which had been sent from Holland. The edifice had a chandelier and candle sconces and two low galleries. The first church in New Amsterdam was of stone, and was seventy-two feet long.

A favorite form of the Dutch churches was six or eight sided, with a high pyramidal roof, topped with a belfry and weather vane. Usually the windows were so small and of glass so opaque that the church was very dark. A few of the churches were poorly heated with high stoves perched up on pillars, the Albany and Schenectady churches among them, but all the women carried foot stoves, and some of the men carried muffs.

Almost as important as the domine was the *voorleezer,* or chorister, who was also generally the bell ringer, sexton, gravedigger, funeral inviter, schoolmaster, and sometimes town clerk. He "tuned the psalm," turned the hourglass, gave out the psalms on a hanging board to the congregation, read the Bible, gave up notices to the domine by sticking the papers in the end of a cleft stick and holding it up to the high pulpit.

The deacons had control of all the church money. In the middle of the sermon they collected contributions by passing *sacjes.* These were small cloth or velvet bags hung on the end of a pole six or eight feet long. Usually there was a little bell on the *sacje* that rang when a coin was dropped in.

In many Dutch churches the men sat in a row of pews around the wall while the women were seated on chairs in the center of the church. There were also a few benches or pews for persons of special dignity, or for the minister's wife.

There were many other colonists of other religious faiths: the Roman Catholics in Maryland and the extreme Southern colonies, the Quakers in Pennsylvania, the Baptists in Rhode Island, the Huguenots, Lutherans, Moravians. All enjoined an orderly observance of the Sabbath day.

The religious aspect of the life of children, especially in early colonial days, and most particularly in New England, bore a deep relation to their daily round of life. The spirit of the Lord, perhaps the fear of the Lord, truly filled their days. Born into a religious atmosphere, reared in religious ways, surrounded on every side by religious influences, they could not escape the impress of deep religious feeling; they certainly had a profound familiarity with the Bible. The universal child's book of that day was the Bible. There were few American children until after the Revolution who had ever read from any book save the Bible, a primer, or catechism, and perhaps a hymn book or an almanac.

The usual method at that time of reading the Bible through was in the regular succession of every chapter from beginning to end, not leaving out even Leviticus and Numbers. This naturally detracted from the interest which would have been awakened by a wise selection of parts suited to the liking of children, and many portions doubtless frightened young children. J. T. Buckingham stated in his *Memoirs* that he read the Bible through at least a dozen times before he was sixteen years old. Some portions, especially the Apocalypse or Revelation of St. John, filled him with unspeakable terror, and he called the enforced reading of them "a piece of gratuitous and unprofitable cruelty." He was careful, however, to pay due tribute to the influence of the Bible upon his literary composition and phraseology. The constant reading of the beautiful English wording of the Bible influenced not only the style of writing of that day, but controlled the everyday speech of the people, keeping it pure and simple.

There was one important reason for the unfailing desire of English folk for the Bible and the

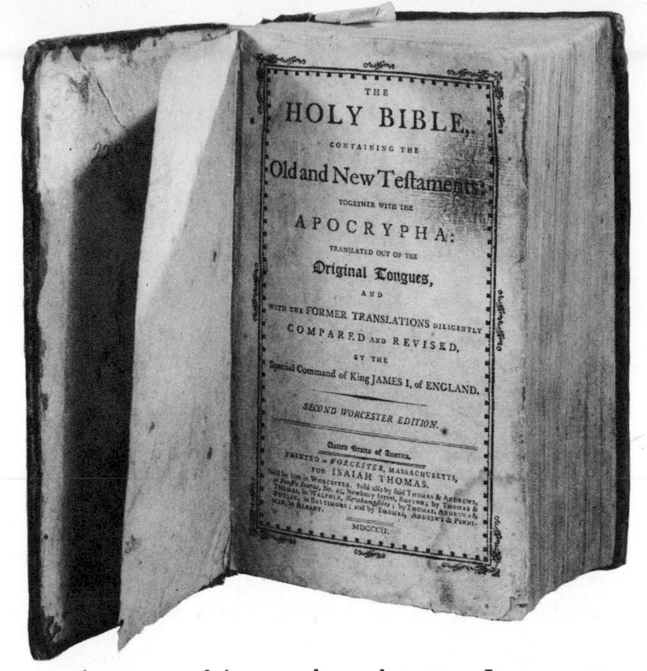
THE

HOLY BIBLE,

CONTAINING THE

Old and New Teſtaments:

TOGETHER WITH THE

APOCRYPHA:

TRANSLATED OUT OF THE

Original Tongues,

AND

WITH THE FORMER TRANSLATIONS DILIGENTLY
COMPARED AND REVISED,

BY THE

Special Command of King JAMES I, of ENGLAND.

SECOND WORCESTER EDITION.

United States of America.

PRINTED AT WORCESTER, MASSACHUSETTS,
FOR ISAIAH THOMAS.

MDCCCII.

From Isaiah Thomas Bible, 1802
(Old Sturbridge Village)

employment of its words and terms. It was not only the sole book with which most English readers were familiar—the book which supplied to them sacred hymns and warlike songs, the great voices of the prophets, the parables of the Evangelists, stories of peril and adventure, logic, legends, history, visions—but it was also a new book. The family of the seventeenth century that read the words of the small Geneva Bibles in the home circle, or poorer folk who listened to the outdoor reading thereof, heard a voice that they had longed and waited and suffered for, and that their fathers had died for. A treasure thus acquired is never lightly heeded. The Pilgrim Fathers left England for Holland before the King James Bible had been published. The Puritans of the Boston and Salem settlements had seen the importation of Geneva Bibles forbidden in England in 1633 and the reading prohibited at their meetings. They reveled in it in their new homes, for custom had not deadened their delight and they were filled with it; it satisfied them; they needed no other literature.

Though Puritanism, anxious and restrictive, denied freedom to childhood, yet the spirit of Puritanism was deeply observant and conservative of family relations. The meager records of domestic life in Puritan households are full of a pure affection, if not of grace or good cheer. The welfare, if not the pleasure of their children, lay close to the heart of the Pilgrims. Their love was seldom expressed, but their rigid sense of duty extended to duty to be fulfilled as well as exacted.

This country was settled at a time when all English people were religious. The Puritan child was full of religious thoughts and exercises, so also was the child of Roman Catholic parents, or one reared in the Church of England. A strict insistence showed itself in all sects in the new world. The "Articles Lawes and Orders Divine Politique and Martiall for the colony of Virginea" were unrivaled by any other code of laws issued in America for their mingling of barbarity and Christianity. No Puritan dared go farther than did the good Episcopalian Sir Thomas Dale. For irreverence to "any Preacher or Minister of Gods Holy Word" the offender was to be whipped three times and thrice to ask public forgiveness.

Another Puritan preacher was so laden with the fruit of the tree of knowledge that "he stoopt for the very children to pick off the apple ready to drop into their mouths." When they came to his study, he would examine them as to "How they walked with God? How they spent their time, what good books they read? Whether they prayed without ceasing?" He wrote to a brother minister in 1657:

"Do your children and family grow more godly? I find greatest trouble and grief about the rising generation. Young people are little stirred here; but they strengthen one another in evil by example and by counsel. Much ado have I with my own family; hard to get a servant that is glad of catechizing or family duties. I had a rare blessing of servants in Yorkshire, and those that I brought over were a blessing, but the young brood doth much afflict me. Even the children of the godly here, and elsewhere make a woful proof."

This minister lived at a time when New England Puritanism in its extreme type was coming to a close, but parents and households thus reared clung more rigidly and exactly to it and instilled in it a fervent hope of giving permanency to what seemed to their sad eyes in danger of being wholly thrust aside and lost.

A strong characteristic of English folk at the time of the settlement of the American colonies was superstition. This showed not only in scores of petty observances but in serious beliefs, such as those about comets and thunderstorms. It controlled medical practice and was displayed in the religious significance attributed to trifling natural events. It was evinced in the dependence on dreams and the dread of portents. Naturally children were imbued with the beliefs and fears of their parents and multiplied the importance and the terror of these notions. It can readily be seen that religious training and thought, joined to hereditary traits and race superstitions, could naturally produce a condition of mind and judgment which would permit such an episode as that known as the Salem Witchcraft.

This was a sad tale but was not peculiar to Salem or to New England. The Salem and Boston settlers came largely from the English counties of Suffolk and Essex, where witches and witch hunters and witch finders abounded, and Salem children and parents had seen in their English homes or heard the tales of hundreds of similar obsessions and possessions.

New England children were instilled with a familiarity with death in still another way than through talking and reading of it. Their presence at funerals was universal. A funeral in those days had an entirely different status as a ceremony from today. It was a social function as well as a solemn one; it was a reunion of friends and kinsfolk, a ceremonial of much expense and pomp, a scene of much feasting and drinking,

A crisis was reached in Boston when funerals had to be prohibited on Sundays because the vast concourse of children and servants that followed the coffin through the streets became a noisy rabble that profaned the sacred day.

Boys were often pallbearers at funerals of their companions. Little girls were pallbearers also at the funerals of their childish mates, and young unmarried girls at those of their companions. Dressed in white with uncovered heads, or veiled in white, these little girls made a touching sight.

Religious expression naturally found its highest point in Puritan communities in the strict and decorous observance of Sunday. Stern were the laws in ordering this observance. Fines, imprisonment, and stripes on the naked back were dealt out rigorously for Sabbath breaking. The New Haven Code of Laws with still greater severity enjoined that profanation of the Lord's Day, if done "proudly and with a high hand against the authority of God," should be punished with death. This rigid observance fell with special force and restriction on children. A loved poet, Oliver Wendell Holmes, wrote of the day:

"Hush, 'tis the Sabbath's silence-stricken morn,
No feet must wander the tasselled corn,
No merry children laugh around the door,
No idle playthings strew the sanded floor.
The law of Moses lays its awful ban
On all that stirs. Here comes the Tithing-man."

There were many public offices in colonial times which we do not have today. One of these is that of tithing-man; he was a town officer and had several neighboring families under his charge, usually ten, as the word "tithing" would signify. He enforced the learning of the church catechism in these ten homes, visited the houses, and heard the children recite their catechism. These ten families he watched specially on Sundays to see whether they attended church and did not loiter on the way. In some Massachusetts towns he watched on week days to keep "boys and all persons from swimming in the water." Ten families with many boys must have kept him busy on hot August days. He inspected taverns, reported disorderly persons, and forbade the sale of intoxicating liquor to them. He administered the "oath of fidelity" to new citizens and warned undesirable visitors and wanderers to leave the town. He could arrest persons who ran or rode at too fast a pace when going to meeting on Sunday, or who took unnecessary rides on Sunday, or otherwise broke the Sunday laws.

Within the meetinghouse he kept order by beating out dogs, correcting unruly and noisy boys, and waking those who slept. He sometimes walked up and down the church aisles, carrying a stick which had a knob on one end, and a dangling foxtail on the other, tapping the boys on the head with the knob end of the stick, and tickling the face of sleeping church attendants with the foxtail.

It was inevitable, since the colonization of America was in the day of Puritanism, that the first modern literature known by American children should be the distinctive literature of that sect and period. A special book for children was written by Cotton Mather, whose sayings were very dull in prose and must have been more so in verse. It was called, *Old Mr. Dod's Sayings; composed in Verse, for the better Help of Memory; and the Delightfulness of Children reading them, and learning them, whereby they may be the better*

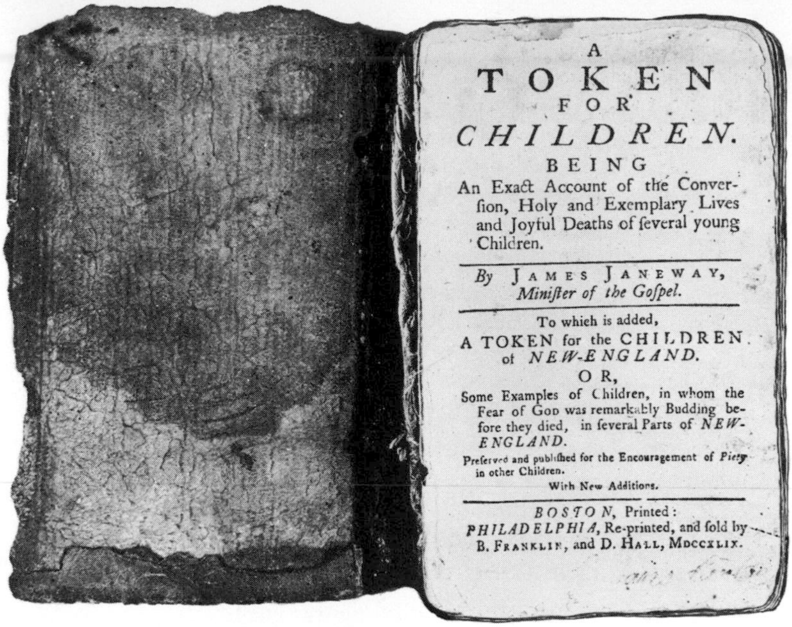

A
TOKEN
FOR
CHILDREN.
BEING
An Exact Account of the Conversion, Holy and Exemplary Lives and Joyful Deaths of several young Children.

By JAMES JANEWAY,
Minister of the Gospel.

To which is added,
A TOKEN for the CHILDREN of *NEW-ENGLAND.*
OR,
Some Examples of Children, in whom the Fear of GOD was remarkably Budding before they died, in several Parts of *NEW-ENGLAND.*
Preserved and published for the Encouragement of *Piety* in other Children.
With New Additions.

BOSTON, Printed:
PHILADELPHIA, Re-printed, and sold by
B. FRANKLIN, and D. HALL, MDCCXLIX.

From A Token for Children, *1749*
(The Free Library of Philadelphia, rare book department)

ingrafted in their memories and Understanding. The Puritan preacher also wrote *Good Lessons for Children, in Verse.*

Doubtless the most popular and most widely read of all children's books in New England was one whose title page runs thus: *A Token for Children, being an Exact Account of the Conversion, Holy and Exemplary Lives and Joyful Deaths of Several Young Children, by James Janeway. To which is added A Token for the Children of New England or Some Examples of Children in whom the Fear of God was remarkably Budding before they died; in several Parts of New England. Preserved and Published for the Encouragement of Piety in other Children.*

The first portion of this book was written by an English minister and was as popular in England as in America. The entire book with the title as given went through many editions both in England and America. In spite of its absolute trustfulness and simplicity of belief, it is a sad commentary on the spiritual conditions of the times. The New England portion, written by Cotton Mather, is even more severe. Young babes chide their parents for too infrequent praying and have ecstasies of delight when they can pray *ad infinitum.*

Another child's book, by James Janeway, was *The Looking Glass for Children.* There had been a previous book with nearly the same title. Janeway's book was certainly popular, perhaps because in was in verse, and children's poetry was very scanty and rare in those days. It was reprinted many times, and parts appeared in selections and compilations until the nineteenth century. A few lines run thus:

> "When by Spectators I behold
> What Beauty doth adorn me
> Or in a glass when I behold
> How sweetly God did form me,
> Hath God such comeliness bestowed
> And on me made to dwell
> What pity such a pretty maid
> As I should go to Hell."

A book of similar title was *Divine Blossoms, a Prospect or Looking Glass for Youth.*

The lack of poetry may also account in some degree for the astonishing popularity of a poem which appeared in 1662, written by a Puritan preacher named Michael Wigglesworth, and entitled, *The Day of Doom; or a Poetical description of the Great and Last Judgment.* This "epic of hell-fire and damnation" was reprinted again and again and was sold in such large numbers that it is safe to assert that every New England household, whose members could read, was familiar with it. It was printed as a broadside, and children committed it to memory. Teachers extolled it; ministers quoted it.

Thomas White wrote a book for children which certainly comes under the head of religious books, though its pages held also those frivolous lines "A was an archer who shot at a frog," etc. This dreary volume was entitled a *Little Book for Little Children.* It contained accounts of short-lived and morbid young Christians, much like those of James Janeway's book. One child of eight wept bitter and inconsolable tears for his sins. One wicked deed was lying. His mother asked him whether he were cold. He answered "Yes" instead of "Forsooth," and afterward doubted whether he really was cold or not. Another sin was whetting his knife on the Sabbath day. This book also had accounts of the Christian martyrs and their tortures. It was an English book, first reprinted in Boston in 1702. An edition of *Pilgrim's Progress* was printed in Boston in 1681, another in 1706, and an illustrated edition in 1744. Many shortened copies and imitations appeared. One was called *The Christian's Metamorphosis Unfolded.* Another, *The Christian Pilgrim.* Dr. Neale edited it for children, making, says a modern critic, "a most impudent book." Bunyan also wrote *Divine Emblems,* which the young were enjoined to read, and he also "bowed his pen to children" and wrote *Country Rhimes*

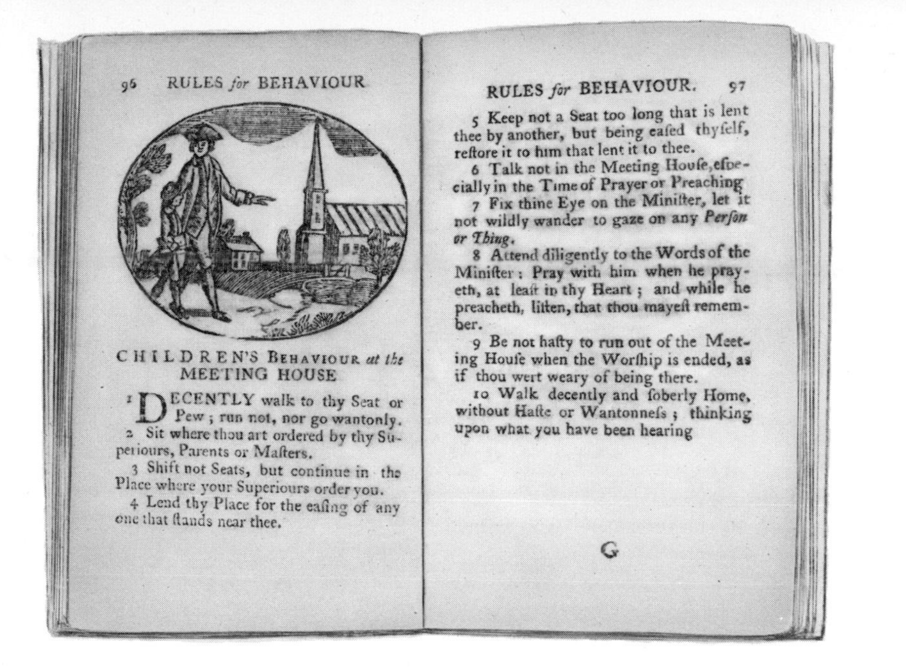

96 RULES *for* BEHAVIOUR

CHILDREN'S BEHAVIOUR *at the* MEETING HOUSE

1 DECENTLY walk to thy Seat or Pew; run not, nor go wantonly.

2 Sit where thou art ordered by thy Superiours, Parents or Maſters.

3 Shift not Seats, but continue in the Place where your Superiours order you.

4 Lend thy Place for the eaſing of any one that ſtands near thee.

RULES *for* BEHAVIOUR. 97

5 Keep not a Seat too long that is lent thee by another, but being eaſed thyſelf, reſtore it to him that lent it to thee.

6 Talk not in the Meeting Houſe, eſpecially in the Time of Prayer or Preaching

7 Fix thine Eye on the Miniſter, let it not wildly wander to gaze on any *Perſon or Thing.*

8 Attend diligently to the Words of the Miniſter: Pray with him when he prayeth, at leaſt in thy Heart; and while he preacheth, liſten, that thou mayeſt remember.

9 Be not haſty to run out of the Meeting Houſe when the Worſhip is ended, as if thou wert weary of being there.

10 Walk decently and ſoberly Home, without Haſte or Wantonneſs; thinking upon what you have been hearing

G

From A Little Pretty Pocketbook, *1787* (*The Free Library of Philadelphia, rare book department*)

for Children. It is an uncouth mixture of religious phrases and similes and very crude natural history.

Pilgrim's Progress was the first light reading of Benjamin Franklin. Other books of his boyhood were Plutarch's *Lives,* Defoe's *Essays upon Projects,* Cotton Mather's *Essays to do Good,* and Burton's *Historical Collections.*

Another book for young people—which might be termed a storybook, though its lesson was deemed deeply religious—was called, *A Small Book in Easy Verse Very Suitable for Children, entitled The Prodigal Daughter of the Disobedient Lady Reclaimed.* It was a poem of about a hundred stanzas, relating the story of a very willful young woman who, on being locked up in her room by her father to check her extravagance, made a league with the Devil, attempted to poison her father and mother, dropped dead apparently on her wickedness being discovered, was carried to the grave, but revived just as the sexton was about to lower her coffin in the ground. She recovered, repented, related her experiences with unction, and lived happy ever after. The title page bears a picture of the devil as a fine gentleman wearing his tail as a sword and having one high-topped cloven-footed boot. This book enjoyed unbounded popularity.

It was similiar in teaching to a chapbook which was entitled *The Afflicted Parents, or the Undutiful Child Punished*. In this tale the daughter gave some very priggish advice to her wicked brother, who promptly knocks her down and kills her. He is captured, tried, condemned, sentenced, and at last executed by two pardoned highwaymen. But upon being cut down he comes to life, pompously discourses at much length, and then is executed a second time, as a warning to all disobedient children.

Death-bed scenes continued to be full of living interest. *The Good Child's Little Hymnbook* represents the taste of the times. One poem is on the death and burial of twins and thus is doubly interesting. Another is on "Dying." The child asks whether he is going to die and "look white and awful and be put in the pithole with other dead people." And yet the preface runs

"Mamma See what a Pretty Book
At Day's Pappa has bought,
That I may at the pictures look
And by the words be taught."

After a time some attempts were made to render the Bible in a form specially for children's reading. One rhymed adaptation was called the *Bible in Verse*.

These Bible abridgments were literally little books, usually three or four inches long, covered with brown or mottled paper. One tiny, well-worn book of Bible stories was but two inches long and an inch wide. It had 250 pages, each of about twenty words.

There was also the famous *Thumb Bible* printed by the Boston book printers Mein and Fleming. *The Hieroglyphick Bible with Emblematick Figures* was illustrated with five hundred tiny pictures set with the print, which helped to tell the story after the manner of an illustrated rebus. Bewick made the cuts for the English edition. Tiny catechisms were widely printed, sought after, and used as gifts to good and godly children. There were also dull little books of parables modeled on the parables of the Bible. These were profoundly religious but were so darkly and figuratively expressed as to be frequently entirely incomprehensible.

An extremely curious and antiquated religious concoction was entitled *History of the Holy Jesus.* The seventh edition was printed in New London in 1754. The illustrations in this stupid little book were more surprising than the miserable text. No attempt was made to represent Oriental scenery. The picture of an earthquake showed a group of toy houses and a substantial church of the type of the Old South in perfect condition, tipped over and leaning solidly on each other. The Prodigal Son returned to an English manorhouse with latticed windows, and the women wore high commodes and hoop skirts. In the picture intended to represent to the inquiring young Christian in New England the Adoration of the Magi, the wise men of the East appear in the guise of prosperous British merchants, in cocked hats, knee breeches, and full-skirted coats with great flapped pockets. They look wisely at the star-spotted heavens, and at a mammoth and extremely conventionalized comet through British telescopes mounted on tripods. The Slaughter of the Innocents must have seemed painfully close at hand when Yankee children looked at the trim military platoons of English-clad infants, each waving an English flag; while Herod, in a modern uniform, on a horse with modern trappings, charged upon them. Perhaps some of the fathers and mothers born in England and in the Church of England had a still more vivid realization of Herod's crime, for it was the custom in some English parishes at one time to whip all the children on Holy Innocent's Day. As Gregory said: "It hath been a custom to whip up the children upon Innocent's Day morning, that the memorie of this murther might stick the closer; and in a moderate proportion to act over the crueltie again in kind."

The History of the Holy Jesus was told by Rev. Mr. Instructwell to Master Learnwell. The book contained also the *Child's Body of Divinity* and some of Dr. Watts's hymns. These *Divine Songs for Children* appear in many forms. The *Cradle Hymn* is the one most frequently seen and it has been extolled as "a perfect lullaby for a child." A curious study it is, showing how absolutely traditional religious conception could usurp the mind and obscure the impulses of the heart. Its sweet and tender lines, which begin

> "Hush my dear, lie still and slumber.
> Holy angels guard thy bed,"

are soon contrasted with the vehement words which tell of the lot of the infant Jesus. At the mother's passionate expressions of "brutal creatures" and "cursed sinners" that "affront their Lord," the child apparently cries, for the mother sings

> "Soft, my child, I did not chide thee,
> Though my song may sound too hard."

This certainly seems an ill-phrased and exciting lullaby but is perhaps what might be expected as the notion of a soothing cradle hymn from a bigoted old bachelor.

Chapter XXI

Colonial Neighborliness

If the first foundation of New England's strength and growth was godliness, its next was neighborliness, and a firm rock it proved to build upon. In olden times there was infinitely greater independence in each household than at present, yet there was also greater interdependence with surrounding households.

The colonist turned to any and all who lived

View of Boston Commons in 1768 (The New York Public Library, Stokes Collection)

around him, and never turned in vain for help in sickness, or at the time of death of members of his household; for friendly advice, culinary aids to a halting appetite, or the preparation for feasting an exceptional number of persons; in short, in any unusual emergency, as well as in frequent everyday cooperation in logrolling, stone piling, stump pulling, wall building, house raising, etc.—all the hard and exhausting labor on the farm.

A logrolling in early pioneer days, in the Northern colonies and in western Virginia and the central states, was a noble example of generous cooperation, where each gave of his best—his time, strength, and good will—and where all worked to clear the ground in the forest for a home-farm for a neighbor who might be newly come and an entire stranger, but who in turn would just as cheerfully and energetically give his work for others when it was needed.

The plantation was the unit in Virginia; in New England it was the town. The neighborly helpfulness of the New England settlers extended from small to great matters; it formed communal privileges and entered into every department of town life. For instance, the town of Gloucester in 1663 granted a right to a citizen for running a small sawmill for twenty-one years. In return for this right the grantee was to sell boards to Gloucester men at "one shilling per hundred better cheape than to strangers." Saco and Biddeford in Maine ordered that fellow townsmen should have preference in every employment. Reading would not sell any of its felled timber out of the town.

There was one curious and contradictory aspect of this neighborliness, this thought for mutual welfare, and that was its narrowness, especially in New England. Just as soon as any group of settlers could call themselves a town, these colonists' notions of kindliness and thoughtfulness for others became distinctly and rigidly limited to their own townspeople. The town was their whole world.

This caused a constant suspicion of all newcomers, especially those who chanced to enter with scant introduction, and made universal a custom of "warning out" all strangers who arrived in any town. This formality was gone through by the sheriff or tithing-man. Thereafter should the warned ones prove incapable or unsuccessful or vicious, they could not become a charge upon the town, but could be returned whence they came with despatch and violence if necessary.

Dorchester in 1634 enacted that "no man within the Plantation shall sell his house or lott to any man without the Plantation whome they shall dislike off." Providence would not permit a proprietor to sell to any "but to an Inhabitant" without consent of the town. New Haven would neither sell nor let ground to a stranger. Hadley would sell no land to any until after three years' occupation, and then only with approval of the "Town's Mind." The harboring of strangers, even of relatives who were not local residents, was a frequent source of bickering between citizens and magistrates, as well as a constant cause of arbitration between towns.

As time passed on and immigration continued, freemen clung closely to their right to keep out strangers and outsiders. From the Boston Town Records of 1714 we find citizens still prohibited from entertaining a stranger without giving notice to the town authorities, and a description of the stranger and his circumstances. Warnings and whippings out of town still continued.

In the Southern colonies conditions differed. In 1656 a Virginia writer could say: "The inhabitants are generally affable, courteous, and very assistant to Strangers (for what but plenty makes hospitality and good neighbourhood) and no sooner are they settled, but they will be visiting, presenting and advising the strangers how to improve what they have, how to better their way of livelihood."

It was the same in the Carolinas. The doors of citizens were open to all decent travelers, and shut to none.

The plantations were in many counties too far apart for any cooperative labor. There were slaves on each plantation to do all the hard work of lifting. But in out-of-the-way settlements the Virginia planters' kindliness was shown in a vast and unbounded hospitality, a hospitality so insatiable that it watched for and waylaid travelers to expend a welcome and lavish attentions upon.

Many general customs existed in the early colonies which were simply exemplifications of neighborliness put in legal form. Such were the systems of common lands and herding. Common lands were set off and common herds existed in many of the Northern colonies. Cowherds or "cow-keeps" were appointed and paid by the town to care throughout the summer for all the cattle owned by the inhabitants. In Albany and New York the cowherd and "a chosen proper youngster"—in other words, a good, steady boy—went through the town at sunrise sounding a horn, which the cattle heard and knew, and they quickly followed him to green pastures outside the town. At sunset they were brought home to the church, and the owners were again warned by the horn of the safe return of their cattle, and that it was milking time.

On Long Island and in Connecticut there were cowherds, calf-keepers, and pound-keepers. The calf-keepers' duties were to keep the calves away from the cows, water them, protect them, etc. In Virginia and Maryland there were cow-pens in early days, and cowherds; but in the South the cattle generally roamed wild through the forests, and were known to their owners by earmarks. In all communities earmarks and other brands of ownership on cattle, horses, sheep, and swine were very important, and rigidly regarded where so much value was kept in domestic cattle. These earmarks were registered by the town clerk in the town records.

Sheep-herds, or shepherds, in colonial days also took charge of the sheep of many owners in herdwalks, or ranges, by day, and by night in sheepfolds built with fences and gates.

Fence viewers were men who were appointed by the town for common benefit to take charge of building and keeping in repair the fences that surrounded the "great lotts," or commons, that is, the enclosed fields which were the common property of each town in which all farmers living near could place their cattle. The fence viewers saw that each man worked a certain amount each year on these "pales," as the fences were called, or paid his share for the work of others. Each farmer or cow owner usually built about twenty feet of fence for each cow which he pastured in the "great lotts." The fence viewers also examined the condition of fences around private lands, noted breaks, and ordered repairs. For if cattle broke through a poorly made fence and did damage to crops, the fence owner had to stand the loss, while if the fences were good and strong, proving the cattle unruly and destructive, the owner of the cattle had to pay. All the colonies were watchful over the safekeeping of fences. In 1659 the Dutch rulers of New Amsterdam ordered that for "stripping fences of rails and posts" the offender should be whipped and branded, and for a second offence he could be punished by death. This seems cruelly severe, but that year there was a great scarcity of grain and other food, and if the fences were pulled down, cattle could get into fields and eat up the growing crops, and famine and death might result.

Sometimes a common field was fenced in and planted with Indian corn. In this case the fence served to keep the cattle out, not in.

Hay wards were, as the name indicates, men to keep watchful care over the growing hay. For instance, in Hadley, Massachusetts, in 1661, the hay ward was to have twelvepence for each cow or hog, two shillings for each horse, and twenty pence for each twenty sheep that he found loose in any field or meadow and successfully turned out. The owner of the animal was to pay the fine. At a later date these hay wards were called field drivers.

Hog reeves were men appointed by the citizens to look after the hogs that roamed the roads and streets to see that all those swine had rings in their noses, were properly marked, and did not do damage to crops.

The neighborly assistance given to new settlers began with a chopping bee, a universal method among pioneers of clearing ground in newly settled districts, or even in older townships in Vermont, New Hampshire, and Maine. Sometimes this bee was held to clear land for a newly married man, or a new neighbor, or one who had had bad luck, but it was just as freely given to a prosperous farmer, though plentiful thanks and plentiful rum were the only rewards of the willing workers.

All the strong men of the township repaired at an early hour to the tract to be cleared and with powerful blows attacked the great trees. A favorite way of bringing the day's work to an exciting climax was by a "drive." This was made by chopping halfway into the trunks of a great group or circle of trees—undercutting it was called—so that by a few powerful and well-driven blows at the monarch of the group, and perhaps a few well-concerted pulls on a rope, the entire group could be felled together, the leader bringing down with his spreading branches his fellows in front of him. It was dangerous work; accidents were frequent; the records of death at logrollings are pathetic to read.

After the trees were all felled, it was no longer a "cut-down" but an "opening." This was made preferably in the spring. The fallen trees were left some months on the ground to dry in the summer

"House Raising," by William P. Chappel, 19th century (The Metropolitan Museum of Art, Bequest of Edward W. C. Arnold, 1954)

sun. In the autumn the tops were set on fire, and the lighter limbs usually burned out, leaving great charred tree trunks. Then came what was known as a piling bee. Usually the half-burned tree trunks were shortened in Indian fashion by burning across with a smaller stick of wood till the long log was in lengths which could be dragged by the farmers with their oxen and horses into vast piles and again set on fire. Another treat of rum accompanied this day's work. The word "logrolling" was often applied to the latter bee, and occasionally the felling of trees and dragging into piles for firing was done in a single logrolling.

Sometimes before the opening was cleared it was planted. The spring rains and melting snows carried the fertilizing ashes deep into the soil. Corn was planted and "dug in"; rye was sowed and "hacked in." The chops were astonishing; the grain grew among the fallen logs and stumps in rioting luxuriance. A stump pulling was another occasion for a friendly bee, to clear off the new field.

Another exhibition of cooperation was in a stone hauling or a stone bee. Some of the rocky fields of hard New England would defy a lifetime of work of one man and a single yoke of oxen. With judicious blasting, many oxen, strong arms, and willing hearts the boulders and ledges were tamed.

A "raising" might be of a church or a schoolhouse, or of a house or barn for a neighbor. All the strong men far and near turned out to help, tools were lent, and many hands and arms made quick work. Often the frame of a whole side of a house —the broadside—was fastened together on the ground. After it was laid out and pinned together, shores of long poles were attached to the plates with ox chains, and it was literally lifted into place by the united strength of the entire band of men and boys. Sometimes women pulled on the rope to express their good will and helpfulness. Then the other sides were put up, and the crossbeams, braces, and studding all pinned and nailed into place. Afterward the huge rafters were raised for the roof. Each man was assigned in the beginning to his place and work and worked faithfully when his turn came. When the ridge pole was put in place, the building was christened, as it was called, by breaking over it a bottle of rum. Often the house was literally given a name.

There is nothing in nature so unnatural, so singular in quality, as the glittering artificiality of the early morning in the country the day after a heavy, drifting, New England snowstorm. It is without life, or atmosphere, or reality; it has nothing but the million reflections of that artificial and repellent sunshine. Then, like a veritable oasis of color and motion in an unmovable glittering white desert, a sound and sight of life appears. Around the bend of the road comes slow and straining down the hill, a long train of oxen with a snow plow "breaking out" the old post road. There is rivalry in the method of breaking. One road-master always used a snow plow, another lashed an ordinary plow on either side of the narrow ox sled, a third used a coarse harrow weighted down with a group of standing boys. The deeper drifts often have to be shoveled out partly by hand. After the road to the tavern is broken, the roads to the schoolhouse, the doctor's house, and the meetinghouse come next.

The roads thus made were not permitted to be cut up by careless use and many townships forbade the use of narrow sleds and sleighs. The roads were narrow at best; often when two sleighs met the horses had to be unharnessed and the sleighs lifted past over each other. On lonely hill roads or straight turnpikes, where teamsters could see some distance ahead, turnouts were made where one sleigh could wait for another to pass.

After the roads were well broken, the time was always chosen where any logging was done to haul logs to the sawmill on ox sleds. An interesting sled, called chebobbin, was used. It was made by a close and ingenious adaptation of natural forms of wood, which made excellent runners, crossbars, etc. They were fastened together so loosely that they readily adjusted themselves to the inequalities of the wood roads. In some localities chebobbin became tebobbin and tarboggin, all three being adaptations in nomenclature, as they were in form, of the Indian toboggan or moose sled—a sledge with runners or flat bottom of wood or bark, upon which the red men drew heavy loads over the snow.

On these chebobbins great logs were hitched together by chains and dragged down from the upland wood lots. Under these mighty loads the snow tracks got an almost icy polish, prime sledding for country sleighing parties.

It was the custom both among men and women to join forces on a smaller scale and have a little neighborly visiting by what was called "change-work." For instance, if two neighbors both were to make soap, or both to make apple butter, or both to make up a rag carpet, instead of each woman sitting at home alone sewing and fitting the carpet, one would take her thimble and go to spend the day, and the two would sew all day long, finish and lay the carpet at one house. In a few days the visit would be returned, and the second carpet be finished. One man could load logs and sled them down to the sawmill alone, but two by "change-work" could accomplish the task much more rapidly and with less strain.

A pleasant custom in New England was sending "tastes of dinner" to friends and neighbors. Covered treasures of housewifery were carried in small amounts, literally "a taste," to tempt tired appetites or lonely diners. The gift of a portion of the over-bountiful supply for the supper of a wedding, a reception, etc., went by the expressive name of "cold party."

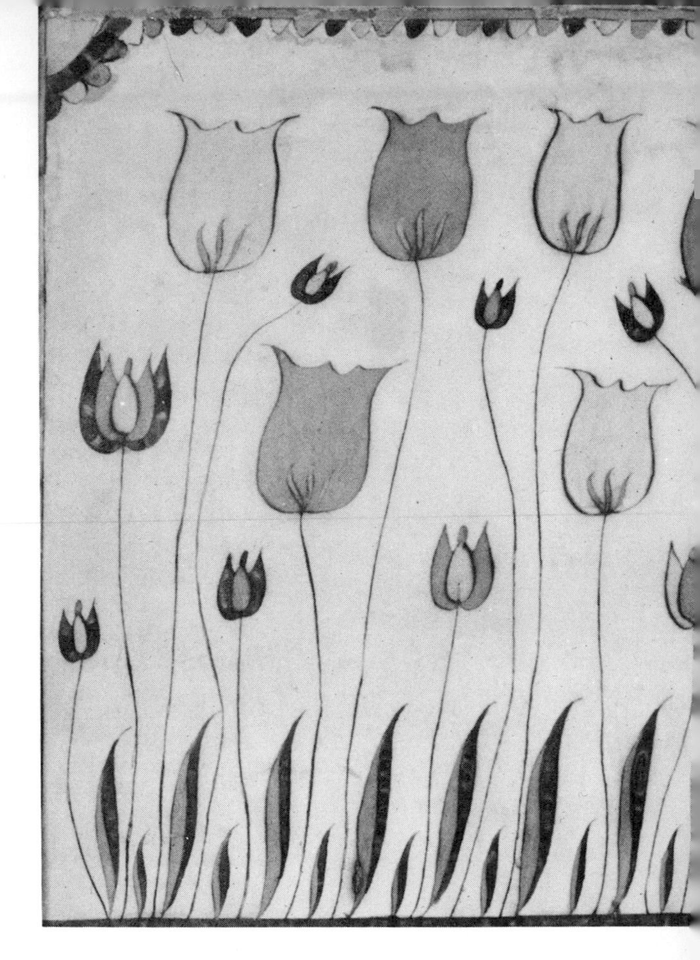

Chapter XXII

Old-time Flower Gardens

A garden was certainly the greatest refreshment to the spirits of a woman in the early colonial days and the purest of her pleasures—too often her only pleasure.

Quickly, in tender memory of her fair English home, the homesick goodwife, trying to create a semblance of the birthplace she still loved, planted the seeds and roots of homely English flowers and

Tulips in a basket, artist unknown, about 1810 (The Henry Francis du Pont Winterthur Museum)

herbs that grew and blossomed under bleak New England skies and on rocky New England shores, as sturdily and cheerfully as they had sprung up and bloomed by the green hedgerows and doorsides in the home beyond the sea.

An account published in 1672 is the earliest and the fullest report of the gardens of our forefathers, after they had tamed the rugged shores of the New World and made them obey the rule of English husbandry. They had "good store of garden vegetables and herbs; lettuce, sorrel, parsley, mallows, chevril, burnet, summer savory, winter savory, thyme, sage, carrots, parsnips, beets, radishes, purslain, beans"; "cabbidge growing exceeding well; pease of all sorts and the best in

From A Pretty New Year's Gift, *1786* (*The Free Library of Philadelphia, rare book department*)

the world; sparagus thrives exceedingly, musk mellons, cucumbers, and pompions." For grains there were wheat, rye, barley, and oats. There were other garden herbs and garden flowers: spearmint, pennyroyal, ground-ivy, coriander, dill, tansy; "feverfew prospereth exceedingly; white sattin groweth pretty well, and so doth lavender-cotton; gilly flowers will continue two years; horse-leek prospereth notably; hollyhocks; comferie with white flowers; clary lasts but one summer; sweet-bryer or eglantine; celandine but slowly; blood-wort but sorrily, but patience and English roses very pleasantly."

Patience and English roses very pleasantly must have shown their fair English faces to English women in the strange land. Hollyhocks, feverfew, and gillyflowers must have made a sunshine in the shady places in the new home. Many of these garden herbs are now common weeds or roadside blossoms. Celandine was "common by fences and among rubbish." Tansy and elecampane grow everywhere. Sweetbrier is at home in New England pastures and roadsides. Spearmint edges our brooks. Ground ivy is a naturalized citizen. It is easy to note that the flowers and herbs beloved in gardens and medicinal waters and kitchens "at home" were the ones transplanted here. "Clary-water" was a favorite tonic of Englishmen of that day.

Not less closely did such old garden weeds as motherwort, groundsel, chickweed, and wild mustard cling. They are old colonists, brought over by the first settlers and still thrive and triumph in every kitchen garden and backyard in the land. Mullein and nettle, henbane and wormwood, are all English emigrants.

The Puritans were not the only flower-lovers in the new land. The Pennsylvania Quakers and Mennonites were quick to plant gardens. Pastorius encouraged all the Germantown settlers to raise flowers as well as fruit.

Among Pennsylvanians the art of gardening reached the highest point. The landscape gardening was a reproduction of the best in England. In the Southern colonies men of wealth soon had beautiful gardens. In New York, before the Revolution, were many beautiful gardens.

A trade in flower and vegetable seeds formed a lucrative and popular means by which women could earn a livelihood in colonial days: A list of names of flower seeds in the *Boston Evening Post* of March 1760 shows exactly the flowers beloved and sought for at that time. They were "holly-hook, purple Stock, white Lewpins, Africans, blew Lewpins, candy-tuff, cyanus, pink, wall-flower, double larkin-spur, venus navelwort, brompton flock, princess feather, balsam, sweet-scented pease, carnation, sweet williams, annual stock, sweet feabus, yellow lewpins, sunflower, convolus minor, catch-fly, ten week stock, globe thistle, globe amaranthus, nigella, love-lies-bleeding, casent hamen, polianthus, canterbury bells,

Prentis Garden
(*Colonial Williamsburg*)

carnation poppy, india pink, convolus major, Queen Margrets." This is certainly a very pretty list of flowers, nearly all of which are still loved, though sometimes under other names—thus the Queen Margrets are our asters.

What cheerful and appropriate furnishings the old-time gardens had; benches full of straw bee-skepes and wooden beehives, those homelike and busy dwelling places; frequently, also, a well-filled dovecote. At the edge of the farm garden often stood the well sweep, one of the most picturesque adjuncts of the country dooryard. Its successor, the roofed well with bucket, stone, and chain, and even the homely long-handled pump, had a certain appropriateness as part of the garden furnishings.

Whiteweed, or oxeye daisy, has been carried intentionally by homesick settlers to many a township.

Chicory or blue weed was, it is said, brought from England by Governor Bowdoin as food for his sheep. It has spread till its extended presence has been a startling surprise to all visiting English botanists. It hurts no one's fields, for it invades chiefly waste and neglected land.

Chapter XXIII

Travel, Transportation, and Taverns

Wherever the earliest colonists settled in America, they had to adopt the modes of travel and the ways of getting from place to place of their predecessors and new neighbors, the Indians. In Maryland and Virginia, New York and Connecticut, travel was almost entirely by boats. Between the large settlements in Massachusetts—Boston, Salem, and Plymouth—travel was also preferably, when the

New Bedford in the early 19th century (The New York Public Library, Stokes Collection)

weather permitted, in boats. The colonists went in canoes, or pinnaces, and in dugouts, which were formed from hollowed pine logs, usually about twenty feet long and two or three feet wide. Both of these were made for them by the Indians. It was said that one Indian, working alone, felling the pine tree by the primitive way of burning and scraping off the charred parts with a stone tool called a celt (for the Indians had no iron or steel axes), then cutting off the top in the same manner, then burning out part of the interior, then burning and scraping and shaping it without and within, could make one of these dugouts in three weeks.

These dugouts usually kept close to the shore, both in calm and in windy weather, though the

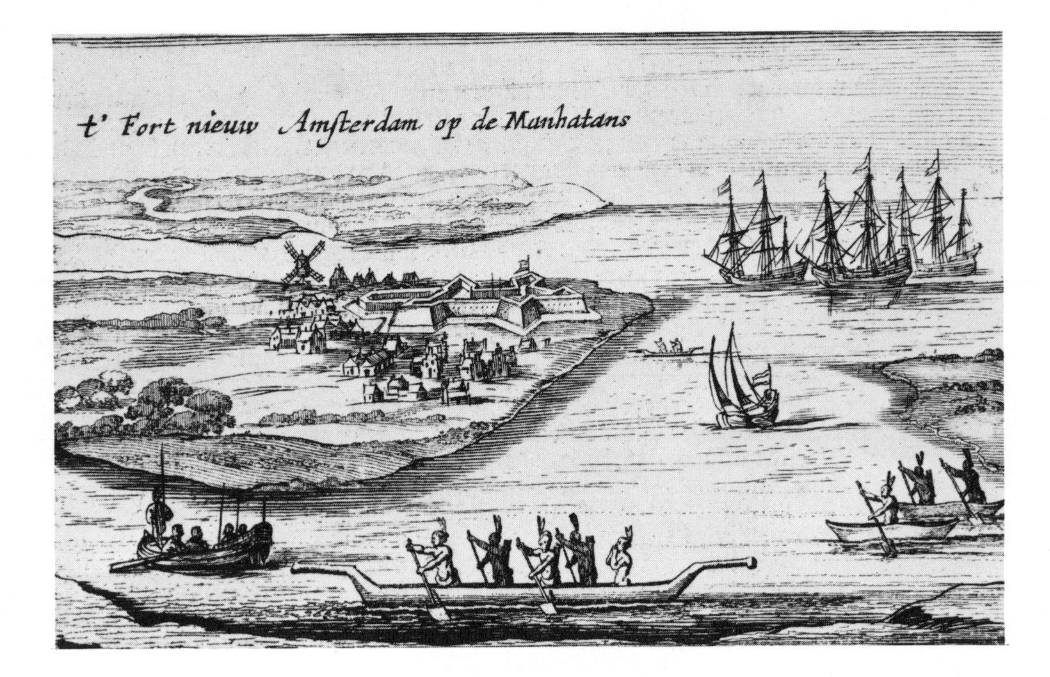

View of New Amsterdam, engraved 1626–1628 (The New York Public Library, Stokes Collection)

natives were not afraid to go many miles out to sea. The lightness of the birch-bark canoe made it specially desirable where there were frequent overland transfers.

Boats and vessels built by the colonists were called shallop, ketch, pink, snow, sloop, batteau, periagua, and gundalow, picturesque with its lateen sail.

The Indians had narrow footpaths in many places through the woods. The narrow streams could be crossed on natural fords or on rude bridges of fallen trees.

These paths were good, though only two or three feet wide, and in many places the savages kept the woods clear from underbrush by burning over large tracts. Some of the old paths are famous in our history. The most famous was the Bay Path, which ran from Cambridge through

Marlborough, Worcester, Oxford, Brookfield, and on to Springfield and the Connecticut River.

When new paths were cut through the forests, the settlers "blazed" the trees, that is, they chopped a piece of the bark off tree after tree standing on the side of the way. Thus the "blazes" stood out clear and white in the dark shadows of the forests, like welcome guideposts showing the traveler his way. In Maryland roads turning off to a church were marked by slips or blazes cut near the ground.

The broader rivers soon had canoe-ferries. The first regular Massachusetts ferry from Charlestown to Boston was in 1639. It carried passengers for threepence apiece. In 1636 the Cambridge ferryman charged but half a penny, as so many wished to attend the Thursday lecture in the Boston churches. We learn from the Massachusetts laws that often a rider had to let his horse cross by swimming over, being guided from the ferryboat; he then paid no ferriage for the horse. After wheeled vehicles were used, these ferries were not large enough to carry them properly. Often the carriage had to be taken apart, or towed over, while the horse had his fore feet in one canoe-ferry and his hind feet in another, the two canoes being lashed together. As soon as roads were built there were, of course, bridges and cart ways, but these were only between closely neighboring towns. Usually the bridges were merely horse bridges with a railing on but one side.

For a century nearly all land travel was on

A view of the State House in Boston in the late 18th century (The New York Public Library, Stokes Collection)

horseback. In 1672 Boston had only one private coach. Women and children usually rode seated on a pillion behind a man. A pillion was a padded cushion with straps which sometimes had on one side a sort of platform stirrup. One way of progress which would help four persons ride part of their journey was what was called the ride-and-tie system. Two of the four persons who were traveling started on their road on foot; two mounted on the saddle and pillion, rode about a mile, dismounted, tied the horse, and walked on. When the two who had started on foot reached the waiting horse, they mounted, rode on past the other couple for a mile or so, dismounted, tied, and walked on; and so on. It was a pleasant custom for friends to ride out on the road a few miles with any departing guest or friend and then bid him Godspeed.

The first regular mail started from New York to Boston on January 1, 1673. The postman carried two portmantles, which were crammed with letters and parcels. He did not change horses till he reached Hartford. He was ordered to look out and report the condition of all ferries, fords, and roads. When he delivered his mail it was laid on a table at an inn, and anyone who wished looked over all the letters, then took and paid the postage (which was very high) on any addressed to himself. It was usually about a month from this setting out of "the post" in winter till his return. As late certainly as 1730 the mail was carried from New York to Albany in the winter by a "foot-post." He probably skated up the Hudson River when the ice was good.

In 1760 there were but eight mails a year from Philadelphia to the Potomac River, and even then the post rider need not start till he had received enough letters to pay the expenses of the trip. It was not till postal affairs were placed in the capable and responsible hands of Benjamin Franklin that there were any regular or trustworthy mails.

The journal and report of Hugh Finlay, a post-office surveyor, in 1773 of the mail service from Quebec to St. Augustine, Florida, tells of the vicissitudes of mail matter even at that later day. In some places the deputy, as the postmaster was called, had no office, so his family rooms were constantly invaded. Occasionally a tavern served as post office; letters were thrown down on a table and if the weather was bad, or smallpox raged, or the deputy was careless, they were not forwarded for many days. Letters that arrived might lie on the table or bar counter for days for anyone to pull over, until the owner chanced to arrive and claim them. Good service could scarcely be expected from any deputy, for his salary was paid according to the number of letters coming to his office. As private mail carriage constantly went on, though forbidden by British law, the deputy suffered.

The post rider between Boston and Newport loaded his carriage with bundles which delayed him long in delivery. He bought and sold on commission along this road, and in violation of law he carried many letters to his own profit. He took twenty-six hours to go eighty miles.

A Pennsylvania post rider, an aged man, occupied himself as he slowly jogged along by knitting mittens and stockings. Not always were mail portmanteaux properly locked; hence many letters were lost and the pulling in and out of bundles defaced the letters.

Of course so much horseback riding made it necessary to have horse blocks in front of nearly all houses. In course of time stones were set every mile on the principal roads to tell the distance from town to town. Benjamin Franklin set milestones the entire way on the post road from Boston to Philadelphia. He rode in a chaise over the road, and a machine which he had invented was attached to the chaise. A number of old colonial milestones are still standing.

The inland transportation of freight was carried on in the colonies on the backs of pack horses. Very interesting historical evidence in relation to the methods of transportation in the middle of the eighteenth century may be found in the ingenious advertisement and address with which Benjamin

Franklin raised transportation facilities for Braddock's army in 1775. Braddock's appeals to the Philadelphia Assembly for a rough wagon road and wagons for the army succeeded in raising only twenty-five wagons. Franklin visited him in his desolate plight, agreed to assist him, and appealed to the public to send to him for the use of the army 150 wagons and 1500 pack horses. For the latter Franklin offered to pay two shillings a day each, as long as used, if provided with a pack saddle. Twenty horses were sent with their loads to the camp as gifts to the British officers. A good and definite list of the load one of these pack horses was expected to carry (as well as a record of the kind of provisions an officer of that day was grateful for) was as follows:

Six pounds of loaf-sugar,
Six pounds muscovado sugar,
One pound green tea,
One pound bohea tea,
Six pounds ground coffee,
Six pounds chocolate,
One-half chest best white biscuit,
One-half pound pepper,
One quart white vinegar,
Two dozen bottles old Madeira wine,
Two gallons Jamaica spirits,
One bottle flour of mustard,
Two well-cured hams,
One-half dozen cured tongues,
Six pounds rice,
Six pounds raisins,
One Gloucester cheese,
One keg containing 20 lbs. best butter.

The wagons and horses were all lost after Braddock's defeat or were seized by the French and Indians.

In Pennsylvania, western Virginia, and Ohio, pack horses in trains, with their gay collars and stuffed bells, filed down the mountain roads to the towns laden with furs, ginseng, and snakeroot and came home laden with salt, nails, tea, pewter plates, etc. At night the horses were hobbled, and the clappers of their bells were loosened; the ringing prevented the horses being lost. The animals started on their journey with two hundred pounds' burden, of which part was provender for horse and man, which was left at convenient relays to be taken up on the way home. Two men could manage fifteen pack horses, which were tethered successively each to the pack saddle of the one in front of him. One man led the foremost horse, and the driver followed the file to watch the packs and urge on the laggards. It is interesting to note that the routes taken by those men, skilled only in humble woodcraft, were the same ones followed in later years by the engineers of the turnpikes and railroads.

As the roads were somewhat better in Pennsylvania than in some other provinces, wagons there soon were far greater in number. Indeed, during the Revolution nearly all the wagons and horses used by the army came from that state. Pennsylvania produced a splendid example of a true American vehicle—the Conestoga wagon, "the finest wagon the world has ever known." They were first used in any considerable number about 1760. They had broad wheel tires, and one of the peculiarities was a decided curve in the bottom, like a galley or canoe, which made it specially fitted for mountain roads. This curved bottom prevented freight from slipping too far at either end when going up or down hill. The body was universally painted a bright blue and furnished with sideboards of an equally vivid red. The wagon bodies were arched over with six or eight stately bows of which the middle ones were the lowest, and the others rose gradually to front and rear till the end bows were nearly of equal height. Over the mall was stretched a strong, white, hempen cover, well corded down at the sides and ends. These wagons could be loaded up to the bows and could carry four to six tons in weight. The rates between Philadelphia and Pittsburgh were about two dollars a hundred pounds. The horses, four to seven in number, were magnificent, often matched throughout; some were all dapple-gray, or all bay. The harnesses, of best materials and appearance, were costly. Each horse had a large supply of deerskin or heavy bearskin trimmed with deep scarlet fringe, while the headstall was tied with bunches of gay ribbons. Bell teams were common; each horse except the saddle horse then had a full set of bells tied with high-colored ribbons.

The wagons were first used in the Conestoga valley, and most extensively used there, and the sleek powerful draft horses known as the Conestoga breed were attached to them, hence their name.

Often a prosperous teamster would own several Conestoga wagons, and driving the leading and handsomest team himself would start off his proud procession. From twenty to a hundred would follow in close row. Large numbers were constantly passing. At one time ten thousand ran from Philadelphia to other towns.

There were two classes of Conestoga wagons and wagoners. The "regulars," or men who made it their constant and only business, and "militia." Militia were farmers or common teamsters who made occasional trips, usually in wintertime, did some carriage for others, and drove but four horses with their wagons. The regulars had broad tires, carried no feed for horses nor food for themselves, but both classes of teamsters carried coarse mattresses and blankets, which they spread side by side, and row after row, on the barroom floor of the tavern at which they "put up." Their horses when unharnessed fed from long troughs hitched to the wagon pole.

The life of the Conestoga wagon did not end with the establishment of railroads in the Eastern states; it penetrated farther and farther west, and at last in its old age it had an equal career of usefulness as the "prairie-schooner," in which vast numbers of families safely crossed the prairies of our Far West.

Four-wheeled wagons were but little used in New England till after the War of 1812. Two-

Detail from engraving of the New Dutch Church, New York, 1731 (The Metropolitan Museum of Art, Photograph by Alfred Tamarin)

wheeled carts and sleds carried inland freight.

By 1773 the Stavers mail coach was plying between Boston and Portsmouth long before England had such a thing. The first stagecoach which ran directly from Philadelphia to New York in 1766—and primitive enough it was—was called "the flying-machine, a good stage-wagon set on springs." Its swift trip occupied two days in good weather. It was but a year later than the original stagecoach between Edinburgh and Glasgow. In 1767 a stagecoach was run during the summer months between Boston and Providence, in 1770 a stage-chaise started between Salem and Boston and a post-chaise between Boston and Portsmouth the following year. Describing a trip between Boston and New York toward the end of the 18th century, President Quincy of Harvard College said:

"The carriages were old and the shackling and much of the harness made of ropes. One pair of horses carried us eighteen miles. We generally reached our resting-place for the night if no accident intervened, at ten o'clock, and after a frugal supper went to bed, with a notice that we should be called at three next morning, which generally proved to be half-past two, and then, whether it snowed or rained, the traveller must rise and make ready, by the help of a horn-lantern and a farthing

"American Stage Waggon," 1798
(The New-York Historical Society)

candle, and proceed on his way over bad roads, sometimes getting out to help the coachman lift the coach out of a quagmire or rut, and arrived in New York after a week's hard travelling, wondering at the ease as well as the expedition with which our journey was effected."

Traveling trunks were small, covered with deerskin or pigskin, studded with brass nails; and each traveler took his trunk under his seat and feet.

The traveler Weld, in 1795, gave testimony that the bridges were so poor that the driver had always to stop and arrange the loose planks ere he dared cross, and he adds:

"The driver frequently had to call to the passengers in the stage to lean out of the carriage first on one side then on the other, to prevent it from oversetting in the deep roads with which the road abounds. 'Now, gentlemen, to the right,' upon which the passengers all stretched their bodies half-way out of the carriage to balance on that side. 'Now, gentlemen, to the left,' and so on."

The growth in stagecoaches and travel came with the turnpike at the beginning of the nineteenth century. In transportation and travel, improvement of roadways is ever associated with improvement of vehicles. The first extensive turnpike was the one between Philadelphia and Lancaster, built in 1792.

Canal travel and transportation were proposed at the close of provincial days, and a few short canals were built. Benjamin Franklin was early awake to their practicability and value. Among the stock owners of the Dismal Swamp Canal was George Washington, and he was equally interested in the Potomac Canal. The Erie Canal, first proposed to the New York legislature in 1768, was completed in 1825.

Until turnpike days all small carriages were two-wheeled; chaises, chairs, and sulkies were those generally used.

Coaches were taxed both in England and America; so we know exactly how plentiful they were. There were as many in Massachusetts in 1750 in proportion to the number of inhabitants as there were in England in 1830.

Coach-building prospered in the colonies; Lucas and Paddock in Boston, Ross in New York, made beautiful and rich coaches. Materials were ample and varied in the New World for carriage-building; horseflesh—not over-choice, to be sure—became over-plentiful; it was said that no man ever walked in America save a vagabond or a fool.

Sleighs were common in New York a half century before they were in Boston. Madam Knights noted the fast racing in sleighs in New York when she was there in 1704.

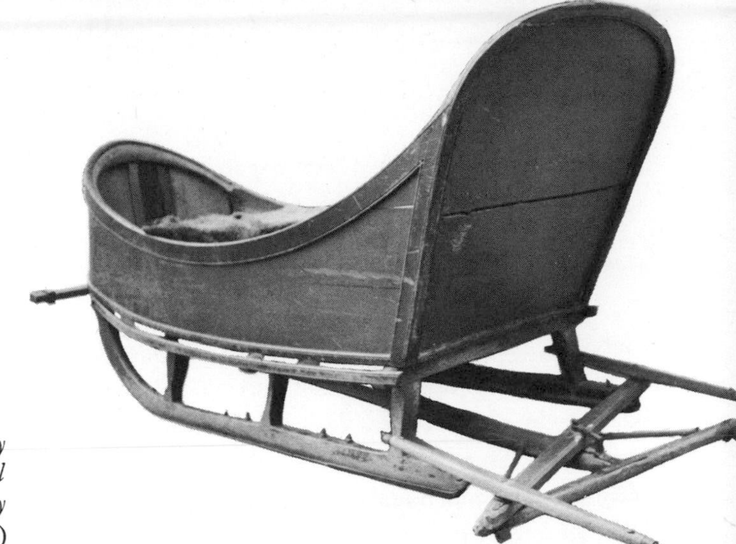

Sleigh, early 18th century (The New-York Historical Society. Photograph by Alfred Tamarin)

One other curious conveyance of colonial days should be spoken of—a sedan chair. This was a strong covered chair fastened on two bars with handles like a litter and might be carried by two or four persons. When sedan chairs were so much used in England, they were sure to be somewhat used in cities in America. One was presented to Governor Winthrop as early as 1646, part of a capture from a Spanish galleon. As late as 1789 Dr. Franklin was seen riding in a sedan chair in Philadelphia.

The building of roads, bridges, and opening of inns show that social interest which marks civilization. Soon inns were found everywhere in the Northern colonies. In New England, New York, and Pennsylvania an inn was called an ordinary, a victualling, a cook-shop, or a tavern, before we had our modern word "hotel."

Board was not very high at early inns; the prices were regulated by the different towns. In 1633 the Salem innkeeper could only have sixpence for a meal. This was at the famous Anchor Tavern, which was kept as a hostelry for nearly two centuries. At the Ship Tavern, board, lodging, wine at dinner and beer between meals cost three shillings a day. At first the tavernkeeper could not sell sack (which was sherry), nor stronger intoxicating liquor to travelers, but he could sell beer, provided it was good, for a penny a quart. Nor could he sell cakes or buns except at a wedding or funeral. He could not allow games to be played, nor singing or dancing to take place.

We know from Shakespeare's plays that the different rooms in English inns had names. This was also the custom in New England. The Star Chamber, Rose and Sun Chamber, Blue Chamber, Jerusalem Chamber, were some of them. Many of the taverns of Revolutionary days and some of colonial times are still standing. A few have even been taverns since first built; others have served many other uses. Every inn had a name, usually painted on its swinging signboard with some significant emblem. These names were simply repetitions of old English tavern signs until Revolutionary days, when patriotic landlords eagerly invented and adopted names significant of the new nation. The scarlet coat of King George became the blue and buff of George Washington, and the eagle of the United States took the place of the British lion.

The signboard was an interesting survival of feudal times, and with its old-time carved and forged companions, such as vanes and weathercocks, door-knockers and figureheads, formed a picturesque element of decoration and symbolism.

Pictorial devices were a necessity because of the general low level of literacy. Gilders, painter-stainers, smiths, and joiners all helped to make the tavern sign a thing of varied workmanship, if not of art.

In Virginia and the Carolinas taverns were not so plentiful nor so necessary, for a traveler might ride from Maryland to Georgia and be sure of a welcome at every private house on the way. Some planters, eager for company and news, stationed servants at the gate to invite passers-by on the post road to come into the house and be entertained. In American cities there was little noise or roistering, no highway robbery, comparatively little petty stealing. The streets were ill paved and dirty, but not foul with the accumulated dirt of centuries as in London. The streets in nearly all cities were unlighted. In 1697 New Yorkers were ordered to have a lantern and candle hung out on a pole from every seventh house. And as the watchman walked around he called out, "Lanthorn, and a whole candell-light. Hang out your lights." The watchman was called a rattle-watch and carried a long staff and a lantern and a large rattle or klopper, which he struck to frighten away thieves. And all night long he called out each hour and told the weather. For instance, he called out, "Past midnight, and all's well"; "One o'clock and fair winds," or "Five o'clock and cloudy skies." In 1658 New York had in all ten watchmen, who were like modern police.

In New England the constables and watch were all carefully appointed by law. They carried black staves six feet long, tipped with brass, and hence were called tipstaves. The night watch was called a bell-man. He looked out for fire and thieves and other disorders and called the time of the night and the weather. The pay was small, often but a shilling a night and occasionally a "coat of kersey." In large towns, like Boston and Salem, thirteen "sober, honest men and householders" were the night watch. The highest in the community, even the magistrates, took their turn at the watch, and were ordered to walk two together, a young man with "one of the soberer sort."

Tavern sign, about 1830 (Old Sturbridge Village)

Index